S0-AHU-649

Regulating Capital

A book in the series

CORNELL STUDIES IN MONEY
Edited by Eric Helleiner and Jonathan Kirshner

For a full list of books in the series,
visit our website at www.cornellpress.cornell.edu.

Regulating Capital

*Setting Standards for the
International Financial System*

David Andrew Singer

Cornell University Press
Ithaca and London

Copyright © 2007 by Cornell University

All rights reserved. Except for brief quotations in a review, this book, or parts thereof, must not be reproduced in any form without permission in writing from the publisher. For information, address Cornell University Press, Sage House, 512 East State Street, Ithaca, New York 14850.

First published 2007 by Cornell University Press
First printing, Cornell Paperbacks, 2010

Printed in the United States of America

Library of Congress Cataloging-in-Publication Data

Singer, David Andrew.
    Regulating capital : setting standards for the international financial system / David Andrew Singer.
        p. cm. — (Cornell studies in money)
    Includes bibliographical references and index.
    ISBN 978-0-8014-4525-5 (cloth : alk. paper)
    ISBN 978-0-8014-7671-6 (pbk. : alk. paper)
    1. International finance. 2. International finance—Law and legislation. 3. International economic integration. 4. Banking law—International cooperation. 5. Securities—International cooperation. 6. Insurance law—International cooperation I. Title. II. Series.
    HG3881.S5365 2007
    332'.042—dc22   2007003491

Cornell University Press strives to use environmentally responsible suppliers and materials to the fullest extent possible in the publishing of its books. Such materials include vegetable-based, low-VOC inks and acid-free papers that are recycled, totally chlorine-free, or partly composed of nonwood fibers. For further information, visit our website at www.cornellpress.cornell.edu.

Cloth printing   10 9 8 7 6 5 4 3 2 1
Paperback printing   10 9 8 7 6 5 4 3 2 1

To my parents

Contents

Preface ix

1. Introduction: Financial Regulators and
   International Relations 1

2. Capital Regulation: A Brief Primer 13

3. Regulators, Legislatures, and Domestic Balancing 20

4. Banking: The Road to the Basel Accord 36

5. Securities: Financial Instability
   and Regulatory Divergence 67

6. Insurance: Domestic Fragmentation
   and Regulatory Divergence 96

7. Conclusion: The Future of International
   Regulatory Harmonization 114

Notes 129

References 143

Index 155

Preface

This book reflects my substantive interests in global financial stability and my theoretical interests in international cooperation. The increasing international integration of national economies—what is commonly known as globalization—generates sobering concerns about the vulnerability of domestic markets to foreign shocks. Some scholars have suggested that there is a crisis in global capitalism, evidenced by the increased occurrence of speculative currency attacks, banking instability, and stock market volatility, and others have advanced far-reaching proposals to reform the global financial "architecture" to bolster financial stability. This book takes a dispassionate step back and analyzes the recent historical record of attempts by financial regulators to cooperate with one another in addressing the challenges of globalization. In some cases, regulators are strong proponents of an international standard that applies a common set of regulations across all countries. In other cases, regulators resist international cooperation and insist on maintaining domestic discretion in their regulatory choices. I find that financial regulators are driven not by international systemic concerns but rather by domestic constraints and the threat of legislative intervention in their activities and mandates. Indeed, financial regulators are reluctant diplomats. With their domestic constituencies and territorially bounded jurisdictions, they are generally hesitant to assert themselves as international actors. Regulators' penchant for international standard-setting emerges only when they are unable to fulfill their domestic mandates with unilateral regulation.

The arguments in this book contribute to ongoing research projects in political science, economics, and public policy. Substantively, the book is a study of the patterns of regulation in the banking, securities, and insurance industries, which constitute the pillars of the global economy. Its historical narratives should generate new directions for research on the viability of global standards and the governance of the global economy. Scholars who advocate international cooperation in response to the specter of global financial instability may benefit from considering the variegated experiences of the regulators chronicled in this book. Analytically, the book challenges the conventional focus on states—and sometimes on legislatures—as the sole actors in international relations. Financial regulators have emerged, albeit reluctantly, as important actors on the world stage. Their activities may seem apolitical at first glance, but it would be unwise to assume that they are insulated from political pressures. The analytical framework presented here illuminates the political incentives that regulators have to "go it alone" at the domestic level or to cooperate with their foreign counterparts.

This book is the culmination of several years of research beginning in the Department of Government at Harvard University. I was blessed from the start with an exceptional group of advisers: Lisa Martin, Jeff Frieden, and Devesh Kapur. I offer my sincere thanks to all three, as well as my apologies if this book does not do justice to the quality of their collective input. Lisa Martin kept me on track during my research and provided crucial guidance and criticism on my research design and theoretical arguments. She was both insightful and patient as she read successive drafts of the book and always filled the margins with questions, suggestions, and challenges. I am convinced that no one provides better feedback than Lisa, and I can only hope to avail myself of her sharp eye in the future. Jeff Frieden was a tough critic and challenged me to clarify my theoretical contributions and to impose a more transparent organizational structure in my empirical analyses. More important, Jeff taught me about international monetary and financial relations and gave me an appreciation for the affinities between economics and political science. He has had, and no doubt will continue to have, the strongest intellectual influence on my research and pedagogy. Finally, Devesh Kapur was a constant source of inspiration and made sure that my research stayed focused on real-world concerns. During our frequent conversations, he was always brimming with new ideas, and he encouraged me to expand my gaze beyond the narrow confines of the existing political science literature. He also looked after my personal well-being and kept me motivated during the darker periods of my research. I feel fortunate to have worked with him and even more fortunate now to call him a collaborator and friend.

I have many friends and colleagues to thank for their contributions to this project. As any writer knows, it takes a village to make a book. I offer special thanks to Ethan Bueno de Mesquita and Mark Copelovitch for providing comments and feedback at various stages of my research. Ethan was especially helpful in challenging me to think more rigorously about my theoretical arguments. I also thank Kim Olson, formerly of the New York Federal Reserve, for valuable feedback on the banking chapter, and especially for challenging my assessments of the Basel II agreement. Robert Gibbons, of the International Insurance Foundation, read the insurance chapter and provided an insightful reaction. For helpful guidance, feedback, criticism, and support, I thank Gabe Aguilera, David Bach, Bear Braumoeller, Lawrence Broz, Dan Carpenter, Fotini Christia, Warren Coats, Ben Deufel, James Fowler, Dan Gingerich, Dan Ho, Layna Mosley, Joseph Sanberg, Allan Stam, Matt Stephenson, participants of the Weatherhead Center graduate student lunch and the Harvard Government Department Political Economy seminar, and my friends at Quincy House. I also thank the participants of the 2005 PROGRES seminar in Geneva for teaching me about international insurance regulation.

This book was completed at the University of Notre Dame and the Massachusetts Institute of Technology. Notre Dame was a delightfully congenial place to draft the final chapters. I offer my thanks to Alexandra Guisinger and David Nickerson for their support during my two years there and my appreciation to Keir Lieber and Dan Lindley for their guidance during the initial stages of the review process. I gratefully acknowledge the research assistance of Jon Bischof. I also thank my new colleagues at MIT for welcoming me (a month early) to the faculty in June 2006.

The field research for this project was conducted in 2002 and 2005. I interviewed nearly forty current and former regulators and industry executives in Basel, Boston, Geneva, London, New York, and Washington, D.C. I agreed to respect their anonymity, but I offer them my thanks for their candor and insight. Administrators at the Bank of England, the U.K. Financial Services Authority, and the Bank for International Settlements were helpful in arranging meetings during my visits in the summer of 2002. Betsy Roberts, of the Financial Stability Institute at the BIS, was especially generous with her time during my visit and read the penultimate draft of the banking chapter nearly four years later.

For financial support during the various stages of this project, I thank Harvard's Weatherhead Center for International Affairs, Center for European Studies, and Center for American Political Studies; and Notre Dame's Institute for Scholarship in the Liberal Arts.

It was a delight to work with Roger Haydon of Cornell University Press. I thank Roger for his efficiency during the review process and for his own counsel about the manuscript. I also thank Eric Helleiner and an anonymous reviewer for detailed and insightful comments on the entire manuscript, which have improved the book in countless ways.

My final acknowledgments go to my family. My brother, Jonathan, watched me toil on this project from a distance but kept a close eye on my mental health. His encouragement and enthusiasm helped to remind me that academia is a rarified environment that I should not take for granted. I enjoyed weekly phone conversations with my grandfather, Henry, who was fascinated by my research and equally eager to hear my prognostications about interest rates on bank accounts in Fort Lauderdale. He passed away before he could read these words—but if he were still with us, I know he would proudly brandish this book to his friends at every opportunity, no doubt to their dismay. I owe special thanks to my partner, Steve, whom I met during my third year of graduate school and who has been with me ever since. Meeting Steve was the best thing that ever happened to me. He, coincidentally, taught me a lot about bank regulation, but more important, he provided constant support and made sure I never lost my sense of humor. Finally, I owe my thanks to my parents, Bob and Harriet, for always encouraging me to ask questions and challenge conventional wisdom. They have helped me to navigate the twists and turns of my career and have waited patiently for me to show them something that I have written. I dedicate this book to them. They have done so much for me already; it's okay if they don't read it.

DAVID ANDREW SINGER

Cambridge, Massachusetts

Chapter 1

Introduction: Financial Regulators and International Relations

Dramatic episodes of financial instability have become increasingly common in the global economy. Since the collapse of the Bretton Woods international monetary system in the early 1970s, the movement of capital has become both more international and more volatile. In the early 1980s the debt crisis in Latin America roiled the global economy and nearly brought down some of the world's most venerable commercial banks. Later in the decade the "Black Monday" stock market crash in 1987 reverberated throughout the largest securities markets, from New York to London to Tokyo. More recently, speculative currency attacks on several Asian countries in 1997 led to wide-scale economic contraction throughout the region, along with fears of "contagious" crises in other countries. Even insurance markets are subject to cross-border influences. The September 11, 2001, terrorist attacks—which constituted one of the largest insured losses in history—created financial strain on insurers throughout the world, and their aftermath served as a reminder that insurance market instability can have a global reach.

Episodes of global financial instability lead inexorably to heated debates about rules and regulations. If the collapse of a financial institution in one country can lead to the sequential collapse of financial institutions in other countries, then should these institutions all be subject to the same regulations? Some scholars and policymakers believe the answer is a resounding yes, at least with regard to a set of minimum prudential standards.[1] However, there is no global financial regulator to set these standards. Financial markets have certainly become internationalized, but national regulators—such as the U.S. Federal Reserve and the Japanese Ministry of Finance—retain the ability to set the rules in their own jurisdictions. Therein is the pre-eminent tension in international finance: the interdependence of financial markets challenges the domestic locus of regulatory policymaking.[2] Global markets, it seems, require global regulation.

This is a book about global regulation in the three traditional pillars of finance: banking, securities, and insurance. Global regulation in these areas implies cooperation (or "harmonization") among national regulatory agencies, generally within international forums such as the Basel Committee (for bank regulators), the International Organization of Securities Commissions (IOSCO), and the International Association of Insurance Supervisors (IAIS). The emphasis throughout the book is on capital at the level of industry and firms. Firm-level capital requirements—also known as capital adequacy—are at the foundation of the debates over international financial standards. To mitigate the possibility of a cross-border domino effect in financial instability, firms must hold enough capital to sustain themselves against outside shocks. Capital adequacy regulations, however, go to the heart of a financial institution's operations and can affect profitability, foreign competitiveness, corporate strategy, and even survivability. Negotiations over capital adequacy, whether at the domestic or global level, are therefore invariably contentious.

This book focuses on the capital adequacy negotiations of regulators in the world's most powerful financial centers in the 1980s and 1990s, namely, the United States, the United Kingdom, and Japan. Developments within the European Union are also addressed where appropriate. The choice to focus on these countries implicitly acknowledges the importance of market power in international regulatory harmonization.[3] Clearly, the preferences of, say, Swedish financial regulators will be far less consequential than the preferences of regulators from larger markets. However, I emphasize throughout the book that power alone does not dictate national preferences. Indeed, regulators in the United States—representing the world's largest financial market—have found themselves advocating international standards at certain times and opposing them at others.

I focus on two related puzzles. The first, high-level puzzle is that international regulatory standards have emerged in some financial industries and not in others. The most prominent regulatory standard is the 1988 Basel Accord, which established an international capital adequacy rule for the banking industry.[4] Policy analysts often herald the Basel Accord as an exemplar for other industries, both within the financial realm and beyond.[5] Political scientists and legal scholars note its importance as an international agreement between unelected bank regulators and therefore as a new form of global governance.[6] Yet a similar agreement has not emerged in the securities industry—despite vigorous negotiations in the late 1980s and early 1990s—or in the insurance industry.

The second puzzle sits at the core of this project: why are certain regulatory agencies strong proponents of international standards whereas others are adamantly opposed? This puzzle captures the variation within each financial industry. During the Basel Accord negotiations, for example, the U.S. Federal Reserve and the Bank of England were the leading advocates of an international capital adequacy standard for banks whereas the Japanese Ministry of Finance (MOF) was a vocal opponent. A similar set of negotiations over capital standards for securities firms resulted in a different configuration of preferences, with the United Kingdom's Securities and Investments Board the aggressive leader and the U.S. Securities and Exchange Commission and the MOF in the opposition. Finally, insurance regulators, with few exceptions, have yet to assert themselves as proponents of international standards. The two puzzles—variation in the emergence of standards across industries, and variation in the preferences of regulators toward international standards—cannot be examined in isolation. Indeed, a compelling explanation of outcomes across industries requires an explanation of the preferences of individual regulators.

Financial regulators in the developed world must maintain a precarious balance between the regulated industry's stability and competitiveness. Costly regulations, such as firm capital requirements, may be necessary to prevent financial instability and to shield regulators from the scorn of elected leaders. However, in a global economy such costly regulations can prove inimical to the international competitiveness of the domestic industry.[7] As a result of this tension, regulators must continuously adjust the stringency of their regulations—tightening with bouts of financial instability, loosening as foreign competitors gain market share—to maintain a politically acceptable balance.[8] In most cases, the cycle of regulatory adjustment occurs quietly and unilaterally. However, when a regulator faces exogenous shocks to stability and competitiveness simultaneously, it is unable to adjust appropriately without asserting itself on the international stage. Through *international regulatory harmonization*, regulators can impose sufficiently stringent regulations on domestic financial institutions—and shore up stability—while relaxing the international competitive constraint that normally prohibits such costly tightening.[9]

A primary goal of this book is to analyze the rise of financial regulators as international actors. Indeed, regulators have been called the "new diplomats" because of their increasing visibility on the international scene.[10] However, I part company with past observers by focusing on variation in regulators' preferences for international harmonization. Just as the enormous body of scholarship on international relations has grappled to explain *variation*—in war and peace, alliance formation and dissolution, and state preferences over a variety of issues—so too should the emerging scholarship on transgovernmental relations focus on variation in regulators' preferences and behavior across borders. The contemporary empirical record demonstrates substantial differences in regulators' patterns of cooperation and discord. Negotiations within the Basel Committee, IOSCO, and IAIS provide ample evidence of variation in regulators' desires to coordinate their policies. Clearly, not all regulators are at the vanguard of international cooperation; in fact, some are vehemently opposed to tying their hands with an international standard. And contrary to conventional power-politics arguments, U.S. regulators—representing the world's largest financial markets—are not always eager to assert themselves (and their rules) on the world stage. The "new diplomats" are an irresolute bunch, and this fact has not yet received adequate attention in the field of political science.[11]

Why do some regulators take the lead in establishing international regulatory standards while others adamantly resist? First, it is important to note that the creation of an international standard ties the hands of a regulator by limiting its ability to adjust to changing domestic (or international) circumstances. Given the importance of regulatory adjustment in avoiding political pressure and enhancing competitiveness, no regulator will voluntarily accede to an international standard without careful consideration of its domestic environment. I argue that regulatory agencies are more likely to press for international harmonization—and assert themselves as international actors—when they are in a precarious position domestically. When financial instability, such as firm collapses and asset market volatility, occurs alongside a rising competitive threat from foreign financial sectors, regulatory agencies face angry pressures from all sides. An attempt to tighten regulations domestically will simply augment the competitive position of foreign firms, yet doing nothing will render the domestic industry unstable and spark the indignation of consumers and politicians. The regulator's weakness stems from the fact that it is not able to adjust to its environment unilaterally by modifying the stringency of its regulations. In short, preferences for international harmonization emerge only when a regulator is unable to balance stability and competitiveness with unilateral domestic regulation. A regulator under fire at home is more likely to emerge as an aggressive player on the international scene—and a strong advocate of international standards—than a regulator presiding over stable and competitive financial institutions.

International Regulatory Harmonization

There are several excellent country studies of domestic financial regulation in the global economy. For example, Steven Vogel and Henry Laurence, in separate books, chronicle and compare the regulatory changes in the United Kingdom and Japan brought about by the globalization of financial markets.[12] Vogel in particular notes that foreign competition created pressures to deregulate financial services but also led to counteracting pressures to "re-regulate" markets with new prudential regulations.[13] Frances Rosenbluth also analyzes Japanese regulatory reform and argues that financial institutions themselves were the driving force behind domestic market liberalization. These prior studies underline a key theme of this book—the difficulties that regulators face in balancing competing interests in a global economy—but their purpose is not to address regulators' international activities.[14] This book could therefore be viewed as the *international* extension of the literature on financial regulatory policymaking in the developed world.

The literature on international regulatory harmonization in the global economy is dominated by studies of the Basel Accord, an agreement that established a global capital adequacy standard for internationally active banks (and the subject of chapter 4 of this book).[15] Many scholars and industry representatives view the accord—established by bank regulators from the G-10 countries in 1988—as a public good that promotes global financial stability. Ethan Kapstein, for example, argues that regulators from the industrialized world developed a shared understanding of the risks of undercapitalized banks and created the accord to address a worldwide market failure in the wake of the less-developed country (LDC) debt crisis in the early 1980s.[16] When applied beyond the specific case of banking regulation, Kapstein's argument implies that regulators will seek international regulatory harmonization when they can realize joint gains from a global standard.[17] This logic is pervasive not just in analyses of regulatory harmonization but in the study of international institutions more generally. Robert Keohane's seminal study of international cooperation emphasized the functional purpose of international institutions, which enable countries to realize mutual benefits in an otherwise conflictual environment replete with information asymmetries, transaction costs, and enforcement problems.[18] In short, the functionalist framework attributes the creation of an international institution to the underlying global need that it putatively addresses.[19]

From an analytical perspective, functionalist approaches are less successful in explaining variation in the emergence of international regulatory standards because nearly any standard—actual or proposed—can be justified on international functionalist grounds. More important, functionalist arguments are not helpful in explaining cross-national variation in regulators' demands for international standards within a given industry. For example, some scholars believe that banks are especially vulnerable to systemic instability, with the ineluctable result being the creation of international prudential regulation. As demonstrated in chapter 4, however, such a functionalist view cannot explain the stark variation in preferences among the major powers for international standards *within* the banking sector.[20]

Because of the widespread association of banking markets with systemic risk—the possibility of a cross-border contagious spread of losses across financial institutions with harmful effects on the real economy—scholars have overlooked cross-border risks in other financial markets, such as securities and insurance.[21] In theory, systemic risk in banking may be especially severe, but this is not to say that such risk does not exist in other areas.[22] Important episodes of systemic instability in banking, securities, and insurance demonstrate that they alone are not capable of explaining the resulting patterns of international regulatory cooperation or discord.

In the broader literature on cooperation, scholars such as Geoffrey Garrett and Stephen Krasner have added sophistication to the functionalist argument by acknowledging the distributional nature of most international institutions.[23] Even when we assume mutual gains from cooperation, there may be many ways of dividing up the benefits among the participants. This complication to the functionalist logic incorporates additional concepts such as ideas, beliefs, and focal points, which can guide politicians to agree on an acceptable distribution of welfare gains. Institutions, according to these arguments, still address global problems and enhance the welfare of all participants, but their distributive effects necessarily complicate any discussion of their origins.

Thomas Oatley and Robert Nabors have taken the distributional effects of institutions one step further, challenging the assumption of mutual gains and the functionalist logic of earlier scholarship.[24] They argue that international institutions may be "redistributive," intentionally reducing the welfare of at least one participating country. Redistributive institutions are proposed by politicians who find themselves in the uncomfortable position of appeasing two opposing groups in the electorate. If voters demand the promulgation of policies that will hurt import-competing producer groups, politicians can propose an international institution that shifts the costs of these policies onto foreign competitors. They can therefore satisfy voters by enacting the appropriate policies but protect the competitive standing of producers by coercing foreign countries into adopting the same policies. Oatley and Nabors apply this framework to the Basel Accord, arguing that it represents the particular interests of U.S. politicians, who were eager to respond to voter demands for stricter prudential regulations for banks without harming domestic competitiveness with Japanese rivals. The authors specifically reject the idea that the agreement constituted a global public good or that it was created to address a growing systemic risk problem in international banking.

An important shortcoming of a legislature-focused argument is that it attempts to analyze a transgovernmental phenomenon with an intergovernmental framework: Oatley and Nabors focus on the legislature as the final decision maker when in fact the main actors in international regulatory harmonization are regulatory agencies. If these agencies create international standards without the need for domestic legislative ratification, then an analysis should proceed by examining variation in regulators' incentives. It is unreasonable to assume that regulators respond to electoral pressures in the same way—or with the same alacrity—as elected officials. Moreover, analysts who seek evidence of the legislature's direct involvement in a regulator's international negotiations will often be unsuccessful.[25] Regulators themselves are surprised at the suggestion that the legislature may have directed them to seek international regulatory agreements.[26] The institutional structure of legislatures, with their committees, voting systems, leadership structures, and party systems, is designed with the explicit goal of balancing the competing interests of the electorate.[27] If the U.S. Congress, for example, sought international agreements every time it imposed costly legislation on the public, then members of Congress would be the most visible actors in international relations! But as Anne-Marie Slaughter notes, legislators lag far behind regulatory agencies in their international activities and remain rather parochial in their outlooks.[28] Legislatures in fact have a variety of tools at their disposal to balance competing interests unilaterally. Costly legislation can be counterbalanced by other legislative incentives, such as subsidies, tax policies, or "pork-barrel" spending, to name a few.

Oatley and Nabors's emphasis on redistribution is nevertheless a significant contribution to the study of international regulatory harmonization. The theoretical framework I develop in chapter 3 is compatible with the view that international institutions may be redistributive and therefore not inherently Pareto-superior to policymaking in the absence of harmonization. This view is also advocated by Beth Simmons, who argues that the process of harmonization reflects dominant-country interests rather than international systemic concerns.[29] However, I am moot on the question of the public-good character of international regulatory agreements. I argue that regulators seek international regulatory harmonization when exogenous shocks preclude their ability to satisfy the dueling pressures for competitiveness and stability simultaneously. Such circumstances may arise due to systemic market failures, in which case an international agreement would have the characteristics of a public good. But international regulatory agreements may provide a mechanism for countries to shift costs onto their competitors rather than address an underlying global systemic problem. Both scenarios are possible, and both are compatible with my framework.

This project builds on the literature by developing a framework to explain variation in regulators' demands for international standards. I show that functionalist arguments are not helpful in explaining this variation since global problems such as systemic risk and instability would predict the emergence of standards across nearly all areas of finance. Competing arguments that purport to explain one particular outcome—namely, the Basel Accord—are similarly not helpful in explaining variation either within that case or across other cases. Instead, I focus on the key actors—regulatory agencies—and their relationship with their respective legislatures and domestic industries in an environment of global competition.

Before we proceed, a note of clarification is in order. International regulatory harmonization is a broad topic, and this book does not pretend to address all of its applications and intricacies. For example, I do not cover regulatory areas such accounting rules, auditing standards, and data transparency. My focus is on the creation of global standards rather than on international memoranda of understanding that facilitate ad hoc cooperation in areas such as securities fraud and other criminal activity. Substantively, my emphasis is on capital, and therefore on the stability of financial institutions, rather than on consumer protection or the fight against illicit activity. And as should be clear, I focus on the role of public-sector regulatory agencies that have been delegated responsibility by the government rather than on private standard-setting organizations or industry self-regulation.[30]

Financial Regulation and International Relations

Why study international financial regulation? Regulation at the domestic level is often designed to address market failures, in which the unfettered activities of firms and consumers result in unfavorable outcomes. For example, the decentralized decisions of banks and their clients may lead the former to lend too aggressively, thereby putting the stability of the financial sector—and the entire economy—at risk. The prevalence of market failures in domestic financial markets provides incentives for governments to step in, as necessary, by establishing financial regulations. With the globalization of financial markets, market failures have moved to the international level. Examples such as the 1987 stock market crash, which roiled financial markets in New York, London, Tokyo, and throughout the rest of the world, demonstrate that financial instability in one country can affect many other countries that are tied together in the global economy. However, addressing international market failures is not as straightforward as in the domestic case. International financial regulation, in short, requires international cooperation. Governments—more specifically, regulators—must coordinate their regulations to mitigate international market failures, and history has shown that international cooperation does not emerge without considerable effort. The creation of international financial regulation is therefore always striking.

The emergence of regulators as international actors has important implications for the study of international relations (IR). Much theorizing in IR scholarship has focused on the international interaction of government leaders or heads of state and on the foreign policy decisions of elected leaders. These actors are accountable to various interest groups, political parties, and domestic constituencies and must take these pressures into account when negotiating with other countries. They may also face institutional constraints in a two-level game scenario, such as the requirement that their international policies are ratified by the domestic legislature.[31] In the political-economy tradition, analyses of political decisions can therefore proceed with an examination of the distributional consequences of policy outcomes, the influence of interest groups and voters, and the institutional structures through which these influences are translated into decisions. But when the goal is to explain the behavior of financial regulators in the developed world, the building blocks of an explanatory structure must be altered. Financial regulators are not elected by voters—indeed, they may not even be selected by the current government.[32] Furthermore, their international agreements do not require domestic ratification. This is not to say that regulators are accountable to no one; rather, the nature of their accountability—and the resulting constraints on their discretion—must be modeled differently than in standard analyses of political decisions. Unlike the decision makers in a typical two-level game, regulators are international actors *because* of domestic constraints rather than international actors *constrained* by domestic politics.

At the international level, agreements between regulators are a notable exception to the trend of "legalization in world politics."[33] The literature on legalization points to the increasing use of domestic legal principles in international institutions. Legally binding treaties have become commonplace, and international organizations—such as the World Trade Organization, the European Court of Human Rights, and the Law of the Sea Tribunal—routinely impose judgments that must be carried out by member states.[34] Regulatory agreements in international finance, on the other hand, are not legally binding, and enforcement and interpretation are largely left to market pressures. There is no "World Capital Organization" to govern international financial affairs, and no dispute-settlement mechanisms that states can use to resolve conflicts.[35] In the language of the legalization literature, international financial regulatory agreements are prime examples of "soft law": they have low levels of "obligation" (in the sense that they are not legally binding between regulators) and do not delegate enforcement or implementation authority to a third party.[36] However, contrary to the expectations of the legalization literature, the costs of violation may be extremely high due to market pressures: a country that chooses to disregard a global financial standard may face capital flight, a loss of competitiveness, and a crisis of confidence.[37]

The absence of legal treaties and third-party enforcers belies the fact that international regulatory agreements can be extremely binding on state behavior. Sovereignty costs—defined broadly as the loss of state authority over decision making in a particular area—may therefore be quite high, since regulators relinquish their discretion to change domestic regulations once they have signed onto a global standard.[38] The market, rather than an international organization or third-party enforcer, is delegated the authority to monitor compliance, and its powers can exceed those of even the most influential enforcement and adjudication bodies. A key implication of this discussion is that international regulatory agreements may involve substantial contracting costs. Negotiations over financial regulations are therefore drawn out and often acrimonious. The current negotiations over the revised Basel Accord on bank capital adequacy (discussed in chapter 4) are a prime example. Soon after the accord's promulgation in 1988, regulators realized that its capital rules were rather crude and inefficient. Negotiations have been under way for several years to modify the accord's mechanism for matching a bank's capital with its level of risk, but progress has been slow due to the need for public comment periods and quantitative impact studies, not to mention multifarious conflicts among regulators. The Basel Committee expects that the revised accord will be implemented by year-end 2007, or nearly twenty years after the original agreement was introduced.[39]

At a more descriptive level, the international activity of financial regulators is consistent with the rise of "transgovernmentalism": international relations between substate and private actors, as opposed to government leaders and heads of state.[40] Owing to the increasing international integration of national economies, new, more flexible governance structures—based on informal networks of government officials—are needed to address common problems. Slaughter notes that the emergence of substate government officials on the international stage gives the modern state a "hydra-headed" character.[41] In most cases, these substate actors are not given specific mandates to cooperate with their foreign counterparts; rather, their international activity occurs organically as a result of their inability to accomplish their domestic goals unilaterally in the face of globalization.

Analytically, the literature on transgovernmentalism (and on global governance more generally) attempts to explain the level—state, substate, or private—of international governance in different issue areas.[42] This book takes that level as given for international regulatory cooperation. My focus is on the patterns of cooperation among regulators rather than the broader characteristics of regulatory cooperation vis-à-vis other forms of governance.[43] Financial regulators have become one of the most prominent "heads" in the hydra-headed modern state, so the political science discipline is clearly overdue for an analysis of their behavior on the international scene.

The Plan of the Book

In the next chapter, I provide a brief primer on financial regulation, focusing on the issue of capital requirements for banks, securities firms, and insurance companies. A discussion of the costs and benefits of capital requirements reveals a trade-off between bolstering financial stability and enhancing international competitiveness. That trade-off is at the heart of the analytical framework developed in chapter 3. The framework builds on the notion of a principal-agent relationship and details the circumstances that prevent regulators from adequately reconciling the trade-off unilaterally. In short, I argue that regulators are more likely to emerge as proponents of international standards when exogenous shocks to domestic financial stability and international competitiveness occur simultaneously. In such circumstances, a regulator finds itself under intense pressure from both politicians and the financial sector and faces the prospect of embarrassing legislative intervention. A regulator's push for the creation of an international regulatory standard arises as a strategy to reconcile the dueling domestic pressures of stability and competitiveness and—in extreme cases—to ensure its survival.

I explore the observable implications of the analytical framework in the case studies in chapters 4–6, which are informed by more than forty interviews with regulators and industry executives.[44] Chapter 4 discusses capital regulation in the banking industry and the negotiations leading up to the 1988 Basel Accord. I pay particular attention to the variation in regulator preferences for international harmonization and demonstrate how regulators' domestic environments shape their positions as international actors. The final outcome of the negotiations—an international capital adequacy standard for banks—is not puzzling once the positions of the main actors are understood.

In chapter 5 I focus on the negotiations over a capital adequacy standard for securities firms, which took place just after the Basel negotiations. Despite its clear parallel with the banking case, the securities case has been largely overlooked by political scientists. Again, I concentrate on the varying preferences of regulators toward international harmonization, and I chronicle the exogenous shocks to their domestic environments that condition their demands for (or resistance to) an international standard.

Chapter 6 explores the case of international insurance regulation, with a focus on capital requirements for reinsurance firms. The reinsurance industry has received short shrift in studies of the global economy, so I begin by describing the industry and its international reach. Insurance regulators have only recently emerged on the international scene, and thus far their efforts at international harmonization have been quite modest. Rather than single out a specific set of negotiations, I analyze regulators' responses to financial instability and show that they have heretofore been able to maintain the domestic balance between stability and competitiveness through unilateral regulation.

Chapter 7 summarizes my findings and discusses possible extensions, methodological improvements, and additional hypotheses. It also revisits the issue of regulators as international actors and offers a typology of regulatory harmonization to guide future research.

Chapter 2

Capital Regulation: A Brief Primer

Before proceeding to the analytical framework, let us examine the purposes of financial regulation and the costs and benefits that regulation imposes on financial institutions and the global economy. This chapter explains the various risks assumed by financial firms, the role of regulation—especially capital adequacy requirements—in mitigating these risks, and the consequences of regulation for firm competitiveness and profitability.

Financial Institutions and Risk

The purpose of any financial system is to channel funds from savers to borrowers, thereby enabling those with productive investment opportunities to avail themselves of much-needed capital. This process is fraught with difficulties. With few exceptions, individuals and businesses cannot siphon these funds to themselves on their own; instead, they require the assistance of a financial intermediary—generally, a bank or securities firm. If these intermediaries had perfect information about borrowers, savers, and the condition of the economy around them, then the financial system would operate seamlessly with minimal risk. But at the heart of any financial system is the problem of *asymmetric information*, in which one party to a transaction has more (and more accurate) information about its own status than another party. Business managers who rely on bank lending are more knowledgeable about their own revenue streams, market conditions, and organizational integrity than are their bank credit officers. Similarly, corporations that seek to raise capital through securitized financing are more aware of the factors that could change their stock and bond prices than are the financial institutions that initially purchase the securities or trade them on the secondary markets. The presence of asymmetric information in virtually every financial transaction implies that financial institutions must assume a degree of risk in their lending, financing, and underwriting activities. When financial institutions assume risk, the users of those institutions—governments, corporations, and individual consumers—also assume a degree of risk since the safety of their own capital may be at stake. A bank failure affects the fortunes of not only the bank's managers but also its debtors and depositors.

Insurance companies facilitate the channeling of excess funds from savers to borrowers by allowing individuals and corporations to shield themselves from the risk of financial losses. For example, an airline will not borrow funds to purchase new aircraft unless it can cede the attendant financial risks of malfunction or catastrophic loss to an insurance firm. Insurance firms are not traditional financial intermediaries because their purpose is not to provide financing for their clients. But even more than banks and securities firms, insurers are well versed in the problems of asymmetric information. Clients are more knowledgeable about their propensities to generate insurance claims than are their insurers. A sudden spate of costly insurance claims could cause an insurance firm to collapse, affecting not only the firm's shareholders but also the firm's other clients with outstanding (and unrealized) claims.

Fortunately, banks, securities firms, and insurers are in the business of taking risks in the face of asymmetric information.[1] The risks of bank lending are obvious: banks lend money directly to businesses, governments, and individuals, thereby incurring *credit risk*: the risk that borrowers will fail to repay their loans.[2] Insurance firms, which provide a market for pure risk, are most concerned about unexpected claims and unforeseen environmental risks (such as terrorism and natural disasters). For securities firms, the risks may be less obvious, but they are no less severe. Securities firms underwrite new issues of marketable securities, serve as market makers in the secondary markets, and often engage in their own speculative trading. In these activities, firms assume *market risk* for as long as it takes them to sell any securities in their inventories.

As an example of market risk, consider a securities firm that agrees to underwrite an offering of stock by XYZ Corporation. XYZ, like most firms that seek to raise capital, does not have the capacity to issue securities directly to customers because it has no seat on a stock exchange, no national (or international) sales force to sell the securities, and no base of clients or investment managers to absorb the sale. Just as a homeowner who wishes to sell her house seeks the help of a real estate agent, so too does a corporation seek the help of a securities firm when it wishes to raise capital. However, unlike a real estate agent, who never assumes an ownership position in the house, the securities firm actually buys the securities from the corporation. In a so-called firm commitment, the securities firm purchases all the stock from XYZ for resale to the public. The firm's profit from this transaction consists of the difference between the price paid to XYZ and the price charged to the public. The securities firm faces market risk from the time it takes possession of the XYZ stock until it is sold to the public, which could be anywhere from a couple of days to several weeks. If the market value of XYZ's stock were to plummet during this period, the securities firm could incur a substantial loss. Similar losses are also possible long after the public offering since the securities firm must continue to make a secondary market in the security and therefore must hold a substantial number of shares in its own account. Sudden swings in securities prices therefore have a dramatic effect on the value of securities firms' assets, which makes market risk a constant concern for the securities industry.[3]

The risks to financial institutions are not limited to asymmetric information. Often there are adverse changes in the financial environment, such as volatility in interest rates and exchange rates, that cannot be predicted by any one party. *Foreign exchange risk* arises when a firm's long or short position in a foreign security may be adversely affected by a change in the exchange rate.[4] If a foreign currency depreciates (or appreciates) at a time when a firm wishes to sell (or purchase) a security denominated in that currency, the firm will incur a financial loss. *Interest rate risk* has similar characteristics since unexpected changes in interest rates affect profit margins and the value of a firm's equity.[5] Unexpected changes in asset prices, which may be influenced by interest rates and exchange rates, contribute to *liquidity risk*, which arises when a firm has difficulty finding a buyer for its securities or other assets. If a firm's assets are not sufficiently liquid—that is, if it is not possible to convert them into cash or cash equivalents without significant loss—then the firm may not have sufficient resources on hand to pay its current obligations.

And finally, financial institutions of all kinds face *operational risk* due to the possibility of failures in internal control systems, managerial malfeasance, technological snafus (such as computer viruses), and fraud. Although financial institutions are invariably designed to manage (and profit from) credit and market risks, they are not designed to benefit from internal control problems or fraudulent employees. Financial managers and regulators have paid closer attention to operational risk in recent years, largely as a result of the growing functional and technological complexity of financial institutions. Activities such as mergers and acquisitions, foreign outsourcing, and e-commerce challenge the efficacy of firms' internal processes and increase the probability of unforeseen financial losses.

The Link between Risk and Capital

The willingness of firms to assume such a broad range of risks allows for the transfer of surplus capital from savers to borrowers, enabling the economy to grow through investment. Financial institutions build the costs of some of these risks into their services. For example, banks lend funds at interest rates that take into account the risk of default by borrowers. Securities firms impose a spread between the price paid to a corporation for securities and the price charged to the public, and this spread can vary as a function of the financial strength of the corporation. And of course, insurance firms charge higher premiums for riskier clients. Financial institutions also maintain a certain level of capital and reserves to cushion against possible losses brought on by borrower default, asset price volatility, unexpected claims, or any of the adverse events already discussed. A firm's capital is therefore like an insurance policy, protecting the firm against exogenous shocks and the risks of financial intermediation.

What constitutes a firm's capital? Although the analogy of "money under the mattress" is notionally helpful, capital is an accounting concept that encompasses stockholders' equity, cash reserves, and a variety of other funding sources. There is in fact no universally accepted definition of capital; in some countries, for example, short-term subordinated debt—repayable to the lender only after other debts with a higher claim have been satisfied—is considered part of a firm's core capital base, whereas in other countries only more permanent forms of capital are included in the definition. The amount of a firm's capital (however defined) is important *relative* to its financial obligations. Banks and insurance firms with extensive portfolios require more capital to protect themselves against financial loss than institutions with small portfolios. Similarly, a securities firm that underwrites large public offerings and maintains a market for a variety of stocks must hold more capital to cushion itself against market risk than a firm with more modest financial obligations.

Capital, just like an insurance policy, is expensive. When a bank holds funds in a loan-loss reserve rather than lending those funds profitably to customers, it incurs a substantial opportunity cost. Since capital is important relative to financial obligations, a firm that seeks to be well capitalized may require a contraction in its revenue-generating lending portfolio or underwriting activity. On the other hand, a firm that seeks to bolster its profits has incentives to hold less capital relative to its obligations. A firm's trade-off is therefore between mitigating the risks of involvement in the financial markets and expanding its revenue stream through additional financing and underwriting activities. In other words, the trade-off is between stability and competitiveness. Capital provides a cushion against risk, but at a significant cost.

Capital Decisions: The Role of Regulation

When the risks of financial activity cause a financial institution to collapse, the firm's managers and shareholders face a financial loss. However, the collapse may also influence the fortunes of the firm's customers as well as other financial institutions and their managers. Financial institutions do not consider these "spillover effects" in their decisions, creating a problem for policymakers: in the absence of regulation, financial institutions do not internalize the systemic consequences of their financial health when deciding how much capital to hold.

To understand the nature of this problem, consider the potentially grave systemic consequences of the failure of a bank. A bank failure can reverberate throughout a community, leading to bank runs and additional failures. Asymmetric information is again the culprit, causing bank depositors to fear that their bank could suffer the same fate as the failed bank. Corporate clients that relied on the failed bank for credit lines and ongoing financing would find themselves in a temporary credit crunch, which could slow investment and harm profits. In a worst-case contagion scenario, a bank collapse could lead to a string of failures, an economic slowdown, and widescale financial panic.[6]

The systemic consequences of insurance market instability arise from the linkages connecting insurance coverage, claims payments, and economic activity. The failure of an insurance company can lead to financial losses for clients with outstanding claims, which could in turn affect business investment decisions. A more realistic possibility is that insurance market instability could limit the availability of coverage for certain assets or activities—such as oil tankers or the construction of skyscrapers—which could in turn cause economic slowdowns in particular sectors. Homeowners and business owners in the coastal regions of Florida that were hit by successive hurricanes in the summer of 2004 are acutely aware of the real effects of insurance scarcity.

Insurance company insolvencies can be potentially inimical to the banking sector if the two industries are closely tied. In many countries commercial banks are permitted to operate insurance subsidiaries and to sell insurance coverage alongside typical banking products. In the United States the Gramm-Leach-Bliley Act of 1999 abolished the longstanding Glass-Steagall prohibition against the affiliation of banks, securities firms, and insurance companies, paving the way for the creation of massive financial holding companies with affiliates in each of the three areas. The collapse of an insurance affiliate could weaken the capital base of the holding company, thereby affecting the stability of the banking and securities affiliates.

The collapse of a securities firm can also lead to a severe disruption in the economy, although through different contagion channels than in the case of banks. If a securities firm goes bankrupt, there is an increased probability that its outstanding obligations to other broker-dealers will go unrealized. If these other firms are not adequately capitalized, they could default or collapse, creating an ever larger circle of bankruptcies in the securities industry. A more likely channel for systemic disruption is through changes in asset prices. A large securities firm must hold substantial quantities of stocks and bonds in order to maintain liquid markets and satisfy the needs of its clients. If the firm were to run into sudden and severe financial trouble, it would sell off its inventory of securities, thereby flooding the market and leading to a sharp drop in securities prices. The capital bases of other securities firms would plummet along with the stock market decline, causing further liquidation of inventories and exacerbating the market crash. Corporations whose day-to-day cash flow relies on commercial paper—short-term debt instruments with maturities ranging from 2 to 270 days—and other capital market offerings would find themselves floundering for alternative sources of capital. In a worst-case scenario a spiral of securities firm failures would cause the collapse of the payments system and drag the rest of the financial system, including banks, into chaos.[7]

To be sure, these doomsday scenarios are unlikely. In developed economies, deposit insurance for customers of banks and securities firms, and insurance guaranty associations, help maintain public confidence in the financial system, and modern information technology allows financial institutions to settle their mutual obligations quickly. Nevertheless, the point remains: the behavior of banks, securities firms, and insurers influences the profits and stability of other firms and can affect the health of the overall economy. When a financial institution collapses, the costs are borne not just by the firm's shareholders but also by other firms and the rest of the economy.

The spillover effects of financial collapse create strong incentives for the regulation of capital requirements. When deciding how much capital to hold relative to their financial obligations, financial institutions do not internalize the negative externalities of collapsing. As Federal Reserve Bank of Chicago president Michael Moskow notes, "Instances may occur where the costs and benefits to an individual agent associated with a particular action may diverge from the costs and benefits to society."[8] The decision calculus for a financial institution is based on profitability, expanding market share, and increasing shareholder value, not on the possible contagion effects of a firm collapse.[9] Firms with international clients also take into account the capital allocation decisions of their foreign competitors, since cross-national differences in capital adequacy can help or hinder a firm's competitive standing. From a firm's perspective, the costs of failure are roughly equivalent to the loss in shareholder value and the costs to the firm's managers and employees. In the absence of government-mandated requirements, a financial institution will generally hold less capital than would be optimal from a societal (i.e., aggregate welfare maximizing) standpoint.

Banks, securities firms, and insurers view capital reserves as necessary for their prosperity and stability. In the event of severe adverse conditions, however, regulators view capital quite differently.[10] For banks and insurers, the regulator's goal is to enable the firm to weather adversity and thereby protect depositors' funds, clients' coverage, and public confidence in the financial system. Capital levels should be sufficient to absorb losses and enable the institution to continue as a going concern.[11] For securities firms, capital regulations are designed to allow a firm to wind down its operations in an orderly manner in the event of severe market losses. This process would include selling off marketable securities, repaying any outstanding obligations, and shutting down operations with sufficient warning to the market.[12] Note that although capital requirements are designed to prevent insolvency and default for all financial firms, in the event of severe trouble banks and insurers should stay standing whereas securities firms should wind down.

Toward an Analytical Framework

Chapters 4, 5, and 6 discuss the evolution of capital regulation in banking, securities, and insurance. A broad theme emerges: capital requirements are not popular with financial institutions. Historically, financial institutions have generally resisted the imposition of capital regulation, which goes to the heart of their financial operations. With the globalization of financial markets beginning in the 1960s and 1970s, capital became an even more important concern for firms that found themselves in competition with foreign rivals. Financial institutions that adopted an aggressive stance, with a relatively low level of capital to cushion against risks and exogenous shocks, could often outbid and outcompete their foreign counterparts with more conservative capital positions. Regulators, with good intentions in mind, found themselves with their own trade-off: mitigating the risk of financial collapse by imposing stiff capital requirements, or easing those requirements and enhancing the international competitiveness of the domestic financial sector. This trade-off is at the center of the analytical framework developed in the next chapter.

Chapter 3

Regulators, Legislatures, and Domestic Balancing

The globalization of capital markets complicates the role of financial regulators in the developed world. On the one hand, regulators must be sensitive to the competitive implications of regulatory policy. Cross-country discrepancies in financial regulation have significant ramifications for the competitiveness of financial firms. In the highly price-sensitive realm of finance, strict regulations can cause domestic firms to lose market share to foreign firms in less-regulated jurisdictions. On the other hand, regulators are responsible for safeguarding the stability of national financial markets and must impose appropriate prudential regulations on financial institutions. These regulations are costly, but without them firms may be encouraged to assume undue risks, such as maintaining low capital reserves, issuing high-risk loans, or adopting aggressive underwriting strategies. Globalization also raises the specter of systemic disruption—a global financial crisis initiated by the failure of financial institutions in one or more countries.[1] With these dueling pressures for competitiveness and stability, it is no wonder that regulators are rarely discussed without mention of their uncomfortable "dilemmas."[2]

In this chapter I develop an analytical framework for explaining the policy positions of the world's most powerful financial regulators toward the creation of international regulatory standards. The framework assumes a simple principal-agent relationship between a legislature (or other elected body) and a regulatory agency.[3] The regulator-as-agent has discretion to enact regulatory policy within certain boundaries implicitly set by the legislature. If the regulator fails to maintain the minimum required levels of financial stability and international competitiveness, it faces legislative intervention or related career costs. The framework demonstrates that exogenous shocks to stability and competitiveness make it difficult for the regulator to satisfy the legislature. In such circumstances, international regulatory harmonization—that is, the creation of an international regulatory standard—becomes an attractive means for the regulator to reclaim its precarious domestic balance between stability and competitiveness. In short, the regulator's precarious domestic position prompts an international solution.

The final step in the explanation—the role of market power—is both critical and uncontroversial. Banking, securities, and insurance are concentrated in a small handful of countries with very powerful regulators. International regulatory harmonization will clearly not occur without the affirmative efforts of these regulators, who control access to their domestic markets and can use their market leverage to impose their regulatory preferences on other countries. I return to this issue at the end of the chapter.

Analytical Framework

There is a considerable literature on the politics of bureaucratic decision making, focusing especially on regulatory agencies. The emphasis of this literature is on explaining the domestic policies of U.S. agencies in light of influences from Congress, voters, industry, and other agencies or branches.[4] The framework presented here borrows some of the fundamental elements of this literature but adds an international dimension. With the globalization of financial markets, regulators have new strategies at their disposal that were never officially sanctioned by elected officials, including the ability to enter into agreements with their foreign counterparts. The potential for international agreements implies that regulators have a new way of working within the constraints on their policymaking.

The analytical framework begins with the observation that elected leaders in the developed world delegate the authority to regulate and supervise the financial industry to regulatory agencies. The delegation of such an important responsibility should come as no surprise: financial regulation requires a level of expertise not commonly found in elected bodies.[5] Moreover, legislatures themselves are not able to devote enough time to supervise the financial sector, given their other policy priorities and the exigencies of electoral politics. In addition, legislatures may have incentives to delegate responsibility as a means of shifting blame in the event of a financial crisis.[6] Clearly, no legislator wants to be held personally accountable for a meltdown in the banking (or securities or insurance) industry.

The legislature's delegation of regulatory responsibility to a regulatory agency results in a principal-agent (PA) relationship.[7] The agency (or the "agent") is generally capable of making frequent modifications to the regulatory environment for firms—such as altering prudential supervisory protocols, tightening capital adequacy rules, and changing reporting requirements—but rarely are these changes prompted by observable pressure from elected officials.[8] However, if the outcome of a regulator's policy choices runs counter to the interests of elected leaders, the legislature—as the principal—can intervene and enact new policies.

Political intervention, in its various guises, is the bane of a regulator's existence.[9] When politicians attempt to influence regulatory policy directly—for example, by holding hearings and publicly criticizing the decisions of regulators, or by legislating new regulations—they threaten the agency's autonomy and prestige.[10] Intervention may also affect regulators' future job prospects, especially for an agency head who is forced to resign. The prospect of intervention by legislators therefore creates *ex ante* constraints on a regulator's range of policy choices, which ensures that the principal can maintain some control over the agent. Regulators will use all strategies at their disposal to minimize the possibility of intervention.

I assume that legislatures will intervene in either of two circumstances. First, a bout of financial instability characterized by firm failures, asset price volatility, or a general crisis of confidence will create enormous pressures on elected leaders to intervene. For example, the collapse of Enron and Worldcom in the United States in 2002 prompted Congress to create a new supervisory body, the Public Company Accounting Oversight Board, which effectively removed a degree of authority from the Securities and Exchange Commission.[11] More generally, legislators feel pressure to reform the regulatory environment when a financial institution fails in their district. Legislatures, in short, demand a certain threshold of stability in the financial sector to appease their constituents.

Second, pressure from the financial sector itself creates incentives for legislative intervention when regulations are deemed too onerous compared to those in foreign jurisdictions. The clamor of financial institutions generally rises soon after the imposition of new regulations, such as the tightening of bank capital requirements in the United States and the United Kingdom in the 1980s (see chapter 4). Increasing competition from foreign countries makes the financial sector especially sensitive to cross-national regulatory differences. The fear of losing jobs, profits, and market share to foreign firms creates strong incentives for legislative intervention. And the preferences of the financial sector—the source of generous campaign contributions and other forms of political support—no doubt weigh heavily on legislators' minds.

To minimize the possibility of legislative intervention, the regulator must take into account the legislature's preferences. Regulations that are too lax (e.g., low minimum capital levels for financial institutions) will ultimately contribute to faltering firms and a crisis of confidence among voters, triggering a swift intervention by elected officials. On the other hand, in an open economy with competitive financial markets, regulations that are too strict will put domestic firms at a competitive disadvantage with foreign firms. No regulator wants to be held responsible for crushing an industry under the weight of onerous regulations. Regulators therefore must walk a fine line between stability and competitiveness. As Ingo Walter notes, "In going about their business, regulators continuously face the possibility that 'inadequate' regulation will result in costly failures, on the one hand, and on the other hand the possibility that 'overregulation' will create opportunity costs in the form of financial efficiencies not achieved, or in the relocation of firms and financial transactions to other regulatory regimes."[12]

Regulators' delicate balancing act creates a limited zone of acceptance—or what can be called a *win-set*—for regulatory policy.[13] If stability or competitiveness falls below certain thresholds, the benefits to the legislature of intervening will outweigh the costs.[14] I derive the win-set in figure 1. The two graphs depict the effects of regulatory stringency on competitiveness and stability, respectively. The horizontal axis on both graphs represents the regulator's realistic range of policy choices, from lax to stringent.[15] For simplicity, I depict each relationship as linear: as regulations become more stringent, competitiveness declines and stability increases. Stability can be thought of as the probability that a firm will collapse as a function of the current regulatory environment. A higher level of stability therefore indicates a lower probability of collapse. Competitiveness refers to the relative costs of conducting business in the financial sector compared with foreign financial sectors, as a function of the current regulatory environment. A higher level of competitiveness indicates a less costly environment.[16] These relationships, of course, do not hold in the extremes: a potentially unstable financial sector will most likely not be a competitive one. However, within a realistic range of regulatory policy choices for developed economies, the simple trade-off depicted in these graphs is reasonable.

The regulator's choice of policy depends on its own preferences vis-à-vis the trade-off between stability and competitiveness. A regulator in one country might be especially inclined toward competitiveness as a result of domestic pressures from politicians and industry or because of some aspect of the institutional environment. Rosenbluth and Schaap (2003), for example, argue that regulators will be biased in favor of stability-enhancing prudential regulation if their political systems create incentives to appeal to the

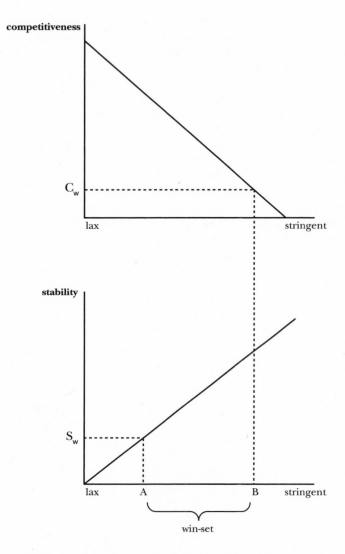

Figure 1. The Trade-off between Stability and Competitiveness:
The Effects of Regulatory Stringency

median voter, as in single-member districts. On the other hand, regulators in countries with "centrifugal" electoral institutions, namely, proportional representation, will be more inclined to acquiesce to the financial sector's interests in regulatory laxity at the expense of broader stability concerns.

Regardless of their initial policy positions, regulators are constrained on both dimensions by the prospect of legislative intervention. In figure 1 the regulator's win-set is demarcated by minimum thresholds for stability (S_w) and competitiveness (C_w) on the vertical axes. These thresholds correspond to regulatory policy choices on the horizontal axis. To maintain a level of competitiveness above C_w, the regulator must enact a policy that is no more stringent than point B, as indicated by the vertical dotted line. Regulations more stringent than B will lead to a loss of market share to foreign firms, triggering political intervention and career costs for the regulator. Similarly, to maintain stability above S_w, the regulator must enact a policy that is no more lax than point A. Regulations to the left of this point will lead to a crisis of confidence in the financial system, triggering a response by the legislature. The space to the right of A and to the left of B represents the regulator's win-set.

The framework thus far assumes that a win-set exists at the status quo. Indeed, if a win-set did not exist, the legislature would not delegate authority to the regulatory agency. The exact size and location of the win-set, however, cannot be generalized across different countries or regulatory environments. Clearly, some regulators have larger win-sets than others, and some regulators are more responsive to financial-sector preferences than others. For example, regulators that are considered "captured" in the Stigler-Peltzman sense will have preferences more in line with the regulated industry and might therefore err on the side of regulatory laxity rather than strict prudential regulation.[17] The importance for this framework is not the status quo characteristics of the win-set but rather the circumstances that lead the win-set to shrink or disappear.

The Win-Set and Exogenous Shocks

When a win-set exists, regulators can use their discretion to set regulatory policy within the threshold points. However, exogenous shocks in the regulator's environment can shift the thresholds toward each other, reducing the size of the win-set or eliminating it altogether. To facilitate a discussion of changes to the win-set, figure 2 transforms the trade-off depicted in figure 1 into a standard indifference-curve diagram. The downward-sloping line is the regulator's feasibility constraint, which shows the possible combinations of stability and competitiveness obtainable for the regulator, given its sole tool of regulatory stringency. Since there is a trade-off between stability and competitiveness, the feasibility constraint slopes downward.[18] Also

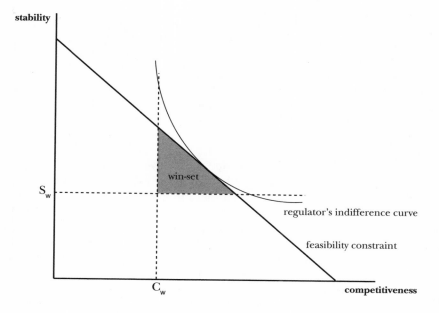

Figure 2. The Regulator's Win-Set

included are the win-set thresholds from figure 1, represented by a point along each axis. To stay within the win-set, the regulator must obtain a level of stability above S_w and a level of competitiveness above (i.e., to the right of) C_w. The shaded region bounded by S_w, C_w, and the feasibility constraint constitutes the win-set. The curved line is the regulator's indifference curve, which represents the combinations of stability and competitiveness that make the regulator equally satisfied. For simplicity, the diagram includes only the indifference curve that is tangent to the feasibility constraint; the point of tangency is the regulator's policy choice.

Exogenous changes to the regulator's environment lead to changes in the size of the win-set. For example, in the event of a high-profile failure of one or more financial institutions, regulators have incentives to enact more stringent regulations simply to reclaim the status quo level of stability. The U.S. savings and loan (S&L) crisis in the late 1980s is representative: as S&Ls throughout the country began to fail, the public became aware that the existing regulatory environment was insufficient to ensure the stability of neighborhood thrifts. Voters were not well informed of the specifics of thrift supervision, but the series of S&L insolvencies made it clear that more stringent regulations were needed to shore up stability. An exogenous shock to stability causes the regulator's feasibility constraint to shift: to maintain the status quo level

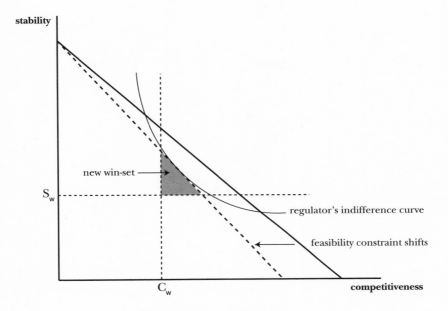

Figure 3. Exogenous Shock to Stability

of stability, the regulator must enact more stringent regulations. Since the enactment of more stringent regulations also adversely affects competitiveness, the feasibility constraint becomes steeper, as shown in figure 3.

Shocks to stability often occur when there are innovations and structural changes in financial markets, resulting in increased risk for financial institutions. In the S&L example, one of the most salient changes was an increase in interest rates, which created tremendous pressure on S&Ls to find higher-yielding assets. Stability shocks may also occur as a result of stock market crashes (if they lead financial institutions to become unstable), fraud and malfeasance, natural disasters, and acts of terrorism.

After an exogenous shock to stability, the win-set shrinks as the feasibility constraint shifts downward. The regulator can no longer obtain the same level of competitiveness for a given level of stability because the shock requires a tightening of regulations. Note also that the legislature's preferences over stability do not change, but the exogenous shock alters the regulatory policy needed to maintain the prior degree of stability.

A similar shrinking of the win-set occurs in the event of a shock to competitiveness. Such a shock would occur if domestic firms incurred an abrupt loss of market share to foreign firms with less stringent regulations. An example is the rise of Japanese banks in the 1980s, facilitated by their relatively

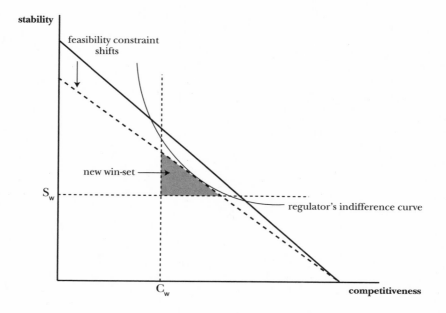

Figure 4. Exogenous Shock to Competitiveness

lax regulations compared with their Western counterparts. The increasing stringency of capital requirements in the United States and the United Kingdom allowed Japanese banks to offer extremely competitive pricing on world markets and therefore to attract a growing share of the market for syndicated lending. An exogenous shock to competitiveness has the effect of flattening the feasibility constraint for the adversely affected domestic financial sector, as shown in figure 4. This shift implies that less stringent regulations—and therefore a lower degree of stability—are required to maintain the prior level of competitiveness. The win-set therefore shrinks, as indicated by the smaller triangular shaded region.

What happens if the regulator faces dual shocks to stability and competitiveness? As depicted in figure 5, the feasibility constraint shifts toward the origin, indicating that it is not possible for the regulator to obtain the status quo levels of stability and competitiveness simultaneously. Dual shocks also increase the probability that the regulator's win-set disappears entirely, as in figure 5. With no win-set, it is not possible for the regulator to obtain the minimum thresholds for stability and competitiveness to ward off political intervention and guard his or her career prospects. Of course, it is theoretically possible that the win-set could disappear based solely on a shock to stability or competitiveness, but the occurrence of the two shocks together

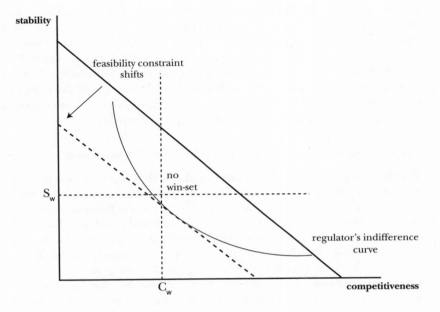

Figure 5. Simultaneous Shocks to Stability and Competitiveness

increases both the magnitude of the shift in the feasibility constraint and the possibility that the win-set will disappear entirely.

The absence of a win-set necessarily implies that the legislature will intervene in some fashion. But it also raises the question how and why the government would intervene if it is impossible to obtain satisfactory levels of stability and competitiveness. Regardless of the constraints on regulators, it may be in elected leaders' best interests to publicly castigate regulators for outcomes deemed unsatisfactory. Regulators can be hauled in front of legislative committees and interrogated, and in some circumstances legislative pressure can lead to their dismissal. Note also that the win-set applies to regulators, not legislatures. Regulators are generally limited to one policy tool—regulatory stringency—to affect stability and competitiveness whereas legislatures have other tools at their disposal: they can enact trade barriers, subsidies, and tax breaks to bolster firm competitiveness, or they can repeal costly legislation such as interest rate ceilings or restrictions on bank lending. These options are not available to regulators. The legislature can also reverse a crisis of confidence in the financial system through a highly publicized change in the structure of the regulatory agency. For example, the legislature can create a new regulatory body with oversight and enforcement powers, such as the Public Company Accounting Oversight Board, created as part of the Sarbanes-Oxley Act of 2002. In more extreme cases, the legislature can abolish an agency entirely and create a new one in its place. Such was the case in the aftermath of the S&L crisis, when Congress dismantled the existing S&L regulator—the Federal Home Loan Bank Board (FHLBB)—and created the Office of Thrift Supervision.[19] It was certainly possible for Congress to institute substantive regulatory changes within the existing FHLBB, but the creation of the OTS constituted a signal to the public of a new, more prudent regulatory environment.[20]

The Shrinking Win-Set and International Regulatory Harmonization

The circumstances depicted in figure 5 indicate that regulators are powerless to protect themselves unless they can create—or, more realistically, *preclude the disappearance of*—a win-set by effecting a shift in the feasibility constraint. Such a shift can be achieved through international regulatory harmonization. If cross-national differences in regulation have competitive implications, then smoothing over these differences affects the competitiveness of firms, either positively or negatively, depending on the stringency of regulations before international harmonization. This is important when domestic firms are losing market share to foreign firms in less stringent regulatory environments. It is also important when shocks to stability require the enactment of more stringent regulations that would put domestic firms at a competitive disadvantage with foreign rivals. If international regulatory harmonization is possible at the more stringent level, then the regulator can bolster stability without harming domestic competitiveness. More generally, a regulator is more likely to seek international regulatory harmonization when its win-set is shrinking due to exogenous shocks. An inability to fend off domestic political pressures leads the regulator to seek an international solution.

Consider the threshold points in figure 5. Ideally, the regulator wishes to increase the stringency of regulations to obtain the minimum stability threshold, S_w, but without harming domestic competitiveness. If the regulator can successfully push for international regulatory harmonization at this more stringent level, then the competitive effects of the more stringent regulations will be minimized. In other words, the feasibility constraint will shift upward—indicating a change in foreign regulations that have competitive implications for domestic firms—thereby creating a viable win-set for regulatory policy. The effects of international regulatory harmonization are depicted in figure 6.

Hypotheses

This analytical framework yields observable implications about regulators' demands for international regulatory harmonization. First, I expect

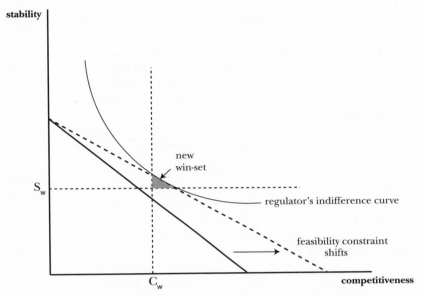

Figure 6. New Win-Set after International Regulatory Harmonization

international regulatory harmonization to be initiated by regulators themselves, not by legislatures. This is an important implication of the principal-
agent framework. Regulators demand global standards as a means of
addressing domestic political pressures. Although the threat of legislative
intervention creates constraints on the regulator, the legislature itself does
not dictate the regulator's strategy. The legislature may in fact express
opposition to an international agreement, as shown in the Basel case in
chapter 4, or remain largely aloof, as in the International Organization of
Securities Commissions (IOSCO) case in chapter 5.

Second, a regulator is more likely to seek international regulatory harmonization when it faces dual shocks to stability and competitiveness. When
less stringently regulated foreign firms are capturing market share from domestic firms, the regulator could enact lax standards in line with the foreign competitor, but such a policy choice would be deleterious in an already
unstable financial environment. International regulatory harmonization addresses the competitive distortions caused by the difference between foreign
and domestic regulations, simultaneously allowing the regulator to bolster
domestic stability. On the other hand, when domestic firms are dominant
and face minimal competition from foreign firms, the domestic regulator
will be unlikely to press for harmonization. The regulator's preference for an
international solution arises out of its position of weakness, not of strength.

The framework presented here is not designed to capture all the nuances of regulatory policymaking in the industrialized world. Rather, it is intended to be broadly applicable to any political environment in which a regulator is granted authority by a popularly elected body. Certain regulators are more insulated from political pressures than others, and not all regulators have the same scope or mandate. These sources of variation are deliberately overlooked by the model in exchange for a more general account of regulatory politics in an international context.

Finally, the analytical framework explains why regulators demand international harmonization, not how they achieve it. Understanding how domestic political and institutional constraints shape preferences is the first step in a more theoretically complete analysis of the circumstances under which regulators will create international standards. Once we understand who wants what and why, we are in a much better position to explain harmonization outcomes using variables such as market power and the coercion of international institutions.[21] In the cases in this book, the final outcomes— a global regulatory standard for banking, a fractious negotiation without resolution for securities, and only nascent efforts at harmonization for insurance—are not particularly puzzling once we understand the preferences of the negotiations' key participants. I focus on explaining the regulatory positions of the world's most powerful financial centers. Thus the importance of market power is implicit in my case selection, and I invoke market power explicitly—and, I believe, uncontroversially—to link preferences to outcomes in each case study.

Methodology and Case Selection

There are many challenges in empirically validating a theory of regulator preferences toward international regulatory harmonization. Unlike the final outcomes of international negotiations—such as the creation of a global standard or a decision to terminate discussions without an agreement—the measurement of what regulators "seek" is not immediately clear. However, a focus on outcomes of negotiations as the dependent variable is not practical at this time. The phenomenon of international regulatory harmonization is quite new in political economic history, and very few negotiations have been formally resolved. There is no doubt that regulators will continue to negotiate international standards with their foreign counterparts and that eventually scholars will develop a database of final outcomes—including whether an international standard was created or not and the substance of the standard. At this time, however, many negotiations are in their early stages, including negotiations over accounting, corporate governance, financial crime, and even capital adequacy. It would simply be premature to explain the variation in the outcomes of these negotiations, especially given the paucity of cases available to analyze.[22]

A focus on regulator preferences as the dependent variable has two main advantages. First, there is significant variation in preferences within cases. In any given set of negotiations, there are generally two or three economically powerful countries (including the United States) whose preferences are particularly salient. The differences in preferences among these participants are critical to our understanding of regulatory cooperation. Second, the domestic circumstances of regulators are generally transparent to all participants in a negotiation, thereby making it very clear where each regulator stands.[23] Regulators' behavior during negotiations, including speeches at meetings and conferences, statements to the press, and the publication of agency position papers, makes it evident whether the regulator is pushing for or resisting an (indeed, *any*) international agreement. In the cases discussed in this book, observers may disagree over the rationale behind regulators' positions, but the positions themselves are not in question.

In the remainder of the book, I explore the consistency of the analytical framework presented here with three cases representing the banking, securities, and insurance industries, respectively. For the banking and securities chapters, I focus on regulators' negotiations over international capital adequacy standards in the late 1980s and early 1990s. The banking negotiations led to the landmark Basel Accord, which remains the most prominent example of international regulatory harmonization and the subject of several articles and book chapters in the political science literature.[24] However, scholars have largely overlooked the parallel negotiations over capital standards for securities firms during the same period. The oversight is not puzzling: securities regulators were not successful in creating a capital standard, and thus the negotiations represent a negative case.[25] For my purposes, the two cases capture across-case and within-case variation and thus are ideal for exploring the observable implications of the analytical framework presented here. In addition to the fact that a standard emerged in banking and not in securities, each case reveals important variation in regulators' preferences for an international standard. In the Basel negotiations the U.S. Federal Reserve and the Bank of England were the primary proponents of a global capital adequacy standard, with the Bank of Japan and the Japanese Ministry of Finance constituting a vocal opponent. In the securities negotiations the United Kingdom's Securities and Investments Board led the charge for an international capital adequacy standard whereas the U.S. Securities and Exchange Commission and the Japanese Ministry of Finance were allied in their opposition.

The final case explores the nascent efforts to create international standards in the insurance industry, focusing in particular on capital requirements for reinsurance firms. Unlike the banking and securities chapters, there is no particular negotiation to analyze. Instead, I focus on insurance regulators' environments in the United States and the United Kingdom (the largest insurance markets) over the past twenty years and on the efforts of regulators to balance the needs for stability and competitiveness when confronted with exogenous shocks.

By exploring three cases involving capital adequacy regulations, I can more easily isolate the variables that drive my argument—exogenous shocks to stability and competitiveness—and hold constant other variables that might otherwise be deemed relevant. Thus the three cases involve regulations designed to minimize the risks borne by financial institutions—specifically, the risk of insolvency due to adverse economic circumstances or management malfeasance. In addition, the cases involve the creation of a global standard that would arguably influence "systemic risk," the risk of cross-border shocks and global financial instability. They therefore provide a convenient test of functionalist arguments that regulators respond to the need for global stability. Finally, the cases focus on efforts to create international standards in the same period, beginning after the breakdown of the Bretton Woods system in the 1970s, so that global macroeconomic conditions are held roughly constant.[26]

The supporting evidence in the cases is bolstered by more than forty interviews with current and former regulators and industry executives in London, Basel, Geneva, and New York from 2002 to 2005. These interviews were off the record except where noted.

On a final note, patterns of international cooperation between any set of actors may be influenced by international institutions and organizations. It would, of course, be ill-advised to examine patterns of multilateral tariff reductions without taking into account the rules set forth in the General Agreement on Tariffs and Trade (GATT) and the dispute-settlement mechanisms of the World Trade Organization (WTO). In the financial regulatory arena, there are a number of international institutions that facilitate regular interactions among regulators. Three in particular—the Basel Committee, IOSCO, and IAIS—are discussed more thoroughly in the chapters that follow, but they are not privileged in the analysis. The international organizations of the transgovernmental regulatory network, including the three addressed in this book, are not constituted by treaty and are not granted agency—legal or otherwise—to act in international affairs.[27] They have skeleton staffs, often consisting of fewer than ten people, and generally exist to facilitate interaction among their members at scheduled intervals throughout the year. To the extent that these organizations help to shape international regulatory outcomes, they are addressed in the analysis. But ultimately, a compelling explanation of regulator behavior must be grounded in domestic politics (including domestic institutions) and the domestic ramifications of globalization.[28]

The detailed case studies are designed to show how the analytical framework can improve our understanding of regulators' decisions in an international context. In each case, I trace the effects of shocks to financial stability and international competitiveness and show how each influences the preferences of regulators in international negotiations over regulatory harmonization. I also demonstrate that regulators themselves are the initiators of harmonization and that elected leaders are important in providing constraints on regulatory policy. In so doing, I also hope to shed light on existing arguments about regulatory cooperation—both the arguments that are supported by the cases and those that require careful reconsideration.

Chapter 4

Banking: The Road to the Basel Accord

In late 1987 central bankers from the Group of Ten (G-10) countries announced the creation of an international capital adequacy standard for commercial banks, now known as the Basel Accord. Scholars have heralded the agreement as a landmark in international financial cooperation and have sought to explain why the agreement was created.[1] Often overlooked in these analyses are the substantial differences in regulator preferences during the negotiations leading up to the accord. The U.S. Federal Reserve Board and the Bank of England were aggressive in their attempts to create an international standard in the face of enormous technical barriers and, more important, stiff resistance from the Japanese Ministry of Finance. The Basel Accord is indeed a prominent example of cooperation between regulators, but the genesis of the agreement was characterized by discord and protest. The stark variation in regulator preferences is the most interesting—and puzzling—aspect of the Basel story.

The goal of this chapter is to explain the preferences of regulators toward international harmonization of bank capital adequacy requirements in the 1980s. Using the framework developed in chapter 3, I argue that regulators sought international regulatory harmonization when two conditions occurred concomitantly: a decline in confidence in the stability of banks due to bank failures, and an abrupt loss of market share to foreign firms facing less stringent regulations. Only under these circumstances did regulators demand international harmonization as a means of enacting sufficiently stringent regulations to shore up financial stability without harming the competitiveness of their domestic financial sectors. For regulatory agencies, seeking an international agreement—and thereby becoming international actors—was a strategy that emerged only after unilateral regulatory adjustments over several years failed to maintain an acceptable balance between stability and competitiveness. My focus in this chapter is on the three countries whose regulators played the most important roles in the story of the Basel Accord: the United States, the United Kingdom, and Japan. These countries also represent the world's largest banking markets. The United States and the United Kingdom both experienced concomitant shocks to financial stability and competitiveness during the 1980s whereas Japan's banking sector grew increasingly competitive and avoided the bouts of instability of its Western rivals.

I begin with an overview of global banking markets in the 1970s, when regulators faced challenges stemming from rising interdependence and international competitiveness. I then analyze in more detail the domestic developments in the United States, United Kingdom, and Japan that determined the stance of each country's regulators toward international harmonization. A pattern emerges in these narratives: regulators continually adjust the stringency of prudential regulations in response to changes in bank stability and competitiveness. Regulators can maintain relatively lax capital requirements as long as banks remain stable. Regulators can counter a possible rise in instability with more stringent regulations, but they must be sensitive to the competitive effects of regulatory changes. Changes in bank legislation—especially deregulation that enhances banks' profitability—can offset the competitive effects of increasing regulatory stringency, but rising instability might require regulatory changes whose competitive implications are too great to bear. As regulators face a shrinking win-set for regulatory policy, they look to the international arena for a solution. I conclude the chapter with a review of the wide-scale criticism of the 1988 capital adequacy agreement and discuss the recent efforts by regulators to create a new global standard—known as Basel II—to address the shortcomings of the original agreement.

Global Banking in the 1970s

The 1970s were a dynamic period for international financial markets. President Nixon effectively ended the Bretton Woods system of fixed exchange rates by closing the gold window in 1971, ushering in an era of exchange rate volatility and increasing capital mobility.[2] Foreign exchange markets grew tremendously as financial institutions and other internationally oriented firms sought to minimize the risks of adverse exchange rate movements—or indeed to profit from them through speculation and arbitrage.

And new financial markets in less developed countries (LDCs), especially in Latin America, began to open their borders to private investment and trade after decades of relative closure.

International banking markets led the way in the evolution of global finance. Between 1964 and 1980, the compounded growth rate of international banking was over 30 percent per year.[3] The world's largest banks were inundated with cash from OPEC member countries after the oil price hikes of 1973 and 1979 and aggressively sought out new clients in the previously insulated LDC markets. The increasing international activity of U.S. banks is telling: between 1970 and 1980 the number of U.S. banks with foreign branches increased from 79 to 159, with total foreign assets increasing from $53 billion to $340 billion.[4]

International credit markets were generally stable in the 1970s. Banks were confident in their ability to gauge sovereign risk without stringent protocols or the "checklists" of creditworthiness common in domestic lending.[5] Indeed, the risks of foreign lending seemed low. Citibank chairman Walter Wriston famously quipped that "countries don't go bankrupt," a statement supported by Citibank's exceptionally small losses on outstanding foreign loans during the decade.[6] But as banks' exposure to the third world grew to unprecedented proportions, public debate gradually began to focus on the vulnerabilities of the banking system to external shocks.[7] Payment difficulties and debt restructurings in Zaire, Peru, and a handful of other LDCs in the mid and late 1970s highlighted the risks of sovereign lending and served as "anticipatory tremors" of the severe debt crisis that would soon follow.[8]

One of the first manifestations of the risks of international banking markets occurred not due to default but instead through a seemingly isolated instance of imprudent foreign exchange trading. In 1974 Bankhaus Herstatt in Cologne, Germany, was declared insolvent by German regulators after it engaged in a series of high-risk foreign exchange plays. In retrospect, the collapse of a bank engaged in foreign exchange trading should have surprised no one. Banks were struggling to adapt to the new system of floating exchange rates after nearly thirty years of relative currency stability. The risk of financial loss to a bank due to currency trading was clear, but banks were lured by the prospect of substantial financial gain. Given bankers' lack of experience in currency speculation and risk management, it was inevitable that at least one bank would make a critical (and ultimately fatal) mistake. But the global financial community was not prepared for what would happen next. After the Herstatt collapse, foreign exchange trading ground to a halt as traders grew concerned that their foreign counterparts would not follow through on their obligations. Banks around the world—such as Morgan Guaranty in the United States and Hill Samuel of the United Kingdom—found themselves in a "payments debacle" and struggled to claim the funds owed to them by Herstatt and other banks.[9]

Trading eventually picked up again, but confidence in the payments system was badly shaken. After the crisis it took more than three years for foreign exchange activity to return to its 1974 peak.[10]

The Herstatt crisis was a jarring lesson for regulators on the potential risks of global banking markets. The crisis came on the heels of a similar occurrence in the United States—the failure of the Franklin National Bank of New York in May 1974—which wreaked havoc on the Eurocurrency markets and made foreign exchange markets even more vulnerable to the Herstatt shock.[11] Regulators had no choice but to emerge from their previously insulated domestic jurisdictions and acknowledge the need for international regulatory cooperation. By the end of the year the central bank governors of the Group of Ten (G-10) industrialized countries (plus Luxembourg) established a committee to address the pressing need for new and better rules for global banking markets.[12] Housed at the Bank for International Settlements (BIS) in Basel, Switzerland, the Standing Committee on Banking Regulations and Supervisory Practices (now called the Basel Committee) took on the task of coordinating and harmonizing the prudential regulations of its eleven member countries. This was no small feat. The second chairman of the Basel Committee, Peter Cooke, notes, "There was, in effect, a supervisory vacuum in this new global market which needed to be filled. Neither the supervisors, nor indeed the banks themselves, had fully appreciated the degree to which the banking environment was changing in character and the new and increasing risks involved in international business. Supervisors were still very much domestically oriented within the framework of different national banking systems."[13]

The domestic orientation of regulators is a constant theme in this analysis. It would be a mistake to imply that the genesis of the Basel Committee was the first in a series of multilateral accomplishments brought about by a group of like-minded regulators to safeguard global financial stability. The impetus for the creation of the committee, in fact, came from the United Kingdom, and its first two chairmen (Sir George Blunden, 1974–76; Peter Cooke, 1977–88) were regulators from the Bank of England. London was the capital of the Euromarkets and hosted a sizable group of foreign banks and subsidiaries. By 1980 foreign banks accounted for more than half of all bank assets in the United Kingdom.[14] Without international regulatory cooperation, London was powerless to monitor and supervise these banks, leaving itself vulnerable to a domestic financial crisis in the event of a foreign bank failure.[15] The Bank of England was understandably resistant to bailing out a large foreign bank, but in the absence of an agreement about international supervisory responsibilities, the bank would have no choice but to serve as the lender of last resort for any institution on its soil. The bank's governor, Gordon Richardson, also wanted an "early warning system" so that regulators could take appropriate measures before a crisis began.[16]

When Governor Richardson proposed the creation of the Basel Committee to the G-10 in 1974, the United States was particularly receptive.[17] Like London, New York was host to a substantial number of foreign banks and therefore shared many of the Bank of England's concerns about supervision and bailout responsibility. The branches and agencies of foreign banks held $38.2 billion in assets in the United States in 1975.[18] Regulators from the United States and United Kingdom also shared an uncomfortable trade-off between battling instability and enhancing the attractiveness of their markets to foreign institutions. London and New York, along with a handful of other financial centers, competed against each other for investment from multinational banks, and London in particular was insistent on maintaining its status as the pinnacle of offshore finance. It was certainly possible for regulators to enact strict regulations to shield their markets from crises in other markets, but unilateral responses would invariably give a competitive advantage to financial entrepôts with less stringent regulations.[19]

With central bankers from the United Kingdom and the United States leading the charge, the Basel Committee worked quickly to reach an agreement on global banking supervision. The secretive committee kept no record of these negotiations, so it is difficult to ascertain the policy positions of the various regulators. However, the vagueness of the resulting agreement, known as the Concordat of 1975, hints at significant underlying discord among the negotiators. The Concordat established a set of rules that central banks should follow in bailing out troubled banks. One of the most important rules is that parent banks should be held responsible for the financial difficulties of their foreign branches, thus absolving the domestic central bank of lender-of-last-resort responsibility.[20] Yet the Concordat does not provide the details and clarity necessary to serve as a viable guide to managing banking crises. Ethan Kapstein notes that the absence of clearly defined rules—such as a protocol for determining when a faltering bank should receive central bank support—renders the agreement ineffective.[21] The central bankers themselves echo the modesty of the accomplishment. In a Bank of England publication, Basel Committee chairman George Blunden downplayed any hope of international regulatory harmonization, instead stating that the goal of committee members was "to learn from each other and adapt the best features of each other's systems for inclusion in our own systems."[22]

The Concordat is significant as the first attempt by regulators to create a regulatory regime for international banking markets. It also marks the emergence of regulators as international actors with institutionalized patterns of communication. During the negotiations over the Concordat, and several times each year from then on, regulators met with their foreign counterparts to share information and expertise, building mutual trust and camaraderie. The importance of this network should not be under-estimated. Joan Spero, writing just a few years after the creation of the Basel Committee, comments, "This contact and trust have made possible an informal but important international early warning system for international banking."[23]

Nevertheless, the importance of this network should not be overesti-mated either. The Basel Committee is not a monolithic actor that proclaims the latest consensus views on banking regulation. The relative secrecy of the committee's meetings hides the enormous degree of dissent among its participants. The vagueness of the Concordat is one reflection of this dis-sent, as is the thirteen-year period that elapsed before the committee's next significant accomplishment, the Basel Accord on Bank Capital Adequacy, in 1988.[24] Regulators might indeed share information in a club-like inter-national network, but they also maintain substantially different regulatory environments in their home jurisdictions. The exigencies of their domestic environments determine their policies at home and their proclivities to-ward international cooperation.

The Growing Trade-off for Regulators

The growth of the worldwide market for commercial banking continued into the 1980s, with banks' activities becoming increasingly global on both the asset and liability sides. On the liability side, banks expanded their networks of foreign branches and attracted increasing amounts of local currency deposits. These foreign branches compete directly with local banks and must lure depositors with competitive prices (i.e., interest rates and fees) or expertise in particular industry niches. On the asset side, banks expanded their lending portfolios through their foreign branches as well as through cross-border lending to private clients and foreign govern-ments. The latter in particular gained importance through the early 1980s as governments sought the help of banks for post–Bretton Woods balance-of-payments financing. Governments also used their clout in the credit mar-kets to secure financing for private and quasi-governmental borrowers such as utilities, airlines, and trading companies.

The international competitiveness of a national banking sector is a function of a variety of factors, including reputation, industry expertise, pricing, and personal connections.[25] The importance of each of these fac-tors depends on the particular banking activity in question. Cross-border lending is driven primarily by relationships between lending officers and borrowers. Banks depend on their branches and affiliates to maintain regular contact with prospective borrowers and to collect information on their changing financial needs. Banks also benefit from referrals from investment banks and financial advisers, thus creating an additional set of relationships that influence a bank's foreign lending revenue. Relationships with other banks are also critical since syndicated credit facilities—involving several banks working in concert—are the most common form of cross-border lending. Pricing, of course, is important for potential borrowers, but the syndication process is generally not characterized by bidding wars by a large number of banks. Clients are interested in maintaining long-term relationships with banks and are more likely to choose banks in which they have existing credit agreements and solid relationships with loan officers rather than banks that offer the lowest prices. But for new clients without these long-standing relationships—especially those in LDCs—competitive pricing by the banks is essential.

In contrast, pricing is always critical for lending to local clients and attracting local currency deposits in foreign branches. The typical individual depositor has every incentive to seek the best interest rates and lowest fees. Individuals can change banks without concern for long-term financial consequences, and even corporate clients must look at bank prices rather than relationships with bank employees as the primary factor in selecting a bank. Foreign branches must therefore attract local depositors by offering competitive interest rates on savings accounts and certificates of deposit, low fees for transactions and account maintenance, and competitive terms for loans and other credit arrangements. Local banks have to follow suit or face a steady decline in their depositor bases.

The battle over prices was exacerbated by the rising threat from non-bank financial institutions, especially money market mutual funds. These alternative investments often offered higher returns than bank savings accounts with a comparable level of stability. In 1986 the ten largest mutual fund managers in the United States had a combined total of more than $350 billion under management, compared with total deposits of just over $1.9 trillion for all commercial banks.[26]

With competitive pressure coming from all sides, commercial banks struggled to maintain their market share. The pressure led to a number of innovations in the banking industry, including the development of "contingent liabilities" that are not delineated in a bank's balance sheet. Examples of these "invisible" items include letters of credit and note issuance facilities, in which banks ensure the availability of credit to clients over a stipulated period of time. Banks also sought higher-yielding assets, which meant extending loans to riskier clients. And to keep prices competitive, they felt pressure to issue more credit as a percentage of their capital bases than ever before. Competitive pressure, it seemed, was also leading to the potential for great instability for banks around the world.

Faced with this turbulent climate for the banking industry, many regulators were worried. Regulations designed to ensure the stability of banks, such as capital adequacy requirements, had the unfortunate side effect of harming banks' competitiveness with foreign rivals unless other countries adopted those requirements as well. Yet if regulators failed to react to the growing possibility of financial instability, the result could be a banking crisis at home and the humiliating political intervention that no doubt would follow.

The 1982 Debt Crisis

The magnitude of the challenges faced by regulators was evident in the 1982 debt crisis, which revealed just how aggressive commercial banks had become in their quest for growth.[27] Mexico alone had borrowed more than $23 billion from U.S. banks, an amount equal to approximately 46 percent of the total capital bases of the top seventeen U.S. banks.[28] When Mexico and other countries in Latin America defaulted on their loans, banks in the United States, the United Kingdom, and Japan were threatened with insolvency. Ultimately, the IMF had to step in to support the faltering economies of the LDCs and enable them to repay their loans.

The debt crisis was no doubt a jarring experience for regulators, and its significance in contemporary economic history should not be underestimated. Lending to LDCs virtually dried up after the crisis, resulting in nearly a decade of economic stagnation for Latin America and other emerging markets. But the importance of the debt crisis in the evolution of bank regulation has been overstated in the literature. Regulators, of course, reacted immediately after the crisis, but over the next few years new changes in banking markets took hold and led to further modifications in the regulatory environment, ultimately leading to varying pressures for international regulatory harmonization some five years later. As John Heimann, former chairman of the U.S. Office of the Comptroller of the Currency (OCC), is fond of saying, "Regulators are like bloodhounds chasing greyhounds."[29] Banking markets change quickly, and it is misleading to assert that the debt crisis was the driving force behind regulatory policymaking for the remainder of the decade.

In 1983, in the immediate aftermath of the debt crisis, the U.S. Congress passed the International Lending Supervision Act (ILSA), which linked an increase in the U.S. IMF quota (required as part of the IMF bailout of the LDCs) with a directive to regulators to impose capital adequacy requirements on U.S. commercial banks. The legislation also stated that regulators should "encourage" foreign regulators to maintain or strengthen the capital bases of their own internationally oriented commercial banks.[30] Some scholars have argued that the passage of the ILSA led directly and ineluctably to the Basel Accord, and they therefore analyze the ILSA's domestic origins to explain international regulatory harmonization.[31] This argument is at best incomplete. First, international regulatory harmonization is not a unilateral phenomenon, notwithstanding the power of the United States. The origins of the ILSA do not speak to the domestic environments in the other major financial markets, especially the United Kingdom and Japan. Second, there is a five-year gap between the passage of the ILSA in 1983 and the creation of the Basel Accord in 1988. During the negotiations over ILSA, Congress was adamantly in favor of new capital adequacy regulations for U.S. banks, arguably reflecting voters' desire to make the banks take responsibility for their lending behavior during the debt crisis.[32] As the Basel Accord was being finalized in late 1987, however, Congress began to vocalize its concerns about the competitive ramifications to U.S. banks of an international capital adequacy standard—and indeed began to speak out *against* the agreement. For example, Congressmen Charles Schumer (D-NY) and Norman Shumway (R-CA) circulated a memo to the House Banking Committee that questioned the competitive implications of the Basel agreement.[33] Schumer in particular stated, "I am concerned that unanticipated and unnecessary effects of the regulations may seriously jeopardize the international competitiveness of American banks."[34] The irony is unmistakable: in 1983 the House Banking Committee mandated the imposition of domestic capital adequacy standards and encouraged international regulatory harmonization through the ILSA, but just five years later that same committee began holding hearings on the competitive implications of the Basel Accord.[35] It seems clear that Congress had strong influence on regulator behavior, but the evidence does not support the assertion that the Basel Accord emerged as a result of a directive in the ILSA.

Moreover, when U.S. regulators broached the subject of capital adequacy standards at a Basel Committee meeting in 1983, other regulators were dismissive.[36] At the time, countries mandated substantially different capital requirements, replete with idiosyncratic measurement techniques and risk management protocols. Regulators could not agree on the definition of *capital,* let alone devise a minimum capital standard. The nascent deliberations in the Basel Committee quickly lost steam. After the U.S. Federal Reserve made its annual legislative report in 1984, legislators also seemed less interested in "encouraging" international harmonization, as they had done in the ILSA.

Another, more common argument is that the debt crisis led to a convergence of views among regulators that bank capital requirements were needed on a global scale; the global "market failure" evidenced by the crisis led to an international agreement to rectify the problem.[37] This argument overlooks the contentiousness of the negotiations leading up to the Basel Accord. As discussed later in this chapter, regulators came to the negotiating table with different preferences over harmonization. The debt crisis may have brought regulators to the table, but other factors must explain the significant variation in their policy positions.

The regulator's trade-off—balancing financial stability and competitiveness—was not of the same magnitude for all regulators either in the wake of the debt crisis or in the months leading up to the Basel Accord. Certain national banking systems remained stable during the 1980s and gained the upper hand in the global competition for bank market share. Other banking systems began to experience shrinking market shares and infringement by foreign competitors as they simultaneously braced for bank failures and a loss of confidence in the banking system. The delicate balance between financial stability and competitiveness determined the decision calculus for regulators.

Rising Instability and Declining Market Share: The United States

Banking markets in the United States suffered a severe bout of instability during the 1980s. There was an extraordinary increase in the number of bank failures, reminiscent of the Great Depression of the 1930s. Between 1980 and 1988 the Federal Deposit Insurance Corporation (FDIC) intervened in nearly one thousand banks to provide financial assistance or to manage their orderly closure.[38] At the same time, banks were quickly losing business to nonbank financial institutions, especially money market mutual funds. Even more troubling was the loss of market share to branches of foreign banks, especially the Japanese. The combination of these factors—declining stability and competitiveness—determined the policy stance of U.S. regulators in the negotiations over a global standard for capital adequacy.

Banking Instability in the 1980s

There is no single cause for the rapid increase in the number of U.S. bank failures during the 1980s.[39] Banks no doubt collapsed for a variety of reasons, including exchange rate volatility, interest rate fluctuations caused by the aggressive anti-inflationary monetary policy of Fed chairman Paul Volcker, imprudent lending and management malfeasance, and the assumption of greater risk as a result of increasing competitive pressures from foreign banks and alternative financial instruments. Volatility in the prices of energy, real estate, and agricultural products also contributed to the overall trend in bank failures.[40]

Proximate causes aside, banks were intrinsically vulnerable to collapse at the beginning of the decade because of their low capital levels. During the 1970s there were no specific minimum capital requirements for banks. Instead, regulators placed banks into "peer groups" and established informal target capital ratios for the banks in each group. Regulators adjusted these targets for individual banks based on their market circumstances and particular needs.[41] With such a loose regulatory burden, bank capital levels steadily declined from the post–World War II period into the 1970s. Capital-to-asset ratios of the large commercial banks declined from approximately 10 percent in the 1950s to less than 4 percent in the mid-1970s.[42] Indeed, the definition of capital was left largely to the discretion of the banks themselves. For example, many banks included subordinated debt—repayable to the bank only after other debts with a higher claim have been satisfied—as an indistinguishable part of their capital bases, along with more permanent forms of capital like common and preferred stock and loan-loss reserves.[43]

Low capital levels, combined with the exogenous changes in banking markets already discussed, made bank failures more likely. Thirteen insured banks failed in 1975, compared with an average of five banks annually for the prior five years (table 1). More important was the size of the banks that failed. A year earlier, in 1974, disbursements from the Federal Deposit Insurance Corporation's deposit insurance fund exceeded $2.4 billion, more than the combined total for the prior twenty years. By the end of the decade it was becoming common to see FDIC disbursements in excess of $500 million annually, indicating that the nation's larger, more established banks were not immune from insolvency due to mismanagement or adverse economic changes.

The increasing incidence of bank failures was not lost on bank regulators. But the benefits to stability of any regulatory reaction had to be weighed against the costs to competitiveness, especially in light of the precarious market position of banks at the beginning of the 1980s. In 1978 Congress created the Federal Financial Institutions Examination Council (FFIEC) to develop uniform prudential regulations across the three commercial bank regulators: the Federal Reserve Board, the Office of the Comptroller of the Currency, and the Federal Deposit Insurance Corporation.[44] The FFIEC established a task force in 1979 to study the issue of uniform capital adequacy standards, but the banking industry was aggressive in its opposition to any attempt to codify capital requirements.[45] The OCC, which was contemplating a stricter definition of capital that would exclude subordinated debt, abandoned its effort in 1980 as a result of this opposition and even *eased* its informal capital requirements for the banks under its jurisdiction.[46] Nevertheless, regulators could not remain quiescent for long in light of the growing instability of the national banking system. In December 1981 the three U.S. bank regulators announced a set of formal guidelines for capital adequacy for the banks under their jurisdictions, with the notable exception of the politically powerful multinational banks.[47] The FDIC adopted a

TABLE 1.
U.S. Bank Failures and FDIC Disbursements, by Year,
1965–1997

Year	Failed banks	Disbursements (thousands of dollars)
1997	1	25,546
1996	5	169,397
1995	6	717,799
1994	13	1,224,797
1993	41	1,797,297
1992	122	14,084,663
1991	127	21,412,647
1990	169	10,816,602
1989	207	11,445,829
1988	280	12,163,006
1987	203	5,037,871
1986	145	4,790,969
1985	120	2,920,687
1984	80	7,696,215
1983	48	3,807,082
1982	42	2,275,150
1981	10	888,999
1980	11	152,355
1979	10	90,351
1978	7	548,568
1977	6	26,650
1976	16	599,397
1975	13	332,046
1974	4	2,403,277
1973	6	435,238
1972	1	16,189
1971	6	171,646
1970	7	51,566
1969	9	42,072
1968	3	6,476
1967	4	8,097
1966	7	10,020
1965	5	11,479

Source: Based on FDIC 1998, 66.

simple minimum equity capital-to-asset ratio of 5 percent; the OCC and the Fed adopted more complicated rules based on different types of capital and different sizes of banks.[48] These rules constituted the first formal capital requirements in the history of U.S. banking.

Despite the early efforts of regulators, bank failures continued to rise into the 1980s. More than forty banks failed in 1982, and this number increased dramatically over the following years (see table 1). Regulators responded by cautiously tightening capital adequacy requirements every two or three years in spite of stiff resistance from the banking industry. In 1983 this resistance was manifest in a court case against the OCC itself. The First

National Bank of Bellaire challenged the OCC's authority to impose capital requirements, arguing that the regulator was infringing on the bank's ability to govern itself based on its own management expertise and was harming its profitability.[49] The courts agreed with Bellaire, but Congress quickly reestablished the authority of the OCC (and the FDIC and Fed) to impose capital requirements in the 1983 ILSA. The ILSA also legislated more stringent capital requirements than were announced by the three regulators in 1981, largely as a result of the 1982 debt crisis.[50] Included under these new requirements were the large multinational banks, which had previously been successful in lobbying for exemptions from all formal capital requirements.[51]

The next round of tightening by the regulators occurred in 1984–85 in the wake of the failure of Continental Illinois, then the seventh largest bank in the United States.[52] Continental was arguably the most important bank failure in recent U.S. history, and it set the terms for the "too big to fail" debates that continue to this day.[53] The bank had a high concentration of loans to Penn Square Bank, which itself failed in 1982, and a generally aggressive loan portfolio.[54] Rumors began to circulate about Continental's health, eventually leading to an electronic bank run in May 1984—what former FDIC chairman Irvine Sprague calls "the premier run of all time."[55] An FDIC account of the Continental failure states: "As the situation continued to deteriorate, bank regulators were faced with a potential crisis that might envelop the entire banking system."[56] The FDIC was forced to step in with a $4.5 billion rescue package, and the Federal Reserve provided ongoing liquidity support.

Congress was not pleased. The House Banking Committee summoned Comptroller of the Currency Todd Conover and his staff to testify on the collapse of Continental and to explain to the public why regulators allowed the bank to get itself into serious financial trouble. In the days before the hearing Conover braced himself for a tongue-lashing by committee chairman Fernand St. Germain and even arranged to have the hearing videotaped to demonstrate to his employees that he would not "sell them out under fire."[57] The regulators were harshly criticized for their lax supervision, St. Germain calling the OCC "timid" in its regulatory approach.[58]

In response to the Continental failure, the three regulators developed a consensus on the issue of capital requirements and imposed a new minimum capital ratio of 6 percent for banks of all sizes.[59] The Fed announced that most large banks, such as those of Continental's size, would be forced to raise additional capital to meet the new requirements.[60] But even these more stringent regulations were not enough to stem the tide of bank failures. Banks continued to engage in off–balance sheet activities and to make riskier (and higher-yielding) loans in real estate and other areas to make up for the costly capital regulations. More banks failed in the 1985–87 period than in the prior thirty years combined, resulting in Bank Insurance Fund disbursements totaling nearly $13 billion.

The banking sector was on the verge of a major crisis. The FDIC was able to cover all depositors in failed banks, but its insurance fund was at risk of insolvency. Beginning in 1984, the FDIC experienced a shortfall between provisions for insurance losses and annual deposit insurance, and in 1988 it experienced its first operating loss in its history.[61] Price-to-earnings ratios for the large money-center banks declined steadily throughout the 1980s, in part due to investors' fears of bank failures and widespread instability.[62] Congress also began to pay closer attention. A bill was introduced in the House of Representatives in 1986 to facilitate the acquisition of failing banks by healthy banks. One proponent of the legislation stated on the House floor that he was "convinced that a serious crisis could develop" unless steps were taken to mitigate the effects of bank failures.[63] Other members of Congress worried about voters' loss of confidence in the safety of their deposits, with one member warning that the "eyes of federally insured depositors are on us."[64]

Maintaining the Balance: The Competitiveness Problem

The narrative thus far indicates a simple pattern of increasing instability, evidenced by the rising tide of bank failures, accompanied by countervailing increases in regulatory stringency. With the exception of the ILSA, regulators enacted tighter capital requirements without the explicit intervention of Congress. As banks assumed more and more risk, regulators responded by imposing greater capital requirements to prevent insolvency and to decrease the probability of a wide-scale financial crisis. Such constant adjustment was in the best interests of regulators, who did not want to preside over an unstable banking market and risk legislative intervention and public humiliation. The decision to enact more stringent regulations, however, is not an easy one in any circumstances. Regulators had to weigh the benefits of stringency against the costs to bank profitability and competitiveness. Throughout the first half of the 1980s important changes in bank legislation made it easier for regulators to obtain a balance between stability and competitiveness. However, by the mid-1980s a rising competitive threat from Japanese banks accompanied by a steady trend toward disintermediation and alternative investments created an environment in which regulators were hard-pressed to maintain stability without harming bank profitability. It was precisely this environment that led U.S. regulators to seek international regulatory harmonization for capital adequacy.

Soon after the OCC's unsuccessful attempt to issue formal capital adequacy requirements in 1980, Congress—in an unrelated move—passed the Depository Institutions Deregulation and Monetary Control Act

(DIDMCA). The law provided for the gradual removal of Regulatory Q ceilings on interest rates for deposit accounts, in effect since the 1930s. The original intent of Regulation Q was to limit the intense competition between banks that contributed to the banking crisis of the Great Depression, but in more recent times its effect was simply to hinder banks' competitiveness with mutual funds and other investments. With the DIDMCA in place, banks could offer negotiable order of withdrawal (NOW) accounts and set more competitive interest rates to maintain their customer bases.[65] The law also increased the FDIC's deposit insurance limit from $40,000 to $100,000. These new regulations were welcomed by the banking industry since they helped to keep banks on equal footing with money market funds and other competitors.

Two years later, in 1982, Congress passed the Garn St-Germain Depository Institutions Act, which went a giant step further by allowing banks themselves to offer money market deposit accounts. The act represented an aggressive effort by the legislature to maintain the profitability of the nation's banks. Also included in the law was the removal of statutory limitations on real-estate lending and an easing of the restrictions on loans to one borrower from 10 percent of a bank's capital to 15 percent.[66]

Both these acts are part of the trend toward deregulation of the banking system and helped banks to become more profitable in a highly competitive environment. They also made the more stringent capital requirements of the early and mid-1980s more palatable for the banks. With the dismantling of long-standing restrictions on banks' activities, banks were in no position to resist new prudential regulations on the basis of competitive concerns. As instability increased in the early part of the decade, the decision by regulators to impose tighter capital requirements was not unduly hindered by fears of competitive consequences. Congressional action proved to be instrumental in helping regulators to maintain the balance between stability and competitiveness.

Although competitive pressures continued into the second part of the decade, Congress was largely quiescent. An FDIC study of banking in the 1980s concludes that 1982–86 was a period of "legislative stalemate" that produced no new banking legislation.[67] The stalemate was broken in 1987, but the legislation that followed was concerned with the savings and loan crisis and not with the health of commercial banks.[68] Regulators were therefore forced to maintain the balance between stability and competitiveness on their own, and they had to be particularly sensitive to the changing economic environment.

In the latter half of the decade the most salient change was the rising threat from Japanese banks. According to the *American Banker*, by 1987 Japan had nine of the ten largest banks (based on assets) in the world, up from just two banks five years earlier (see table 2). More important,

TABLE 2.
Ten Largest Banks in the World, 1982 and 1987 (millions of U.S. dollars)

Bank	Dec. 1982 total assets	Bank	Dec. 1987 total assets
1. Bank of America	111,897	1. Dai-ichi Kangyo Bank	345,027
2. Banque Nationale de Paris	107,949	2. Sumitomo Bank	322,484
3. Citibank	101,268	3. Fuji Bank	313,115
4. Credit Agricole	96,719	4. Mitsubishi Bank	309,247
5. Barclays	95,064	5. Sanwa Bank	297,708
6. Credit Lyonnais	94,979	6. Industrial Bank of Japan	238,477
7. National Westminister Bank	87,724	7. Norinchukin Bank	229,966
8. Dai-ichi Kangyo Bank	87,193	8. Credit Agricole	214,879
9. Societe Generale, Paris	84,186	9. Tokai Bank	208,281
10. Fuji Bank	84,002	10. Mitsui Bank	192,183

Source: Based on *American Banker* 1989, 128.

the United States was home to a growing number of branches of Japanese banks. Between 1981 and 1988, Japanese branches in the United States experienced a 315 percent increase in total assets, with the most dramatic growth between 1985 and 1988 (table 3). Japanese banks held 8.7 percent of U.S. banking assets at year-end 1986, up from 5 percent in 1982.[69] And in 1985 Japanese international lending outpaced U.S. lending for the first time ever.[70] The growing influence of Japanese banking coincided with a larger trend of foreign direct investment in the United States. Newspapers and magazines were full of articles bemoaning the loss of U.S. sovereignty to Japanese firms; indeed, "Japan-bashing [had] become something of an American pastime."[71]

The rise of Japanese banks created a dilemma for regulators. U.S. bank instability continued to grow, with bank failures becoming even more frequent in the latter part of the 1980s. In a typical example of "bloodhounds chasing greyhounds," regulators almost immediately proclaimed that the new capital requirements announced in 1984–85 were inadequate to counter U.S. banks' increasingly risky lending portfolios.[72] Largely in response to the stringent capital requirements, the leading banks began to shift their international lending activities off their balance sheets through the use of note issuance facilities (NIFs), which ensure borrowers of the availability of funds for a set duration (usually five to seven years).[73] Banks also participated in the market for derivatives, including interest rate and currency swaps, which did not require capital backing. A Federal Reserve Bank of New York study reported a significant increase in the ratio of loan commitments—including NIFs—to adjusted assets (on–balance sheet items) for the top nine U.S. banks. This ratio increased from 35 percent to 43 percent between 1982 and 1985, indicating a substantial shift toward off–balance sheet activity in a short amount of time.[74] Regulators were eager to rein in the banks and avoid any further instability in the banking sector, but they were

TABLE 3.
Location of Assets of Japanese Banks, 1981–1988 (billions of U.S. dollars)

Year ending December	Assets in offices in Japan	Assets in foreign branches		
		Total	U.K.	U.S.
1981	791	233	134	74
1982	811	310	161	97
1983	908	350	178	108
1984	926	421	194	131
1985	1,339	600	257	151
1986	1,927	837	359	208
1987	2,854	1,090	426	252
1988	3,044	1,120	445	307
% Increase				
1981–88	285	381	232	315
1984–88	229	166	129	134

Source: Based on Terrell, Dohner, and Lowrey, 1990.

forced to consider the competitive effects of tighter capital requirements in light of the rise of Japanese banks.

The three regulatory agencies began to study the available options for mitigating the risk of off–balance sheet items and ultimately focused their attention on so-called risk-based capital standards. Under such standards the size of the required capital cushion would be determined by the risk level of a bank's lending activity, both on and off the balance sheet. Regulators would assign each asset or lending activity a "risk weight" based on the probability of default or financial loss. The goal was to encourage banks to hold lower-risk assets, such as government bonds or loans to established corporations, and to discourage the use of riskier off–balance sheet activities.[75] In January 1986 the three agencies officially announced their intention to develop risk-based capital standards and hinted that a final proposal could be ready as early as October.[76] But in a situation reminiscent of the OCC's early efforts at setting more stringent standards in 1980, the major commercial banks were adamantly opposed to the new risk-weighting scheme. Banks already felt that they were at a competitive disadvantage compared with the Japanese, and the extra capital required by the new rules would exacerbate those competitive pressures. A study by Salomon Brothers indicated that the inclusion of standby letters of credit—an example of an off–balance sheet item—in a bank's on–balance sheet assets would decrease the capital ratios of twelve money-center banks by 11 percent.[77] In other words, the new risk-weighting rules would require a substantial increase in the capital bases of most large banks. Banks were particularly concerned that the risk-weighted rules would require them to increase their prices for standby letters of credit. In a 1986 letter to the Federal Reserve Board,

Edward L. Yingling, director of government relations for the American Bankers Association, wrote: "Commercial banks will see this traditionally high credit quality business being provided by others whose capital levels are more attuned to market reality than regulatory edict."[78] Reflecting on these regulatory developments later, Gerald Corrigan, of the New York Fed, said, "We, the Fed . . . had moved farther and faster on that issue than others might have liked."[79]

In principle, members of the banking community were in favor of risk-weighted capital rules, which were seen as far less crude than the capital-asset ratios required under existing regulations. Certain banks, especially small community banks, would actually be able to hold *less* capital under the new regulations.[80] But many banks, with their eyes on their international competition, feared a loss of business to their less-capitalized Japanese rivals. In 1986 Citicorp had a capital-to-asset ratio of 4.73 percent whereas Japan's Dai-Ichi Kangyo, Sumitomo, and Fuji had ratios of 2.38 percent, 2.89 percent, and 2.95 percent, respectively.[81] Given the high opportunity cost of holding capital rather than lending it out, it is clear that Japanese banks would have higher operating expenses if they were to hold the same level of capital as their U.S. competitors.[82] In fact, major Japanese banks would have to raise an additional $20–30 billion to meet the new risk-weighted capital rules.[83] On the differences between U.S. and Japanese regulations, FDIC chairman William Seidman said, "Especially on how much capital a bank must keep on hand, our banks have much stricter rules, which can affect international market share."[84]

With confidence in the banking system faltering with each new bank failure, and a rising competitive threat from Japanese banks, regulators sought to bring the U.S. banking market back into balance through international regulatory harmonization. The strategy was simple: push for a global capital adequacy standard based on the risk-weighted framework, thereby stemming the rising tide of bank failures while mitigating the competitive implications of more stringent regulations.

In summary, U.S. regulators faced a shrinking win-set for regulatory policy. Shocks to stability continued throughout the 1980s as banks failed at an alarming rate, prompting regulators to enact more stringent prudential regulations unilaterally. However, shocks to U.S. competitiveness due to the rise of the Japanese banking sector exacerbated the costs to domestic banks of tighter capital rules. It was becoming increasingly difficult for regulators to choose a regulatory policy that would satisfy the competing needs for stability and competitiveness. This shrinking win-set prompted U.S. regulators to demand an international capital adequacy standard.

In its push for international regulatory harmonization, the United States was fortunate to have an ally in the United Kingdom, which favored harmonization for very similar reasons. Analogous developments in the United ·

Kingdom led to an Anglo-American alliance in the quest for a global capital standard.

Parallel Developments: The United Kingdom

Before 1979 there was essentially no formal regulatory apparatus for the prudential supervision of banks in the United Kingdom.[85] The Bank of England (hereafter "the Bank") granted banks a high degree of independence, delegating informal supervisory responsibility to self-regulatory organizations and banking associations. However, the Bank used "moral suasion" to exercise its oversight authority when necessary. If a bank's behavior deviated from expected practice, the governor of the Bank would send a polite note to the institution's management team which spelled out the proper way of conducting business; and indeed, "no banker in his right mind would buck the Bank of England."[86] Nevertheless, the Bank's relatively lax regulatory environment was said to augment British banks' international competitiveness and ability to adapt to changing market conditions.[87]

The Bank's approach to supervision in the 1970s was far more laissez-faire than the regulatory regime in the United States. The Bank, in fact, did not have a working definition of a "bank," and there was no law or statutory regulation that established the parameters of banking as a business.[88] But the emergence of increasingly stringent prudential regulations in the United Kingdom mirrors the developments in the United States after 1980. The first relevant catalyst for regulatory reform in the United Kingdom was the secondary banking crisis of 1973–75.[89] Secondary banks, also known as "fringe banks" because of their lack of formal recognition by the Bank, suffered a liquidity crisis as a result of imprudent lending decisions and changing macroeconomic conditions. These banks made the classic mistake of borrowing short to lend long without sufficient regard for their liquidity, and they found themselves in serious financial trouble after the government tightened its monetary policy in late 1973.[90] With the secondary banking markets facing imminent collapse, the Bank was concerned about the possible repercussions to the rest of the banking system, including a wide-scale crisis of confidence.[91] It should be no surprise that the Bank's response—along with its "lifeboat" rescue operation of the fringe banks—was to implement more stringent supervisory standards. In 1974, as the crisis was unfolding, the Bank enacted stiffer reporting requirements for all banks and nonbank deposit-taking institutions, which included quarterly reporting of balance sheet data and details on the maturity structure of assets and liabilities.[92] The Bank also increased the formality and frequency of its examinations, which included detailed interviews with bank managers.

Despite these changes, the Bank still did not have statutory authority to supervise the banking sector. The secondary banking crisis highlighted a gaping hole in the United Kingdom's supervisory framework, which was ultimately addressed by the Banking Act of 1979. The act established an authorization process whereby deposit-taking institutions were required to secure a license from the Bank. All authorized banks were then subject to mandatory examinations by regulators. The Bank's supervisory authority finally had the force of law. The actual regulatory regime, however, was arguably no more stringent than during the mid-1970s. One observer noted that the Banking Act of 1979 simply enabled the Bank "to do formally what it had done traditionally informally."[93]

More significant tightening of prudential regulations occurred over the following decade in response to increased bank instability. The formalization of the Bank's supervisory responsibilities proceeded in 1980 with a published statement on bank capital adequacy that established a new "risk-asset ratio" to guide banks' lending activity. This ratio, calculated by assigning capital requirements to groups of assets (i.e., loans and other activities) based on risk to the bank, was the precursor to the U.S. risk-weighting system proposed in 1985–86. Included in these groups of assets were certain contingent liabilities (i.e., off–balance sheet items) such as guarantees and other financing commitments.[94] The new capital requirements were resisted by the banks themselves, which feared a loss of flexibility and competitiveness.[95] Largely as a result, the Bank published the capital requirements as guidelines only and did not prescribe minimum numerical ratios.[96]

Within four years, however, the Bank was reconsidering just how flexible it should be in its supervisory role. The event that shaped the regulatory environment in the United Kingdom during this period was the failure of Johnson Matthey Bankers Limited (JMB) in October 1984.[97] JMB, one of only a select few officially recognized gold dealers in London, had an important position in the bullion market.[98] In 1981 JMB embarked on an aggressive plan to expand the nonbullion side of its business and became heavily involved in real estate and trade finance. Its nonbullion lending increased from £50 million in 1981 to £500 million in early 1984.[99] If this increase in lending had been diversified across a broad range of borrowers, JMB would have been able to ride out any instability in the market. However, the bank's managers made the unfortunate mistake of lending to a small number of clients; one customer received a loan equal to 76 percent of JMB's capital base.[100] When JMB's debtors ran into financial trouble, the bank extended more loans to them and ultimately found itself insolvent.

When details of the JMB affair emerged, confidence in the banking markets was badly shaken, and the public began to pay attention to the arcane issue of bank regulation.[101] The press wondered how regulators could allow a well-regarded financial institution to "get so close to the brink."[102] The Bank of England provided a substantial rescue package, arguing that JMB's collapse would have deleterious consequences for the gold market.[103] Regulators were also concerned that the failure of Continental Illinois in the United States earlier in the year had already jarred global banking markets and that the collapse of JMB would exacerbate an already uncertain domestic banking sector.[104]

The Bank of England found itself in an embarrassing situation, and the future of the Bank's leaders was in doubt. Deputy governor Christopher McMahon was up for another five-year term in late 1984, but the government was reportedly reconsidering his reappointment because of criticism of the Bank's role in the JMB affair.[105] One observer noted that the "row over the handling of JMB erupted into some of the worst-tempered scenes witnessed at Westminster for some years."[106] Under intense pressure from Parliament the chancellor of the exchequer established a committee to investigate the JMB affair and to pinpoint where the Bank of England went wrong.[107] In 1985 the committee issued a report with thirty-four recommendations, many of which found their way into the landmark Banking Act of 1987. Among other things, the act removed the arbitrary distinction between "recognized banks" and other deposit-taking institutions and established a Board of Banking Supervision within the Bank.[108] This new oversight board, consisting of six independent representatives from the banking sector, was tasked with assisting the Bank in its regulatory responsibilities by "providing it with direct access to senior practitioners in the fields of law, accountancy, and commercial banking."[109] The creation of the board was a public rebuke to the historically revered "Old Lady of Threadneedle Street" (as the Bank was commonly called) and created considerable tension between the Bank's staff and Parliament.[110]

Although the Banking Act of 1987 caused embarrassment for the Bank, it did not legislate significant changes in prudential requirements. Instead, its focus was on the process of supervision within the Bank itself. The act required an increase in the number of accountants in the Bank's supervision department and mandated close contact between supervisors and audit committees.[111] The Bank retained discretion over the establishment of capital adequacy guidelines and even over exposure requirements (a primary source of JMB's financial difficulties). But the Bank did not need legislative prompting to effect a change in its own capital adequacy requirements. The shock to stability in the banking system triggered a reevaluation of the Bank's capital adequacy guidelines. In 1985 the Bank modified the 1980 capital framework to include note-issuance facilities with other forms of contingent liabilities, explicitly leaving open the possibility of further refinements in capital rules in the short term.[112]

After this bout of regulatory tightening, the Bank found itself in another difficult situation. The JMB affair left it struggling to reclaim its reputation for maintaining stability and eager to avoid further political intervention. However, the resulting regulatory stringency had substantial ramifications for the competitiveness of British banks. Christos Hadjiemannuil notes:

> By the mid-1980s, the Bank had adopted internally an uncompromising stance, which was reflected in the formalisation and retrenchment of the risk-based measurement; at the same time, however, it was anxious to protect the competitiveness of the British banking industry. Its increasingly strict requirements had put U.K.-incorporated banks at a disadvantage even in the domestic markets, because the supervision of the capital adequacy of overseas banks was normally left to their home authorities.[113]

The Bank felt these competitive pressures directly through intense resistance by the banks to the new off–balance sheet requirements. Bank executive director Brian Quinn said of this set of requirements, "We couldn't get it moving."[114]

At this point the Bank's capital requirements were comparable in stringency with those in the United States, and Citicorp and Barclays had nearly equivalent capital-asset ratios.[115] However, as discussed earlier, Japanese banks operated under less stringent regulations and were encroaching on the market share of the British banking sector. Between 1981 and 1988 Japanese branches in the United Kingdom experienced a 232 percent increase in assets (see table 3). More important, Japanese branches were responsible for a growing proportion of banking assets in the United Kingdom: 13.5 percent, or roughly £41 billion, in 1980, and 26.6 percent, or approximately £242 billion, by 1986 (table 4). The data on particular markets within the United Kingdom are more telling. Between 1983 and 1988 the Japanese market share for lending to U.K. residents increased from 5 percent to 8 percent, with much steeper increases for specific target markets such as

TABLE 4.
Distribution of Total Bank Assets in the United Kingdom,
1980–1988 (billions of pounds)

	1980	1981	1982	1983	1984	1985	1986	1987	1988
U.K.	128.9	169.0	209.2	242.5	271.4	283.0	324.9	352.6	399.8
(% share)	(42.5)	(39.8)	(38.7)	(38.4)	(35.7)	(37.1)	(35.8)	(38.4)	(39.3)
U.S.	60.0	78.3	96.5	102.9	116.3	99.8	99.2	93.1	96.7
(% share)	(19.8)	(18.5)	(17.9)	(16.3)	(15.3)	(13.1)	(10.9)	(10.1)	(9.5)
Japan	40.8	70.1	99.4	122.9	167.6	178.1	241.7	225.8	245.9
(% share)	(13.5)	(16.5)	(18.4)	(19.5)	(22.1)	(23.4)	(26.6)	(24.6)	(24.2)

Source: Based on Fisher and Molyneux 1996, 272. Figures as of December of each year.

TABLE 5.
Total Lending to U.K. Residents by Japanese Banks, 1983 and 1987

Borrower	Market share (%), 1983	Market share (%), 1987
Securities dealers[a]	—	27
Building societies	14	34
Other financial services	6	11
Wholesale distribution[b]	31	37
Manufacturing	3	4
Construction	1	6
Property companies	—	4
Water supply	—	34
Energy companies	13	13
Government services	18	30
Total	5	8

Source: Derived from Bank of England data (available at www.bankofengland.co.uk).
[a] Includes Japanese-owned securities firms and merchant banks.
[b] Includes U.K. offices of Japanese trading companies and wholesale distribution arms of Japanese exporters.

government services and financial institutions (table 5). Indeed, by 1987 Japanese banks were responsible for approximately one-third of all lending to U.K. entities in the areas of water supply, building societies,[116] and wholesale distribution. On a global scale, the rankings (based on total assets) of British behemoths such as Barclays and National Westminster fell precipitously as the Japanese banking sector flourished. In 1981 Barclays and National Westminster ranked sixth and tenth in the world, respectively, but by 1988 they had fallen to fourteenth and seventeenth.[117]

With Japanese banks on the rise in the United Kingdom, the Bank found itself unable to balance stability and competitiveness. Stringent capital standards were necessary to maintain the stability of the domestic banking sector, especially in light of banks' increasing involvement in off–balance sheet lending and other high-risk activities. But these same standards were contributing to a loss of market share to less-capitalized Japanese banks. There was a simple, although potentially difficult, solution: push for international harmonization of capital requirements at the United Kingdom's stringent level. Fortunately for the Bank, regulators in the United States, who were in essentially the same position, were eager to combine forces and make progress toward a global capital standard.

Japanese Resistance and Acquiescence

For purely domestic reasons, the United States and the United Kingdom were each eager to adopt a global capital standard. The American and

British regulators learned of their mutual interest during their regular meetings in Basel and through personal connections.[118] Fed chairman Paul Volcker and his U.K. counterpart, Bank of England governor Robin Leigh-Pemberton, met in late 1986 to discuss their shared concerns about bank capital and were surprised to learn of the "fortuitous alignment of conditions" in their domestic economies that made a bilateral agreement feasible and practical.[119] The two regulators and their staffs quickly devised a capital standard that met each of their needs and announced the bilateral agreement in January 1987. The standard included a common definition of capital and a framework of risk-weighting based on five categories of assets.

The Japanese Ministry of Finance (MOF) was alarmed at these developments.[120] Unlike the banking markets in the United States and the United Kingdom, the Japanese banking sector was a rising star in the world economy and was quickly acquiring market share in the West.[121] Moreover, Japanese banks were historically quite stable. In general, when a Japanese bank found itself in financial difficulty, the MOF and the Bank of Japan stood ready to provide funds or arrange the orderly acquisition of the bank's assets by another financial institution.[122] At the time of the negotiations, no bank in Japan had ever failed and no depositor had lost a single yen.[123] The MOF therefore felt no need to tighten its capital requirements. It faced no exogenous shocks to stability, which was likely at an all-time high as Japanese banks ascended the ranks of the world's largest financial institutions without any sign of instability. Elected leaders therefore had no reason to galvanize and demand more stringent regulations. And as the narrative thus far has already shown, the Japanese faced no exogenous shocks to competitiveness—indeed, the Japanese banking sector was at its competitive zenith. In short, the MOF had a viable win-set for regulatory policy and had no desire for international regulatory harmonization. As one MOF member recalled, "Japanese banks were not interested," and some Japanese bankers thought the Anglo-American agreement was another example of Japan-bashing.[124]

Regulatory developments in Japan in the 1970s and 1980s show a marked absence of the U.S. and U.K. patterns of rising instability matched with increasingly stringent prudential regulations. This is not to say that the MOF adopted a laissez-faire approach. Indeed, the absence of instability in the Japanese market is attributable to the MOF's routine intervention in management decisions and its refusal to allow banks to collapse.[125] Jennifer Amyx notes that the so-called convoy approach to regulation limited competition within the sector, encouraged labor-market stability, and ensured that politicians had little reason to worry about bank failures within their constituencies.[126] The result was that capital adequacy requirements could stray toward laxity without leading to bank failures, since the MOF's safety net would cover up any overt signs of instability.

Throughout the contemporary period the MOF faced significant difficulty in tightening prudential regulations in those rare times when bank instability threatened to become a public issue. One prominent example is the Banking Act of 1982. In the late 1970s the MOF imposed a net-worth-loan rule (a restriction on the amount a bank could loan to one customer) in response to aggressive bank lending in the wake of the 1970s oil shocks.[127] But in the absence of legal authority or sanctioning power, the MOF was powerless to enforce compliance, and banks such as Mitsui openly defied the regulation.[128] In the initial banking law proposed to the Diet in 1980, the MOF requested legal authority to enforce the loan rule. The banking sector vocalized its opposition to the Diet, however, and the MOF's legal authority was quickly excised from the law. Moreover, the MOF's initial net-worth-loan rule of 20 percent was statutorily changed to 25 percent, representing a considerable easing of the regulation.[129]

With this background of historically flexible prudential regulations, Japanese banks were resistant to the imposition of the new risk-weighted capital standard set forth in the Anglo-American agreement of 1987.[130] U.S. and U.K. regulators made it clear that the bilateral agreement was not meant to stand in isolation; rather, it was intended to spur the Basel Committee into promulgating a multilateral capital standard based largely on the Anglo-American formula.[131] The regulators pursued direct talks with the MOF and the regulators of other G-10 countries in an attempt to curry support for the capital standard, pressuring the Basel Committee to respond with a multilateral agreement of its own. Most of this effort was aimed at the Japanese. Gerald Corrigan, head of the New York Federal Reserve during the Basel negotiations, stated bluntly, "The single item on which I place the greatest emphasis relates to . . . the goal of moving Japanese bank capital standards into closer alignment with emerging international standards."[132] Ultimately, the regulators' main tool of persuasion was an implicit threat of excluding Japanese banks from Western markets. As Kapstein notes, "The tacit threat being made was that foreign bank activity could be reduced in the U.S. and U.K. markets unless these banks adopted the new risk-based standard. Since Japanese banks were intent on expanding their activities in New York and London . . . this was a prospect that had to be taken seriously."[133]

An understanding of the preferences of regulators during these negotiations makes the final outcome unsurprising. In late 1987 the Basel Committee announced the creation of a multilateral capital standard—the Basel Accord—which was based largely on the Anglo-American agreement. With the United States and the United Kingdom adamantly in favor of a global capital standard as a result of domestic pressures, Japanese resistance did not stand a chance. Scholars of the Basel Accord agree that the outcome can be explained by a simple acknowledgment of market power, and the analysis presented here is no exception.[134] The framework laid out in chapter 3 provides a clear picture of how regulators actually exercise this power. Why did Japan agree to the Basel Accord? The Bank of England and the Fed were able to threaten Japanese banks with exclusion from Western markets, thereby inducing a shift in the competitiveness of Japanese banks. If the MOF had refused to agree to the accord, banks no doubt would have pressured the Diet to intervene. Under these coercive circumstances, the adoption of more stringent regulations actually *helped* the competitiveness of Japanese banks. Acceding to the Basel Accord was the only way for the MOF to maintain a regulatory win-set and avoid political intervention.

To be sure, the United States and the United Kingdom did not use their market power to foist a global standard onto the industrialized world with complete disregard for the concerns of other countries. Indeed, the final Basel Accord accommodated some of the preferences of the G-10 countries, Japan included. Most of these accommodations pertained to the definition of capital itself. For example, negotiators appeased France by allowing subordinated debt to count as supplementary capital and even eased the burden of Japanese adjustment by allowing a portion of unrealized capital gains on securities to be included in the capital base.[135]

In summary, the preferences of the three countries' regulators toward an international capital adequacy standard can be traced back to changes in their win-sets. For the United States and the United Kingdom, the loss of market share to less-regulated Japanese banks, combined with rising bank instability, made it increasingly difficult for regulators to choose a capital adequacy rule that could satisfy the legislature's demands for stability and competitiveness. Legislative intervention was close at hand in both countries. In the United States, Congress made its concerns felt—through hearings and other public statements—about both the alarming number of bank failures and the loss of market share to the Japanese. In the United Kingdom, Parliament pressured the Bank of England on both the JMB affair and the competitive threat from foreign rivals. For regulators from these two countries, the creation of a global capital adequacy standard was a means to avoid further legislative intervention. A global standard served two purposes: it enabled the United States and the United Kingdom to enact more stringent regulations to shore up financial stability, and it tempered the adverse competitive implications of stricter regulations by creating a level playing field. Japan, on the other hand, was the ascending rival throughout this story, and it did not suffer the growing bank instability of its Western counterparts. It therefore resisted the creation of an international capital standard and acceded to the Basel Accord only after a display of market power by the United States and the United Kingdom.

The Basel Accord was a remarkable accomplishment in the history of financial regulation, and its risk-weighting system for capital adequacy has arguably made global banking markets more stable and competitively balanced.[136] Since its promulgation in 1988, countries outside the G-10 have implemented its requirements for their own banks, despite the fact that the accord was not originally intended to be applicable beyond the developed world. As of 2007, more than one hundred countries abide by the Basel Accord.[137] Basel compliance has become a seal of approval for banking markets in LDCs, which tout the stability of their banks to attract capital from abroad. And scholars of the global financial architecture, who wish to enhance the stability of international finance on a broader scale, point to the Basel Accord as evidence of the feasibility and utility of global financial standards.[138]

Epilogue: Back to the Drawing Board with Basel II

The analytical contribution of this chapter ends with the emergence of the Basel Accord in 1988, but the larger narrative does not stop there. After the promulgation of the accord, two developments occurred: first, the accord quickly became a truly global standard embraced by developed and developing countries around the world; and second, regulators in the Basel Committee—and throughout the developing world—faced pressure from their domestic banking sectors to address some of the shortcomings of the original agreement.

The original accord provided a risk-weighting scheme whereby different classes of assets—such as cash, sovereign debt, mortgages, and corporate loans—were assigned a risk score between zero and 100 percent. These "risk buckets" ultimately formed the denominator of a bank's capital-to-asset ratio, with the stipulation that the numerator must equal or exceed 8 percent. A bank's investment in a sovereign bond from an OECD country was assigned a risk weighting of zero and thus did not enter the denominator. On the other hand, a loan to a private corporation was assigned to the 100 percent risk bucket and therefore entered the denominator in full. Regulatory capital (the numerator) was divided into two categories: Tier 1, consisting primarily of shareholder's equity, and Tier 2, consisting of subordinated debt, loan-loss reserves, and other forms of capital. Of the Basel Accord's 8 percent regulatory capital, a minimum of 4 percent came from Tier 1 capital, with the remainder coming from Tier 2.[139]

At the time, the accord's risk-weighting scheme seemed innovative, and it was no doubt an improvement over the lax (or absent) requirements in place in many banking sectors. And as just mentioned, compliance with the accord soon became a signal to international investors of the creditworthiness and stability of a country's banking sector. However, as the accord became a global standard, regulators and bankers themselves realized that the risk-weighting system was arbitrary, inefficient, and potentially harmful to the broader economy.[140] For example, all sovereign bonds from OECD countries (including emerging-market countries such as Turkey, and later Mexico and Hungary, among others) were assigned the same risk classification despite the obvious variation in credit risk within that group. Likewise, a loan to a large, reputable firm such as General Electric was placed in the same risk bucket as a loan to an obscure, potentially unstable firm. In regard to the broader economy, the absence of capital charges on sovereign bonds caused an investment bias away from corporate lending and toward sovereign lending, arguably causing a private-sector "credit crunch" in the early years of the accord's implementation.[141]

The Basel Committee addressed one shortcoming of the accord soon after its implementation: its exclusive focus on credit risk at the expense of other types of risk. In 1996 the committee issued an amendment to incorporate market risk into banks' capital requirements.[142] Market risk includes potential losses from banks' debt and equity trading activities, as well as foreign exchange and commodities trading. The amendment allowed banks to calculate market risk based on one of two formulas. The first was a standardized set of rules specified in the amendment and known as the "building block" approach. In this approach, banks begin by calculating the specific risks of their debt and equity positions—in other words, "the risk of a loss caused by an adverse price movement of a security due principally to factors related to the issuer of the security."[143] They then add to that measure—as if stacking a block on top of a block—an assessment of general risk arising from broad swings in the entire market.

The second, more innovative approach proved to have important ramifications for the future of the Basel agreement. Known as the "in-house" model, it allowed banks to develop their own proprietary risk-management systems, subject to the supervision of the national regulatory authorities. At the heart of the in-house approach is a "value at risk" calculation, which estimates the amount of capital needed to absorb a minimum price shock equivalent to ten trading days.[144] With this approach, larger banks with sophisticated risk-assessment capabilities could cater their own capital requirements to their particular market risks rather than rely on a one-size-fits-all rule.

The in-house market-risk approach made the 1996 amendment more palatable to banks in the major financial centers, but the other shortcomings of the accord—including the crude risk buckets—remained a source of dissatisfaction for regulators and bankers alike. In 1999 the Basel Committee issued a proposal for a wholesale revision of the accord and followed up with consultation papers in 2001 and 2003.[145] At the foundation of the proposal, now known throughout the financial community as Basel II, are three "pillars" that address the fundamental criticisms of the original accord. The first pillar incorporates the innovations of the 1996 amendment by allowing banks to use either a standardized approach or an in-house system to calculate their capital requirements. For gauging credit risk, the standardized approach introduces, among other things, a private credit ratings system in which capital charges on loans reflect the risk evaluations of rating agencies such as Standard & Poor's and Moody's.[146] Thus a loan to a company rated AAA by Standard & Poor's will require a lower capital charge than a loan to a company rated BBB. Banks with more sophisticated risk-management capabilities can opt for an internal-ratings-based (IRB) approach that allocates capital charges according to in-house risk assessments. Also included in the first pillar of the new accord are capital requirements for market risk (largely unchanged from the 1996 amendment) and operational risk, defined as the "risk of loss resulting from inadequate or failed internal processes, people and systems or from external events."[147]

The second and third pillars of the new accord implicitly acknowledge the shortcomings of the first pillar.[148] The second pillar relates to supervisory oversight and mandates a greater degree of monitoring and supervision of banks' risk profiles. In light of the increase in risk-management discretion granted in the first pillar (for banks choosing the IRB approach), bank regulators must be on high alert for improper risk assessments and should be ready to intervene promptly should a bank begin to manifest signs of undercapitalization. The third pillar addresses market discipline, mandating that banks disclose information on capital structure, organizational structure, and risk management. The goal of the third pillar is to enable shareholders, bondholders, and other counterparties to monitor banks' activities and to punish bank managers for imprudent risk management or malfeasance.

Given that a bank capital adequacy standard already exists, cross-national variation in regulators' preferences over Basel II is not as stark as with the initial accord in the 1980s. Indeed, there was virtual consensus among regulators that the accord must be modified: U.S. Federal Reserve vice chairman Roger Ferguson notes that "there is not much disagreement with the assertion that Basel II should be built on modern techniques of risk management," including complex statistical assessments of risk.[149] That said, there are many possible ways to incorporate modern risk management into the agreement, and the length of the Basel II negotiation period—from the first consultation paper in 1999 to the expected implementation of the agreement in 2008 or beyond—is testament to the difficulties in forging a consensus among the regulators in the Basel Committee.[150]

One stumbling block in the Basel II negotiations is over the treatment of large versus small banks. It is generally understood that small banks do not have the technology or sophistication to adopt an IRB approach to capital adequacy. To the extent that the IRB approach is more flexible than the standardized approach, small banks may be at a competitive disadvantage to their larger, more sophisticated competitors. The competitive implications of Basel II compliance are especially sensitive in the United States, where the Federal Reserve has announced that the new agreement will be a required regulation for only the top ten banks in the country.[151]

Disagreements over Basel II are less important than what the revisions reflect more generally: a relaxation of the original accord's specificity.[152] U.S. Fed vice chairman Ferguson puts the issue more delicately:

> The tradeoff that is at the heart of Basel II is the tradeoff between flexibility and comparability. Allowing banks to calculate regulatory capital in any manner that they see fit would certainly maximize the flexibility of such calculations, but the results would not be comparable across banks and thus the value of the capital standard would be compromised. On the other hand, to focus too rigidly on comparability would require an approach that made no use whatsoever of internal measures of risk or allowed no differences of technique across banks. Such an approach would not be sufficiently flexible and would prevent us from measuring risk as sensitively as necessary. It would inevitably not be much different than the Basel I standard we have today.[153]

Ferguson goes on to call Basel II a "balancing act," which is reminiscent of the balancing required of regulators in the analytical framework presented in chapter 3. Other commentators have stated more bluntly that the Basel II agreement reflects a decrease in regulatory harmonization, given the wide discretion that banks have to "game" the system to their own advantage.[154] At a minimum, Basel II will allow banks to hold less capital relative to their assets than under the original accord. The most recent quantitative impact study conducted by the Basel Committee predicts a 6.8 percent average decline in minimum capital requirements for international active banks in the G-10 countries.[155]

The move toward relaxing the Basel Accord should not come as a surprise. Banks have been remarkably stable since the 1990s. In the United States the recent stability of the banking sector stands in stark contrast to the turbulence of the 1980s. Indeed, not a single bank failed in 2005, and failures were relatively few in number in the first years of the twenty-first century.[156] Likewise, bank failures have been rare in the United Kingdom since the mid-1990s.[157] Thus the original impetus for the Basel Accord—the instability of U.S. and British banks—has largely disappeared. Japanese banks, however, are the exception. Japan saw three important bank failures in the late 1990s in the wake of the Asian financial crisis and Japan's own recession: the Hokkaido Takushoku Bank and the Long Term Credit Bank of Japan in 1997 and the Nippon Credit Bank in 1998.[158] Given the severity of Japan's decade-long economic decline and stagnation, the failure of these banks most likely reflects the underlying poor health of the economy rather than a regulatory failure.

As we can see from this discussion of Basel II, international systemic risk does not drive the creation of international standards. Has the world of international banking somehow become less systemically risky over the past decade, thus triggering the more relaxed Basel II agreement? Have we witnessed a decline in the extent of international ties among banks in the major financial centers and therefore a corresponding decline in the importance of international regulatory harmonization? Clearly, the answer to both questions is no. Instead, regulatory preferences emerge from a domestic balancing act (to use Ferguson's phrase), with stability on one side and international competitiveness on the other. The prolonged period of stability in the G-10 countries has, for now, changed the calculus of national bank regulators, but the tide will no doubt shift back toward increasing stringency if banks' attempts to "game" the Basel II agreement lead to an unfortunate revival of the turbulent banking markets of the 1980s.

Chapter 5

Securities: Financial Instability and Regulatory Divergence

The Basel Accord has captured the attention of political scientists and economists, but it is by no means the only example of an attempt by regulators to harmonize their domestic prudential regulations. In 1987, just as central bankers were finalizing the accord, a group of securities regulators initiated discussions on harmonizing capital requirements for securities firms under the auspices of the International Organization of Securities Commissions (IOSCO). The ostensible motivations of the securities regulators were similar to those of the central bankers: mitigate systemic risk by ensuring that all securities firms were adequately capitalized, and minimize the inefficiencies of cross-national regulatory differences. But behind the rhetoric of global solutions to global problems were the familiar domestic goals of financial stability and competitiveness, which led to marked variation in the preferences of securities regulators toward the creation of an international capital adequacy standard. The United Kingdom's Securities and Investments Board was the most vocal proponent of harmonization during the more than four years of negotiations, whereas the U.S. Securities and Exchange Commission resisted the creation of an international standard. Japan's Ministry of Finance was skeptical of harmonization but maintained a low profile behind the more dominant SEC. In late 1992, after a particularly acrimonious meeting, securities regulators officially abandoned their efforts to harmonize their capital adequacy requirements after it became clear that the SEC was not interested in moving forward.

Why study the seemingly obscure case of the IOSCO capital adequacy negotiations, which did not lead to the creation of an international regulatory agreement? The IOSCO negotiations in fact constitute an important case in the study of regulatory harmonization, largely because U.S. regulators were adamantly opposed to an international standard. If regulatory harmonization is driven by international systemic risk, why did the globalization of securities markets—which no doubt led to increasing levels of interdependence and vulnerability to foreign shocks—not prompt U.S. regulators to advocate for harmonization? Why did U.S. and U.K. regulators, representing the world's largest securities markets, find themselves on opposing sides of the debate?

Advocates of international financial regulation are quick to point to the Basel Accord as an exemplar of international cooperation and to urge policymakers to emulate bank regulators in overcoming national differences to enhance global stability.[1] But regulators themselves are aware of the enormous obstacles to international cooperation and often point to the IOSCO negotiations as an important counterexample to the successful Basel agreement.[2] Studies of regulatory harmonization generally treat the Basel Accord in isolation rather than in the context of a research design that explores variation in a dependent variable of interest, such as final outcomes or regulators' preferences. By bringing in the case of the IOSCO negotiations, this book offers a more compelling explanation of the international behavior of regulators.

This chapter provides an explanation of the variation in regulator demands for an international capital standard for securities firms. As in the previous chapter, I confine the discussion to the regulators from the three most important capital markets in the early 1990s: the United States, the United Kingdom, and Japan. Using the framework developed in chapter 3, I argue that each regulator's position toward an international agreement can be explained by the constraints on the regulator's ability to maintain stability and competitiveness in domestic financial markets. Exogenous shocks to the stability of securities markets and to the competitiveness of domestic securities firms lead to pressures on regulators to adjust the stringency of their regulations. When a firm failure or a bout of asset price volatility rattles the confidence of the public in the stability of securities firms and markets, regulators have incentives to tighten the regulatory environment by requiring new safeguards against instability, such as more stringent capital requirements. On the other hand, the loss of market share to foreign financial sectors with less stringent regulatory environments provides incentives for regulators to relax the stringency of domestic regulations, even though such a move would imply a greater risk of domestic instability. All countries faced at least one type of shock at some point in the 1980s, and regulators responded by changing their respective domestic regulatory environments accordingly. However, when a regulator faced both shocks simultaneously, it found itself unable to adjust the stringency of regulations to maintain both stability and competitiveness. As the specter of legislative intervention increased, the regulator shifted its focus to the international arena in an attempt to find a solution. An international regulatory agreement, if reached, would allow the regulator to enact appropriately stringent regulations to maintain financial stability while avoiding the negative effects on competitiveness that regulatory stringency usually implies.

The SIB's advocacy of harmonization was driven by competitive pressures in derivatives markets from U.S. firms, combined with a heightened sense of the vulnerability of asset prices to shocks from abroad and the precariousness of British securities firms in the wake of the 1987 stock market crash. The United States, as the rising player in derivatives markets, was resistant to the creation of an international standard that would raise the cost of operations for its firms. The SEC was not struggling with the same competitiveness threats as the SIB, and U.S. securities firms retained their reputation for strength and stability after the stock market crash. Japan, on the other hand, was not yet a major force in derivatives markets despite the overall size of its capital markets, and it therefore remained on the margins of the international debate.

The Internationalization of Securities Markets

Securities firms experienced a rapid expansion in their international activities throughout the 1980s and into the 1990s. The expansion is evident in the growth of cross-border securities transactions and the increasing presence of foreign branches and subsidiaries of securities firms in domestic markets. Annual international transactions in equity securities totaled approximately $73 billion in 1979 and rocketed to $1.5 trillion in 1990.[3] By 1993 approximately 25 percent of stock market transactions conducted worldwide involved either a foreign security or a foreign counterparty, up from 10 percent in 1979.[4] Total portfolio holdings of equity and long-term debt securities reached $5.2 trillion by the end of 1997, with the United States, the United Kingdom, and Japan accounting for 68 percent of these holdings.[5] Throughout the 1980s foreign branches of firms such as Goldman Sachs, SG Warburg, and Nomura increased their size and prominence in the major capital markets of New York, London, and Tokyo. As shown in figure 7, the combined market capitalizations of these three countries soared.

The magnitude of these statistics has become familiar to scholars of globalization and to those who follow international economics in the popular press. But knowledge of the increasing prominence of derivatives—especially during the period of investigation for this analysis, the 1980s and

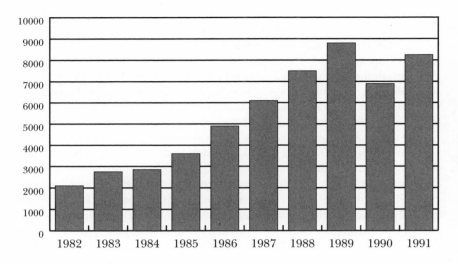

Figure 7. Combined Stock Market Capitalization of the United States, United Kingdom, and Japan, 1982–1991 (millions of U.S. dollars). (Source: International Finance Corporation, *Emerging Stock Markets Factbook,* 1992.)

early 1990s—is not as widespread. Scholars often use data on trade, bank lending, foreign direct investment, and stocks and bonds as evidence of globalizing markets but overlook the veritable explosion in worldwide derivatives activity.[6] Derivatives are financial instruments whose value is based on, or derived from, the value of another security or asset; they include forwards, futures, options, and swaps. The Chicago Board of Trade first developed financial futures contracts in 1975, and other types of derivatives, including stock index futures and interest rate swaps, emerged in the early 1980s.[7] By 1987 the notional amount of total outstanding derivatives contracts based on interest rates and currencies alone was nearly $866 billion, and this figure jumped to more than $5.3 trillion in 1992 and to nearly $100 trillion in 2002.[8] When the full suite of derivative instruments is included, the figures are even more impressive: in 1992 investors traded more than 600 million futures and options on organized exchanges, representing a notional amount in excess of $140 trillion.[9]

The growth of international securities and derivatives markets was a function of a similar set of factors that drove the internationalization of banking: increasing currency volatility due to the collapse of the Bretton Woods fixed exchange rate system, financial and technological innovation, and greater demands for cross-border speculative activities. As capital markets became increasingly integrated, large businesses were no longer confined to domestic stock exchanges for raising capital and sought the help of firms and exchanges in other countries—especially the United States and western Europe—for their funding needs. Businesses also sought mechanisms to shield themselves from the newfound risks of global markets, especially sudden changes in exchange rates, interest rates, and asset prices. Derivatives were either a speculative instrument or a hedging strategy, depending on the requirements of the investor, and enabled businesses to profit from changes in a variety of underlying assets and indexes.

Volatility in interest rates and exchange rates helped to drive the growth of international securities activities, but capital market integration brought its own forms of volatility and vulnerability. New telecommunications and computer technologies enabled investors to buy and sell securities with relative ease, often in response to rumors of economic downturn or a change in government policy. The result was a substantial increase in the frequency of extreme daily price movements in securities markets.[10] Markets with significant foreign investment became vulnerable to the economic and political conditions of investors' home countries, and stock markets around the world were increasingly linked by a common pool of large institutional investors. An inevitable consequence of integration was that markets worldwide began to move in similar directions.[11] The mean correlation coefficient between the New York Stock Exchange and nine major countries increased from 0.35 during the period 1975–79 to 0.43 in 1980–84 and to 0.62 in 1985–89.[12] The interdependence of stock exchanges was especially salient in times of crisis. A sudden plunge in equity prices in one exchange would often reverberate quickly throughout other exchanges, regardless of market fundamentals. The most infamous example is the stock market crash of 1987, which was centered in New York but spread quickly to other markets throughout the world. On October 19, 1987, the Dow Jones Industrial Average (DJIA) dropped 508 points, or nearly 23 percent, constituting one of the most severe shocks in financial history.[13] The next day, Tokyo's Nikkei dropped 14 percent, London's FTSE more than 12 percent, and Hong Kong's market 42 percent.

The interdependence of national capital markets intensified with the growth of the derivatives market. Derivatives—especially the over-the-counter variety purchased directly from financial institutions—are customized contracts designed to meet the particular needs of a client, and they often assemble risks in complex ways.[14] Changes in the prices of disparate assets—from currencies to commodities to securities—can be connected contractually to meet a client's demands for hedging or speculation. As Richard Dale notes, "The trading of derivatives contracts creates close linkages, not only between derivatives and the underlying cash markets, but also between different segments of the cash and derivative markets—thereby opening up new channels for the communication of financial disturbances."[15] Analysts of the 1987 stock market crash point to derivatives as an important contributor to the plunge in securities prices. An SEC report notes that derivatives trading had a negative impact on market psychology on October 19 and that the derivatives themselves—not the underlying assets from which their value is derived—were the initiators of changes in prices in the equity markets.[16]

The interdependence of securities markets became worrisome for regulators. Sudden changes in asset prices could have a substantial effect on the real economy if the market's financial institutions became unstable. If a major securities firm in, say, London were to go bankrupt, the firm's outstanding transactions with broker-dealers in other countries would go unrealized. If these firms were not sufficiently capitalized, they could default or collapse, creating an ever larger circle of bankruptcies worldwide.[17] An influential OECD publication in 1991 stated the problem more starkly: "The extreme systemic threat arising from a collapse of securities prices is that default by one or more large securities dealers will lead to further defaults and that the failures will extend into the core of the banking system and cause a breakdown in the flow of payments in settlement of financial transactions throughout the world."[18]

Fortunately, the stock market crash of 1987 did not lead to such a dire outcome, but the event served as a jarring lesson for regulators about the potential dangers of interdependent markets, spurring a number of research reports on "systemic risk" in securities markets.[19] Regulators were also growing more aware of the risks involved in securities firms' investment strategies, from currency trading and futures to interest rate swaps and other complex derivatives.[20]

Systemic risk was an early catalyst for international cooperation among regulators, but the issue of international enforcement of securities laws—in particular, fighting securities fraud—was more pressing. Securities regulators in the developed world had always placed enforcement of antifraud legislation at the forefront of their mandates. With globalization, enforcement of national laws became increasingly difficult. As Beth Simmons notes, "When trading networks cross multiple jurisdictions, regulators' efforts to access information that would expose fraudulent or highly risky trading activities are greatly complicated."[21] Regulators need information to fight fraud, but financial institutions and legal authorities in other countries may be reluctant to release personal information due to concerns about privacy and confidentiality. Previously insulated regulatory agencies found themselves contacting their foreign counterparts in an effort to coordinate their antifraud strategies.

International meetings of securities regulators were virtually unprecedented until the 1970s, and significant efforts at cooperation began only in the 1980s. In 1974 regulators from North and South America established the Inter-American Association of Securities Commissions and Similar

Organizations, but its vague mandate—to serve as a general forum for regulators in the Western Hemisphere—and lack of interest severely limited its ability to produce significant results.[22] Over the next decade the organization underwent a number of changes, including expanding its membership and changing its name twice, eventually calling itself the International Organization of Securities Commissions (IOSCO) in 1986. By the end of the 1980s IOSCO had a secretariat and headquarters in Montreal, and its membership included regulators from the United States, the United Kingdom, Japan, and forty-five other countries.[23] IOSCO also established a Technical Committee, consisting of regulators from the most developed securities markets, to guide the work of its members.[24] As of 1988 that group included regulators from the United States, the United Kingdom, Japan, West Germany, France, Australia, Canada, Hong Kong, Italy, the Netherlands, Sweden, and Switzerland.[25] Despite its formal structures, regulators understood from the beginning that decisions would be made in the style of the Basel Committee: nominally by consensus but actually dominated by the preferences of the most influential securities markets, namely the United States, the United Kingdom, and Japan.[26]

Unlike the Basel Committee, IOSCO had virtually no accomplishments in its first few years, and the public viewed the organization with cynicism. The *Financial Times* noted wryly that IOSCO "always had the reputation of being a rather sleepy organization whose annual get-togethers gave the opportunity for jamborees rather than jaw-boning."[27] But in 1987, just weeks before the stock market crash, IOSCO's Technical Committee created seven working groups to address specific challenges in international securities markets and make recommendations to the full membership.[28] The creation of these working groups, and the delineation of regulatory challenges that they represented, marked the emergence of IOSCO as a potentially important international organization. Commentators began to make analogies—albeit premature ones—between IOSCO's Technical Committee and the Basel Committee.[29]

The efforts of Working Group 3, tasked with studying the issue of capital adequacy requirements for securities firms, is of particular interest. The group was composed of regulators from the United States, France, Japan, and the United Kingdom and was chaired by Jeffrey Knight of the International Stock Exchange in London.[30] The group focused on the requirements in the member countries of the Technical Committee, which constituted the world's most active securities markets.[31] Expectations for the group were high after the stock market crash, and participants in the negotiations felt increasing pressure to produce an international agreement in light of the accomplishments of the Basel Committee in late 1987.

In 1989 the group issued its first report, which was then approved by the full Technical Committee for presentation at IOSCO's annual meeting.

The report concluded that a common framework was needed regarding the capital requirements of securities firms and should contain the following elements:

1. Liquidity and solvency should be covered by a standard that provides for a firm to have sufficient liquid assets to meet its obligations given the risks a firm faces.

2. Marking of marketable securities and commodities positions to market is necessary to prevent firms from storing up losses and also to give a true picture of a firm's position.

3. Risk-based requirements should cover all the risks to a firm and, in particular, should contain:

    i. a base requirement reflecting the scale of a firm's activities to capture non-measurable risks.
    ii. position risk requirements (for both on and off balance sheet items) reflecting the price volatility of individual securities with provisions for concentrated positions and allowances for risk reduction measures such as hedging.
    iii. settlement risk requirements reflecting the risk of non-performance in a timely manner.[32]

The bottom line was that firms should hold enough capital to exceed the sum of these risk-based requirements.

The 1989 IOSCO report was merely a set of guidelines that set the agenda for further negotiations. The group had yet to decide how to measure capital, let alone what the specific minimum level of capital should be for securities firms. Another obstacle was the relationship between the proposed IOSCO standard and the Basel Accord. Since an increasing number of banks were involved in securities activities, the competitive implications of any new regulations were of critical importance.

The 1989 report on capital adequacy is roughly analogous to the Basel Committee's Concordat in 1975. The report was a critical first step toward the international harmonization of capital adequacy regulations for securities firms, just as the Concordat set the stage for more precise international capital standards for banks. However, the vagueness of both sets of guidelines was symptomatic of the underlying discord among national regulators. Over the next three years the extent of securities regulators' discord would manifest itself in acrimonious meetings and bitter accusations in the press and behind closed doors. At the heart of regulators' preferences was the effect of capital requirements on the competitiveness of their domestic firms. But unlike the Basel case, the most salient issue was not the specification of the minimum capital level itself but rather how that level would be applied to the various divisions and subsidiaries of a firm.

I use the analytical framework from chapter 3 to explain the varying demands for international harmonization from the three major players in the international securities market in the late 1980s: the U.S. Securities and Exchange Commission, the U.K. Securities and Investments Board, and the Japanese Ministry of Finance. I begin with the SIB as the main advocate of an international capital adequacy standard and then discuss the SEC's and MOF's resistance to harmonization. Recall that the dependent variable of this study is regulators' advocacy for or resistance to an international regulatory agreement. To explain this variation, I focus on the type and nature of the exogenous changes to each regulator's win-set. Shocks to stability provide incentives for the regulator to tighten regulations whereas shocks to competitiveness provide incentives for relaxing the regulatory environment. Simultaneous shocks to stability and competitiveness will likely prompt the regulator to seek an international regulatory agreement.

The 1987 stock market crash constituted a more severe stability shock for regulators in the United Kingdom than in the other two countries, decreasing the ability of the SIB to relax the domestic regulatory environment. At the same time, securities markets in the United Kingdom faced an onslaught of competition from better-capitalized and less stringently regulated derivatives providers in the United States. This competitiveness shock added pressure to the SIB, which found itself squeezing its own securities firms with regulations that were burdensome in comparison with the U.S. environment. The SEC and the MOF, on the other hand, endured the 1987 stock market crash relatively unscathed and faced only modest pressure to tighten prudential regulations. U.S. securities firms remained dominant in the late 1980s, and their derivatives offerings allowed them to gain further ground over their British counterparts through the 1990s. The SEC therefore did not experience a competitiveness shock, and its stability shock was relatively minor. Japanese firms remained on the sidelines during the early rise of derivatives and struggled with their own domestically induced troubles (including a dramatic decline in the prices of real estate and securities). The MOF's difficulties were therefore largely domestic in nature and did not involve discrepancies between domestic and foreign regulations or the incursion of foreign firms in Japanese market share.

From the outset, it should be clear that international systemic variables cannot explain the variation in regulators' positions toward harmonization. There is no theoretical reason to believe that the SIB's lone advocacy of harmonization was somehow driven by a desire to mitigate global systemic risk in securities markets. Instead, I focus on the observable implications of the framework presented in chapter 3: bouts of financial instability (such as firm failures and severe volatility in asset prices) and the loss of market share to a foreign rival facing less stringent regulations will prompt a regulator to seek an international regulatory agreement. Therefore, for each country, I examine changes in domestic financial stability and the status of foreign rivals throughout the 1980s and early 1990s.

The SIB's Advocacy of Harmonization

The genesis of the United Kingdom's securities regulator, the SIB, is a prime example of a government's attempt to maintain adequate levels of stability and competitiveness. The hallmark of Prime Minister Thatcher's deregulatory movement was the so-called Big Bang in 1986, a series of reforms designed to liberalize the London Stock Exchange and the United Kingdom's financial sector. The reforms included the abolition of fixed broker commissions, the removal of restrictions on foreign participation, and the end of the forced segregation of brokers and dealers ("jobbers").[33] The reforms increased the competitiveness of the stock exchange and prevented institutional investors from taking their business to more hospitable environments. At the roughly same time, Parliament passed the Financial Services Act, which created the SIB and a formalized system of regulatory oversight. The SIB was charged with drawing up a set of detailed rules for all aspects of the securities industry, including new licensing requirements for stockbrokers, antifraud measures, and prudential requirements for securities firms.[34] The "re-regulation" exemplified by the SIB served to counterbalance the liberalizing reforms of the Big Bang, maintaining the regulatory balance between stability and competitiveness.[35]

That balance became quite precarious in the years following the creation of the SIB. Securities markets in the United Kingdom experienced a jarring bout of instability with the stock market crash of 1987. Although securities firms remained resilient during and after the crash, the bungled initial public offering of British Petroleum (BP) drew the public's attention to the vulnerability of London's merchant banks to exogenous shocks. The market crash, combined with the newly created Basel Accord, placed enormous pressure on regulators throughout Europe to create a set of stringent capital requirements for securities firms—indeed, for all financial institutions—in the European Union. At the same time, London's tradition of consolidated supervision, in which all parts of a firm are subject to prudential regulations, stood in stark contrast to U.S. regulations that applied only to registered broker-dealers and not their parent companies. The U.S. holding companies of broker-dealers were exempt from capital requirements and could therefore offer highly competitive pricing on financial services, especially derivatives contracts, and capture market share from competitors in London. The SIB found itself with a shrinking win-set for regulatory policy. Pressure was high to create a set of stringent regulations for Europe, but the SIB also faced the prospect of a wide-scale decline in London's merchant banks due to foreign competition. The combination of pressures due to stability and competitiveness drove the SIB to advocate an international capital adequacy standard for securities firms. Ultimately, the SIB's inability to maintain a win-set for regulatory policy—for capital adequacy and a variety of other policy areas—resulted in a decision by the British government to overhaul London's regulatory environment with far-reaching legislation and a new regulatory agency.

The Stability Constraint

Stock market volatility increased dramatically in the late 1980s, and the SIB's win-set for regulatory policy began to shrink almost immediately after its creation. The newfound precariousness of British merchant banks and the increasing chance of a firm collapse meant that the SIB did not have the option of easing regulations, despite the liberalization of the Big Bang reforms. London struggled to claim its place as a worldwide financial center, but the SIB had powerful incentives to maintain a stringent regulatory environment to ward off the dangers of financial instability.

When the FTSE index fell nearly 11 percent on October 19, 1987, and more than 12 percent the following day, the timing could not have been worse. The stock market crash occurred in the middle of a £7.25 billion ($12 billion) equity offering, which remains the world's largest public offering of stock. On October 15, just four days before "Black Monday," the British government released details of an offer to sell its remaining 31 percent stake in British Petroleum (BP). Merchant bank N. M. Rothschild was the lead manager of the offering, along with a syndicate of sixteen underwriters in London and a small number in the United States and continental Europe. The underwriters agreed to a pay a price of 330 pence per share of BP on October 14, which, given the stock's trading price of over 360 pence, provided ample opportunity for profit making.[36] However, when the stock market plunged, the subscription process—by which individual and institutional investors commit to purchasing shares of the offering from the underwriters—had hardly begun. The BP offering was therefore almost completely unsubscribed, leaving underwriters with tremendous losses.[37] The share price of BP fell as low as 285 pence, or nearly 14 percent lower than the underwriters' purchase price. As journalist Steven Solomon noted, "Instead of easy profits, the underwriters faced a £1.5 billion ($2.5 billion) bloodbath."[38]

In the hours after Black Monday, securities houses in London urged the British government to suspend the BP offering, arguing that the crash was a clear case of force majeure—an unexpected, overpowering event that should abrogate all existing agreements.[39] They also feared additional losses and firm failures if the market were to fall again later in the month. But the Thatcher government found itself in an uncomfortable political bind. The BP privatization represented Thatcher's overall vision of free market liberalism, and its cancellation would be politically humiliating. On the other hand, if the BP offering continued without government interference, the resulting financial instability could disrupt Thatcher's fragile coalition in favor of further economic reforms. Ultimately, the government found a compromise: the Bank of England set a floor price for the BP shares and allowed underwriters to sell their shares to the Bank. This safety net helped to control the fallout from the offering, but underwriters were nonetheless left with losses totaling some £700 million.[40]

There were no major firm failures in London in the months after the crash, but policymakers were less certain of the stability of British firms on the eve of October 20. In fact, a Bank of England team led by Brian Quinn consulted with the New York Federal Reserve in late October to discuss "the dire situation when a house failed."[41] The sudden collapse of one of London's major securities firms, such as Morgan Grenfell or SG Warburg, would pull the market down even lower and possibly trigger the failure of additional firms, including banks with close ties to the securities industry. The consequences for financial stability and monetary policy could be disastrous.

The SIB, created the year before the market crash, found itself in the middle of this turbulent environment. The market crash constituted an exogenous shock to stability for the SIB, but because of its international scope the shock was qualitatively different from those described in the previous chapter on the Basel Accord. The crash affected all the major markets in Europe, including exchanges in France, Germany, and the Netherlands, as well as financial institutions throughout the EU. Thus, rather than prompt a unilateral response from the SIB, the crash expedited the development of an international regulatory directive for all EU member countries. Negotiations over the Capital Adequacy Directive (CAD) began in the late 1980s with the goal of establishing minimum capital requirements for investment firms, as well as the securities activities of banks. As the representative of the EU's largest capital market, the SIB took the lead in drafting the CAD. The timing was fortuitous: the Financial Services Act of 1986 required the SIB to enact a broad set of regulations for London's securities markets, and the SIB's leadership with the CAD meant that London's domestic regulations could find themselves adopted—with modifications if necessary—by the rest of the EU.

On October 13, 1989, just two years after Black Monday, capital markets experienced another market crash. The Dow Jones Industrial Average fell

190 points, or 6.9 percent, and the Standard and Poor's 500 index fell 6.1 percent. On Monday, October 16, the financial press speculated about a repeat of the 1987 crash, and some financial advisers urged clients to liquidate their holdings before the market completely collapsed.[42] In London, government ministers were reportedly holding their breath before the start of the trading day on Monday morning, fearful that another 1987-type crash could push the British economy "over the brink" into recession.[43] The London Stock Exchange's FTSE-100 index fell 204 points before noon on Monday, but an auspicious opening on Wall Street helped London recover a portion of its losses, and the index closed down just over 3 percent for the day.

As stock market volatility became a common story on the front page of newspapers around the world, the SIB's room to maneuver in regulatory matters was tightly constrained. The Thatcher reforms clearly needed to be counterbalanced by more stringent prudential regulations, as evidenced by the 1986 Financial Services Act and the development of the CAD. But even more salient for the SIB was the potential decline of London's securities firms due to international competition, especially from the United States and western Europe. The growth in the market for derivatives and the increasing dominance of U.S. derivatives dealers would provide the additional impetus for the SIB's advocacy of an international capital adequacy standard through IOSCO.

International Competitiveness and the Rise of Derivatives

London's securities firms never fully recovered from the Big Bang reforms and the 1987 market crash. The Big Bang effectively ended a generation of protected markets and artificially high commissions for investment firms. Small, weakly capitalized brokers and jobbers thrived in the pre-1986 regime but quickly shut their doors or were acquired at fire sale prices after the reforms were announced.[44] Foreign financial institutions, including large U.S. banks and securities firms, were responsible for many of the acquisitions in the mid-1980s. Citicorp, for example, purchased brokers Scrimgeour Kemp-Gee, Vickers da Costa, and Seccombe Marshall Campion, and Chase Manhattan acquired Laurie Milbank and Simon & Coates.[45] Swiss firms were similarly aggressive in targeting British brokers: Union Bank of Switzerland acquired Phillips & Drew, a prestigious London firm, in 1986, followed by broker Moulsdale.[46] Even the larger British firms struggled to adapt to the new, more open economy in the City of London. Morgan Grenfell, one of the largest of London's merchant banks, was acquired in 1989 by Deutsche Bank. By the end of the decade London had secured its place as a formidable rival to New York as an international financial center, and the Big Bang reforms transformed the London Stock

Exchange from a closed "gentlemen's club" into a vibrant and competitive capital market. London's own securities firms, however, found themselves fighting to maintain their independence, or indeed to stay afloat.

The SIB, coincidentally, was in a similar position. The newly created regulator was tasked with establishing a formal regulatory environment for London's securities markets, including stringent rules against fraud and market manipulation. But the newfound foreign competition in the City of London led to increased resistance from domestically based British merchant banks to onerous regulations. The SIB circulated a new rule book in early 1987, and London's self-regulating organizations (SROs) followed soon after with their own rules, which by law had to comply with SIB standards.[47] Steven Vogel notes that these rules incited a "forceful rebellion from City practitioners," who were concerned that the burdensome rules would undermine the efficiency gains from the Big Bang.[48] Within the next few years the SIB came to be viewed by the public as weak and beholden to the interests of regulated firms.[49] The SIB's first chairman, Sir Kenneth Berrill, revealed his agency's precarious position when he referred to it as a "watchpuppy."[50]

While the SIB struggled to maintain a balance between stability and competitiveness after the Big Bang and the 1987 market crash, a new challenge emerged for firms in the City of London with the explosive growth of derivatives. As discussed earlier, New York was the locus for the development of many types of derivatives, and U.S. firms took an early lead in marketing derivatives to financial institutions and other corporate and governmental clients. But by the late 1980s a thriving market for futures, swaps, and other derivatives had developed in London, and British firms became formidable rivals to U.S. firms in the over-the-counter derivatives business.

Competition over derivatives became fierce in the City. The major U.S. securities firms, including Goldman Sachs, Salomon, and Morgan Stanley, established agents in London to garner their share of the international market. By the early 1990s these London-based agents had earned high marks among institutional investors for their range of products and competitive pricing. Goldman Sachs and Morgan Stanley were voted the top overall derivatives providers by investors in a late-1992 Euromoney Publications survey.[51] Other U.S. securities firms in the top twenty included Merrill Lynch (no. 6), Salomon (no. 8), and Lehman Brothers (no. 14). Phillips & Drew, at that point part of Union Bank of Switzerland, was third in the list. The only other U.K. securities firm to make the top twenty was SG Warburg (no. 15), although a few commercial banks, such as NatWest (no. 13) and Midland (no. 17), also made the cut. Data on the derivatives business of firms in the late 1980s and early 1990s are notoriously difficult to find, and the patchy data that do exist—including aggregate notional measurements and numbers of outstanding contracts—are generally not helpful as indicators of international market share.[52] But interviews with regulators and industry executives in London reveal the precariousness of British market share and the wariness of London-based firms toward their rivals in the United States. The word on the street was that Goldman Sachs and Morgan Stanley had a strong grip on the international market and that British firms were struggling to compete.[53]

Derivatives dealing, like bank lending, is conducted in an environment driven by relationships between financial institutions and clients. But just as clients seek to borrow money at low interest rates and favorable repayment terms, they also seek the lowest cost derivatives for their hedging and risk-management needs. The Big Bang reforms and the influx of foreign firms in London intensified the price competition in derivatives markets. Margaret Reid notes the evolution from "relationship" banking to "transaction" banking in the City: "Corporate (company) treasurers want the best terms when they raise cash or place out funds and increasingly go to whoever—whether British or foreign—offers the best 'buy,' rather than just to the merchant banker whose father and grandfather served them."[54] At the beginning of the 1990s it seemed that U.S. derivatives dealers were most likely to offer the best buy.

The competitive advantage of U.S. firms may have been attributable to technical innovation and expertise, operational efficiency, or other structural characteristics of the securities industry, but British firms focused on a key regulatory difference between the United States and the United Kingdom: consolidated supervision. In the United Kingdom, financial institutions (including securities firms) were supervised on a consolidated basis, meaning that all parts of the firm—holding companies, divisions, and subsidiaries—were subject to prudential regulation. Thus any British firm involved in derivatives dealing had to maintain a specified level of capital based on the risk profile of its portfolio. This rule had long been implicit in the Bank of England's regulatory regime, which tended to include securities activity in its umbrella due to the prevalence of universal banking (where commercial banking and securities trading are conducted under one roof). The Basel Accord codified the norm of consolidated supervision for the banking sectors in the G-10 countries, and the EU explicitly extended the rule to securities firms with the 1993 Capital Adequacy Directive.

Unlike firms in the United Kingdom and the rest of Europe, U.S. securities firms were not subject to consolidated supervision. The SEC's Net Capital Rule, adopted in 1975, applied a minimum capital requirement to registered broker-dealers only. All transactions involving "securities," defined by the SEC to include instruments involving ownership positions (such as stocks and bonds), had to be routed through broker-dealers, but derivatives—which either do not involve ownership or involve rights to ownership—were conspicuously absent from the SEC's definition.[55] As a result, securities firms created holding companies and special-purpose affiliates to conduct derivatives transactions, thereby avoiding the SEC's capital requirements. For example, Goldman Sachs and Morgan Stanley had separate "derivatives products companies" (DPCs) through which they effected derivatives transactions.[56] In terms of prudential regulations, these DPCs were almost completely unregulated. In contrast, the broker-dealer divisions of Goldman Sachs and Morgan Stanley faced stringent capital requirements based on their trading books; as the risk profile of their securities holdings increased (based on the risk of market fluctuations and liquidity problems), they were forced to hold more capital to augment their stability.

As discussed in chapter 2, capital requirements are costly for firms. British firms subject to consolidated supervision had to consider the cost of capital requirements when pricing their derivative contracts. U.S. DPCs, on the other hand, were free to balance their derivative portfolios without the imposition of expensive capital requirements and could therefore offer highly competitive pricing to their clients. To be sure, it would be a mistake to attribute the rising market share of U.S. firms solely to the lack of consolidated supervision in the United States. But the imposition of consolidated supervision in the United States would be a serious blow to the profitability of U.S. DPCs and would place the two countries on equal regulatory footing—the so-called level playing field.[57]

The SIB's competitive threat from less stringently regulated firms in the United States counterbalanced the regulator's incentives to enact more stringent regulations to bolster financial stability. As demonstrated by the figures in chapter 3, the SIB's win-set was closing in on both sides. Market volatility, combined with weakly capitalized firms, prevented the SIB from easing London's regulatory burden, but the rising threat from unregulated U.S. derivatives providers made the SIB's regulatory mix untenable.

The SIB and the Push for Harmonization

At the beginning of the 1990s the SIB faced an uncomfortable trade-off. The Financial Services Act of 1986, combined with the stock market volatility of the late 1980s, placed pressure on the SIB to tighten its regulatory requirements for the securities industry. Supervisory procedures such as consolidated supervision and minimum capital requirements were becoming codified in British law and finding their way into the early drafts of the EU's Capital Adequacy Directive (eventually promulgated in 1993), in line with the Basel Accord requirements developed for commercial banks. The SIB also created a new and complex web of regulations to prevent fraud and criminal abuse of London's financial markets. But at the same time, the City of London was struggling to adapt to the new competition from foreign firms, especially the DPCs of major U.S. securities firms. The

SIB, armed with only a financial regulator's limited set of policy tools, faced considerable difficulty in balancing the dueling demands for stability and competitiveness. It came to be viewed as weak and beholden to the securities industry, but at the same time, the legislation that created the SIB—and the SIB's subsequent rule making—was lambasted as anticompetitive and inimical to the continued growth of the City. The SIB, and the sweeping legislation of which it was a part, was pleasing no one. On the Financial Services Act of 1986, London's *Observer* quipped, "Unloved by professional and private investors alike and rejected by its parents, the [act's] long-term survival is far from assured."[58] The financial press routinely referred to the head of the SIB, David Walker, as its "embattled chairman" and questioned his future job prospects in light of the wide-scale resentment of the SIB's rules.[59]

There was little that the SIB could accomplish domestically to maintain a balance between stability and competitiveness and to appease the various interests of elected leaders and industry. Thus its shrinking win-set for regulatory policy led it to look toward the international arena for a solution. The SIB, as the main representative of the United Kingdom in IOSCO, had already championed a 1989 IOSCO report that laid the foundation for an international capital adequacy standard. As discussed earlier, the report—approved by the full Technical Committee at the 1989 annual meeting—was sufficiently vague to accommodate the varying interests of the world's primary securities markets. The SIB was now ready to tighten the language of the report and create a true international agreement on minimum capital levels for securities firms. It led the effort to create an international standard through IOSCO by drafting the initial proposals and marshaling the support of other European countries.[60] Its goal was to pressure the United States to adopt consolidated supervision of its securities firms, thereby hindering the momentum of U.S. DPCs and giving U.K. derivatives dealers a much-needed competitive boost.

Given the competitive pressures on British firms, the SIB's advocacy of an international capital adequacy standard may seem curious to historians of the era. The financial press and academic analyses focused on how the SIB and the U.S. SEC calculated minimum capital requirements, not on how they applied them. The SIB's mandated capital levels, introduced soon after the Financial Services Act of 1986, were flexible and arguably lax in comparison with those in the United States. Initially, the SIB adopted a "simplified portfolio approach," which established capital guidelines based on modern portfolio theory. The goal of the requirement was to ensure that firms had adequate capital to cover one week's fluctuations in securities prices.[61] As work began on the EU's Capital Adequacy Directive, the SIB advocated a building-block approach that allowed firms to maintain lower capital levels if they could match long and short positions in a diversified portfolio.[62] One study of capital adequacy requirements concluded that the SIB's move from the portfolio approach to the building-block approach constituted "negative" progress from a prudential standpoint.[63] But more important was that the SIB's approach was considerably less stringent than the SEC's net capital rule, which had been in place since 1975. Whereas the SIB's approach was based on netting—in which long and short positions could balance each other out—the SEC's approach was "comprehensive," mandating specific amounts of capital for both long and short positions.[64] In short, the SEC's regulations required far higher capital levels for broker-dealers than the SIB's approach.

Beneath the surface of the debates over the SIB's and SEC's regulatory approaches was the more critical issue of how firms are supervised. The SIB's capital requirements, though lower than those in the United States, were applicable to all parts of a securities firm. British firms therefore incurred capital charges for their derivatives trading, which necessarily affected their pricing and the aggressiveness of their portfolios. The SEC, on the other hand, exempted holding companies and other special-purpose entities from their capital rules. It is for this reason that consolidated supervision was an implicit component of the IOSCO negotiations. It is difficult to reconcile the SEC's sole focus on broker-dealers with the content of the 1989 IOSCO report, which emphasized such concepts as "a firm's true position" and an amalgamation of all risks faced by a firm.[65] With the creation of an international capital standard, the SIB expected the SEC and U.S. legislators to cave in quickly and apply the standard more broadly to securities firms. A former regulator in London stated that a global capital adequacy standard—enforced by nearly every other regulator on a consolidated basis—would put the SEC on a clear path toward regulatory supervision of holding companies.[66] The SEC, for its part, had little interest in cooperating with the SIB and became a vocal opponent in the negotiations over international regulatory harmonization.

The SEC's Opposition to Harmonization

Compared with the SIB, the U.S. Securities and Exchange Commission was on solid footing in the early 1990s. Its capital adequacy regime had been in place for some fifteen years and was considered stringent compared with the regulations in other financial markets. Equally important was the strength of U.S. securities firms in the growing international market for derivatives and the overall dominance of New York's capital market. The SEC's comfortable win-set for regulatory policy made it resistant to cooperating with its foreign counterparts. Whereas British regulators were struggling with stability and competitiveness shocks, the SEC faced a relatively comfortable environment of rising market share and financial stability. There was, however, one incident that rattled the SEC to its core: the dramatic collapse of broker-dealer Drexel Burnham Lambert in 1990. The SEC reacted to this stability shock by demanding new monitoring powers over the holding companies and affiliates of registered broker-dealers. This new tightening of regulatory stringency could be accomplished with little effect on the dominant position of U.S. securities firms in the international securities market. Congress heeded the SEC's wishes and legislated the Market Reform Act of 1990, which gave the agency the authority to demand financial information from all divisions of a firm, including its holding company. But Congress and the SEC had no interest in adopting outright consolidated supervision because of the competitive implications for U.S. firms in the international derivatives market. The SEC in particular believed that a crisis like the Drexel collapse could be prevented by increasing holding-company transparency, as legislated in the Market Reform Act, and that more comprehensive prudential supervision was not necessary to maintain financial stability. It was at this point that the SIB began its quest for an international capital adequacy standard with the goal of coercing the United States into imposing capital requirements on derivative products companies. The SEC had inadvertently established the momentum for such a change with the 1990 reforms and therefore had to be especially vocal in its resistance to an international standard.

Stability Shock: The Collapse of Drexel Burnham Lambert

Drexel Burnham Lambert was a pioneer in the development of the market for "junk bonds," bonds issued by corporations with less-than-stable finances and low credit ratings. Under the leadership of "junk bond king" Michael Milken, Drexel aggressively marketed the bonds to insurance companies, pension funds, and mutual funds in the United States and abroad, enabling companies with precarious balance sheets to raise cash for acquisitions and other projects. Milken's high profile and questionable business dealings eventually attracted the attention of federal prosecutors, who indicted him in 1989 on charges of mail and securities fraud and fined the company $650 million—a spectacular sum, even by Wall Street standards. The firm pleaded guilty to felony charges, rendering itself vulnerable to contingent legal liabilities to the New York Stock Exchange and client companies and making it nearly impossible to raise additional capital or find a merger partner.[67] Drexel filed for bankruptcy on February 13, 1990, precipitating a rapid downfall in the junk bond market. The average difference between the yields of junk bonds and government bonds nearly doubled (from 400 to 750 basis points) between mid-1989 and the Drexel collapse, indicating a significant collapse in junk bond prices (which move in the opposite direction of yields).[68] Many of Drexel's clients, which were dependent on junk bonds for their livelihood, went bankrupt soon after Drexel's demise, including Campeau Corporation and Integrated Resources.

From the SEC's perspective, Drexel's collapse was especially worrisome because of the transactions between its broker-dealer and its holding company. Drexel Burnham Lambert, Inc. (DBL), was a registered broker-dealer, subject to regulation by the SEC. Until just a week before the collapse of the firm, DBL was adequately capitalized, meeting the requirements set by the SEC's net capital rule. However, after the imposition of the $650 million fine and the collapse in the junk bond market, DBL's holding company, Drexel Burnham Lambert Group (DBLG), began to siphon capital away from its solvent broker-dealer. The SEC became aware of this transfer only after more than half the broker-dealer's capital—some $400 million—had been depleted and just eleven days before DBLG declared bankruptcy.[69] The incident made it clear to the SEC that the financial well-being of a parent company is crucial to the continued operation of its regulated affiliates. It also highlighted a serious hole in the SEC's supervisory authority: holding companies were not subject to SEC regulations.

SEC chairman Richard Breeden immediately called for a review of the 1975 net capital requirement and pressed Congress to expand the SEC's jurisdiction. Breeden was in a politically delicate position. To maintain public confidence in securities firms, he felt, the SEC needed more information on the financial status of the holding companies of registered broker-dealers. As Breeden stated during a Senate Banking Committee hearing, "If there's a five-alarm fire raging, we think we ought to know about it."[70] However, he had no interest in imposing capital requirements on holding companies. The adoption of consolidated supervision, as in the United Kingdom, would be a serious competitive blow to U.S. firms. Instead, the SEC wanted a middle-of-the-road solution: require holding companies to submit periodic financial reports to the SEC on their balance sheets, cash flow, and transactions with their affiliates. Senators John Heinz (R-PA) and Christopher Dodd (D-CT) agreed with Breeden and introduced a bill that would amend the 1934 Securities Exchange Act by requiring holding companies and affiliated entities of registered broker-dealers to submit periodic reports to the SEC.[71] In its early stages the bill was resisted by a handful of large securities firms that were concerned that the new requirement was one small step away from consolidated supervision.[72] But the momentum of the Drexel failure eventually carried the day: the bill, passed as the Market Reform Act of 1990, constituted a significant change in the supervision of holding companies.[73]

The SEC on the Defensive

Regulators in the United Kingdom watched from afar as the Drexel story unfolded and realized that they had an unprecedented opportunity to press for an international capital adequacy standard that would place British securities firms on equal regulatory footing with those of the United States. In the early stages of the IOSCO negotiations, the SEC seemed to be a willing participant. It supported the United Kingdom's 1989 resolution, which established a set of general guidelines for capital adequacy, and continued the negotiations within IOSCO Working Group 3 beginning in 1990. However, as an international standard began to take shape, the SEC abruptly turned defensive. At a meeting of the IOSCO Technical Committee in July 2002, SEC chairman Breeden suggested that the SIB's building-block approach was fatally flawed, and he monopolized the ensuing discussion to avoid any progress on the issue.[74] He also argued that the SEC's comprehensive approach (which assigns capital requirements to long and short positions) was the only sufficient way to ensure the stability of securities firms in the event of severe market fluctuations. One participant said, "I think the feeling of most of the people at the meeting was that he [Breeden] didn't want an agreement. So he reverted to a hard and fast position which he knew the others couldn't adopt."[75] At the IOSCO annual meeting in October 1992, Breeden was explicit in his resistance to an international agreement. He stated, "We don't see any value to an agreement that ratifies the bottom of the barrel," and he later remarked that he viewed IOSCO as a forum for discussion, not a rule-making body akin to the Basel Committee.[76]

Given the growing awareness of the vulnerability of a registered broker-dealer to the unregulated activities of its parent, the SEC had to be wary of a global capital adequacy standard. Requiring information from holding companies is a clear step toward regulating their activities. The SEC had no interest in expanding its capital requirement to include holding companies; indeed, financial firms made their resistance to such a development clearly felt in Congress during the debates over the Market Reform Act. But in light of Breeden's push for more information from unregulated affiliates, a global capital adequacy standard, intended to address the full range of risks to securities firms, would provide more momentum for the emergence of consolidated supervision in the United States.[77] As these developments unfolded, the SEC—eager to defend its own policymaking discretion and the competitiveness of U.S. securities firms—made its preferences known by unceremoniously pulling out of the IOSCO negotiations.

The Japanese Ministry of Finance: On the Sidelines

The 1980s were a strong decade for Japanese securities firms, just as they were for the banking sector. The Nikkei index experienced a dramatic rise throughout the period, from around 10,000 in 1984 to a zenith of over 39,000 at the end of 1989. Large trade surpluses primed the domestic economy, and high liquidity led to increased speculation in real estate and other investments. As stock prices soared, so did the profits of Japan's large securities firms. The so-called Big Four—Nomura, Daiwa, Nikko, and Yamaichi—reaped the benefits of artificially high commissions and underwriting fees. The oligopolistic structure of the securities industry, in which the Big Four accounted for more than 75 percent of securities transactions, kept domestic competition to a minimum, and long-standing restrictions on foreign participation in the Tokyo Stock Exchange provided insulation from global competitive pressures.

When the October 1987 stock market crash rippled across the developed world, Japanese securities firms were not nearly as concerned about the market as their Western counterparts. Steven Solomon, who chronicled the effects of the crash in the developed world, notes that the "Tokyo establishment remained calm."[78] U.S. and British central bankers scrambled to soothe the markets with commitments of emergency liquidity and encouraged banks to support faltering securities firms with short-term financing. The Bank of Japan, however, was reluctant to alter its monetary policy given its perception of the strength of the domestic economy.[79] Japanese firms did not require additional liquidity; in fact, they were more interested in buffering the losses of their best corporate clients with their own substantial capital bases.[80] The Nikkei bounced back quickly and rose to new heights over the next two years.

For the developed markets of the West, the 1987 stock market crash was a turning point of sorts, a catalyst for the reevaluation of regulatory policy in light of the newfound interdependence of market volatility. The crash therefore serves as a convenient episode to organize the discussions of securities firm regulation in the United States and the United Kingdom. For Japan, however, the turning point came later and involved changes in the domestic economy rather than exogenous shocks from abroad. In 1990 the Nikkei began to drop as dramatically as it had risen over the previous five years. Japan's bubble economy burst as real-estate prices tumbled and business investment contracted sharply. By 1992 the Nikkei average had plunged to around 14,000, a decline of nearly 65 percent from the beginning of the decade. The period of Japanese financial ascendance was largely over, and regulators in the once powerful Ministry of Finance struggled to adapt to a seemingly moribund market. The bursting of the Japanese economic bubble, which coincided with the height of the negotiations over capital adequacy under IOSCO, ultimately had a significant impact on the policy stance of the MOF toward international harmonization.

Throughout the 1980s the MOF maintained informal and ad hoc rules for the prudential operation of securities firms. There were basic guidelines for asset-liability ratios and capital levels, often intended to limit specific lines of business or to serve as barriers to entry for small firms. For example, firms engaged in securities underwriting were required to have a capital stock in excess of ¥3 billion, with total liabilities not exceeding ten times net worth. In addition, ratios of securities owned to net worth could not exceed 40 percent for members of the Tokyo Stock Exchange.[81] More important than these restrictions were the scores of unwritten rules regarding pricing, liquidity, and risk that the MOF could enforce at its discretion. Just as banks in the United Kingdom politely heeded the requests of the Bank of England in the 1970s and 1980s, so too did Japanese securities firms take pains to avoid an uncomfortable encounter with the MOF. The former head of international securities at Nomura Securities stated, with some resentment, "There are so many unwritten rules, called administrative guidelines. Even Nomura Tokyo, a giant, must send people to the MOF before we do anything different. Because we don't want to receive a long sermon from mother, 'You didn't behave.' Then the ball bounces differently."[82]

The gradual liberalization of the Japanese securities market, combined with the increasing international expansion of the Big Four, created new challenges for the MOF. In 1982 the Tokyo Stock Exchange amended its charter to allow foreign membership for the first time, and after a period of nationalistic resistance and diplomatic wrangling, a small group of U.S. and U.K. firms became members in 1986. Foreign membership continued to expand in the late 1980s, with the addition of nineteen foreign members between 1988 and 1990.[83] Conversely, the Big Four expanded their international presence substantially in the late 1980s. For example, the U.S. subsidiary of Nomura had a modest staff of 75 in 1985 but expanded to 625 employees just four years later.[84] By 1989 Japanese securities firms had 231 foreign branches in twenty-two countries.[85] Nomura and Daiwa joined the elite club of primary dealers in U.S. government securities in 1986, with Nikko following suit in 1987. And the liberalizing reforms in Canada, the United Kingdom, and much of western Europe expedited the expansion of Japanese firms into those markets.[86] By 1986 Nomura, Daiwa, and Nikko were among the top ten underwriters of Eurobonds.[87] The dramatic international expansion of the Big Four led many observers to protest their alleged predatory pricing and aggressive tactics.[88] At a more mundane level, the growing foreign presence of Japanese firms led to increased attention to the MOF's regulations. The previously insulated securities bureau of the MOF faced increasing pressure to formalize its prudential regulations, as the United States and United Kingdom had already done.[89]

When IOSCO Working Group 3 was established to examine the issue of capital adequacy for securities firms, the MOF was a willing participant. The growing chorus of resentment toward the Japanese in the West provided every incentive for the MOF to appear cooperative in international financial matters. The 1989 IOSCO resolution, discussed earlier, was general enough to accommodate the MOF's current system of informal prudential rules, but nevertheless the MOF decided to introduce a new set of formal regulations. In March 1989 the MOF issued a codified framework for capital adequacy, in which capital charges would be based on a comprehensive survey of a firm's risks.[90] Capital charges were allocated based on the vulnerability of a firm to changes in asset prices, customer default (i.e., counterparty risk), and operational malfeasance.[91] Given the MOF's regulatory penetration of all financial institutions, there was no way for a firm to avoid these rules through special-purpose corporate entities such as U.S. DPCs and holding-company divisions. The regulatory framework was developed with the assistance of the Big Four and had the quiet support of the securities industry.[92] The framework in fact represented the formalization of the MOF's administrative guidelines and expectations developed over the course of the decade rather than a significant tightening of the regulatory environment. The skyrocketing Nikkei and the healthy profits of the securities industry made the newly formalized regulations almost inconsequential in the short run.

The Japanese securities industry experienced a drastic change with the collapse of asset prices beginning in 1990. The Nikkei plummeted 40 percent in just one year and reached a low point of around 14,000 in 1992.[93] Investors were particularly rattled by the drop in real-estate prices, which fell more than 70 percent throughout the 1990s.[94] The seemingly endless flow of profits that had accrued to the Big Four in the 1980s came to an abrupt halt as investors became more conservative and businesses scaled back their expansion plans. A survey by Teikoku Data Bank found that 130 Japanese securities firms faced a 30 percent drop in operating profits in fiscal year 1990.[95] Underwriting commissions by the top eleven firms amounted to only ¥2 billion in the six months to September 1992, compared with ¥170 billion in the first half of 1990.[96] The ratings agencies began to take notice: Moody's downgraded the long- and short-term debt ratings of each of the Big Four in 1992, with Daiwa and Yamaichi hit especially hard.[97]

In 1991 the industry experienced another jolt with the so-called loss-compensation scandals, in which the Big Four admitted that they had compensated their large corporate clients for losses stemming from the 1987 market crash.[98] Policymakers in Japan and abroad were incensed by the arrogance of the Big Four in protecting their larger clients at the expense of smaller businesses and individual investors. Prime Minister Toshiki Kaifu established a committee to recommend a course of action in the wake of the scandal, and a proposal quickly emerged to establish an SEC-style independent securities regulator to replace the MOF's securities division.[99] The MOF eventually defeated the proposal—which, in Vogel's terms, would have "dismembered" the ministry—after an aggressive lobbying campaign.[100]

The faltering Japanese economy and the securities scandal led to a backlash in Japanese financial expansion abroad, especially in the United

States. The SEC announced that it would put Japanese brokers under closer scrutiny, and the New York Stock Exchange launched its own investigation into the business practices of the Big Four.[101] U.S. institutional investors that previously enjoyed amiable relationships with the Big Four, such as the California Public Employees Retirement System and other state pension systems, promptly closed their accounts and took their funds to other brokers.[102] In response to their shrinking capital bases and bad publicity, Japanese firms began to scale back their foreign offices. Nomura closed three European offices in 1992 and trimmed the staff of its London office, and the rest of the Big Four followed suit.[103]

The retrenchment of Japan's securities industry coincided with the height of the IOSCO negotiations over capital adequacy for securities firms. The SEC and the SIB had staked out opposing positions on the issue, which was particularly contentious because of the significant consequences of an agreement to the international competitive standing of British and U.S. derivatives dealers. The MOF, however, was more interested in the health of the Japanese economy and the revival of domestic asset prices than the exigencies of international competition. The Big Four were losing international market share in equity and debt underwriting and investment management as a result of domestic scandals and eroding capital bases, not because of the regulatory environments of their foreign competitors. Moreover, Japanese firms were not yet major players in the international market for derivatives. The MOF and other policymakers in fact resisted the introduction of derivatives trading in the 1980s; in a particularly memorable episode, the deputy chairman of the Tokyo Stock Exchange threatened to throw an ashtray at the president of the Singapore Exchange, who was moving forward with plans to introduce derivatives trading based on Japanese securities.[104] Even in Japan itself, U.S. firms dominated the futures market in the early 1990s because of their greater expertise and product offerings.[105] To be sure, Japanese firms were not completely disengaged from the derivatives markets. The Tokyo Financial Futures Exchange was established in 1989, and trading volume in stock index futures reached 58,000 contracts per day in 1990.[106] But as suppliers of derivative contracts to institutional investors, Japanese firms were only marginal players. By the end of 1994 the notional amounts of outstanding derivatives for Nikko and Nomura were $53 billion and $134 billion, respectively; the comparable amounts for Solomon Brothers and Merrill Lynch were $1.5 trillion and $1.2 trillion.[107]

As the SIB demanded an international capital adequacy standard based on a relatively flexible "netting" approach, the MOF quietly stood behind the SEC in opposition.[108] The promulgation of an international standard would have a negligible impact on the international competitiveness of Japanese firms in the market for derivatives. If the United States was forced into adopting consolidated supervision, as the SIB had hoped, the resulting jolt to U.S. derivatives dealers would have provided little help to faltering Japanese firms. Derivatives pricing—which for U.S. firms would be greatly influenced by the introduction of capital requirements for derivatives dealers—was not a serious challenge for Japanese firms, which were known to undercut their competitors to gain market share, even if at a short-term financial loss. Rather, Japanese firms were counting on a domestic stock market recovery to boost their profits and expedite their continued international expansion. In terms of the framework developed in chapter 3, the MOF did not experience a competitiveness shock, since any changes to foreign regulations would not affect the market share of Japanese firms. Rather, Japanese firms were losing market share because of the wide-scale collapse of the domestic economy and the highly publicized scandals of the Big Four.

The MOF was also wary of tying its hands with an international capital standard when the Japanese securities industry was in a state of transition. Article 65 of the Japanese Securities and Exchange Law had previously segregated the functions of banking and securities brokerage (similar to the Glass-Steagall Act in the United States), but a 1992 legislative measure allowed banks to establish separately capitalized affiliates to conduct a limited amount of securities business.[109] At the same time, Japan's smaller securities firms were on the verge of collapse, and the Big Four were in no position to acquire them. The MOF told bankers in 1992 that they might be required to extend a "lifeboat" to prevent the disintegration of the securities industry.[110] With the blurring distinction between banking and brokerage, and the increasingly precarious financial position of Japanese securities firms, the MOF had little interest in embracing an international capital standard that would limit its discretion in handling a troubled industry.

The Resolution

The IOSCO negotiations got off to an auspicious start despite the stark divergence in the demands of regulators for an international capital standard. Working Group 3 drafted the 1989 report discussed earlier, which was approved by the full IOSCO membership. Following the resolution, the Working Group continued to meet, ostensibly to tighten up the language of the resolution and move toward a true regulatory standard. In the three years after the 1989 report was published, the IOSCO Technical Committee and the Basel Committee exchanged a number of issue papers in an attempt to arrive at a consensus view of the appropriate capital requirements for any firm conducting securities business. At a meeting in late January 1992 regulators converged on a proposal that would require securities firms to hold capital equivalent to 4 percent of their gross holdings plus 8 percent of their net holdings, after netting out long against short positions.[111] Such a requirement was considerably more stringent than the SIB's current domestic requirements, but the SIB's expectation was that the creation of an international standard would soon lead to the adoption of consolidated supervision in the United States. At the conclusion of the meeting the SIB was optimistic that a formal IOSCO agreement would be forthcoming at the October annual meeting.[112]

The Technical Committee had scheduled one final meeting in July 1992 before the annual meeting, with the intent of drafting a preliminary agreement. As we have seen, however, when it became clear that an agreement was actually taking shape, U.S. regulators, with the backing of the Japanese, abruptly turned resistant.[113] A particularly contentious issue was the extent to which a securities firm should be able to reduce its capital requirement through hedging.[114] The SIB initially backed a plan that would allow a firm to carry 2 percent of the sum of its long and short positions, assuming the firm had a perfectly hedged book as defined in the proposal.[115] This plan was substantially lower than the SEC's existing standard of 15 percent. SEC chairman Breeden said that under the SIB's proposed rules, a major U.S. securities firm would have failed after the October 1987 crash, and he refused to endorse a standard that he called "dangerously low."[116] He also argued that IOSCO should be a "clearing house of ideas" and not a rule maker.[117] The IOSCO annual meeting therefore produced no agreement, and the Technical Committee went back to the drawing board to see if a consensus could still be created. Despite the SIB's protests, however, it was clear that no further progress would be made on the issue without support from the United States and Japan. IOSCO officially abandoned the effort to harmonize capital adequacy regulations in early 1993.[118]

For historians of the era, it is easy to miss the source of the tension between the various regulators. An international standard, after all, would set forth *minimum* requirements for securities firms; regulators who agreed to the standard could always enforce more stringent regulations if they desired. But fueling the tension was the understanding that the United States was precariously close to adopting consolidated supervision, and that the creation of a global standard would provide an additional impetus to the SEC and Congress to change how regulations were enforced in the United States. Leading the charge for harmonization was the SIB, which faced a substantial competitiveness shock from U.S. derivatives dealers and sought to protect itself from political pressure by changing the regulatory environment in the United States. The SEC had the competitive upper hand and a stable securities industry and thus had no interest in acceding to an international standard that could prompt regulatory changes at home. The MOF faced a variety of shocks at home, but foreign regulations were not relevant to the moribund state of the Japanese securities industry. The MOF therefore stood beside the SEC in opposing regulatory harmonization and instead focused its energies on salvaging the domestic financial sector with its own ad hoc system of punishments, rewards, and regulatory changes.

The stability-competitiveness framework indicates that regulators seek international standards when their autonomy is threatened—in particular, when their win-sets are shrinking and legislative intervention becomes more likely. What happens when regulators in such circumstances fail to achieve harmonization? The fate of the SIB after the failed IOSCO negotiations is telling. The U.K. securities industry continued to decline in the early 1990s as foreign firms acquired London's weakly capitalized merchant banks. The distressed investment firm SG Warburg had been seeking a suitor for several years and was finally acquired by Swiss Bank Corporation in June 1995 for a modest $1.35 billion.[119] That same year, Kleinwort Benson accepted a takeover offer of just over $1.5 billion from Germany's Dresdner Bank, and Barings became part of the Netherlands' ING Bank after it suffered $1.4 billion in derivative trading losses.[120] By the end of 1995 only a small number of independent British merchant banks remained in London, including relatively small firms Rothschild and Hambros. Meanwhile, U.S. firms continued to dominate the derivatives market in Europe. These developments helped to boost London's reputation as a global financial center rivaling New York, but the decline in British firms was an unwelcome development for the SIB. The regulator had struggled to maintain the balance between stability and competitiveness from its creation in 1986, and the onslaught of foreign firms in London made this balance nearly impossible to obtain.

In 1997 the chancellor of the exchequer announced a series of regulatory reforms that transformed the British financial sector. The government effectively dismantled the existing SIB and in its place created a new agency—the Financial Services Authority, or FSA—which would gain jurisdiction over banks, securities firms, and other financial institutions with the Financial Services and Markets Act of 2000. A variety of factors were responsible for the elimination of the SIB and the creation of the FSA, including changes in the charter of the Bank of England and the rise of conglomerates with multiple financial functions. However, the analytical framework of this book contributes another reason: the SIB's failure to maintain a win-set for regulatory policy triggered the legislature to intervene and change the regulatory environment. To be sure, capital requirements and competitive pressures in the derivatives market were just one component of the SIB's struggle. In the end, the SIB's inability to strike a balance in all its regulatory areas, including antifraud provisions, licensing restrictions, and prudential regulations, prompted the British government to revamp the entire regulatory system.

When the negotiations over capital adequacy ended without an agreement, regulators' hopes for IOSCO as a rule-making body were shattered.

Regulators in the United Kingdom and the rest of Europe had hoped that a new securities capital adequacy standard would place IOSCO on the same level as the Basel Committee, which had garnered much attention with its heralded accord on bank capital in 1988.[121] Moreover, the threat of stock market volatility and firm bankruptcies grew more acute in the 1990s as the United States, Europe, and Japan faced recessions at home and fervent competition abroad. But ultimately, the specter of financial instability was not a great enough incentive for regulators to converge on an international standard. Instead, regulators were driven by their domestic political circumstances, which varied considerably among the most powerful participants in the negotiations. Given the resistance from the SEC and the MOF, the absence of an international standard is not surprising. Instead, the puzzle addressed by this chapter—indeed, the most intriguing side of the story—is the stark variation in the demands of regulators for international regulatory harmonization.

Chapter 6

Insurance: Domestic Fragmentation and Regulatory Divergence

After the dust of the September 11, 2001, tragedy began to settle, the financial press began to raise the mundane but important question: who is going to pay for this? The attacks constituted the largest insured loss in U.S. history. Two of the world's tallest buildings collapsed, taking with them billions of dollars' worth of equipment, artwork,[1] and other valuables, and reducing more than sixteen acres of prime New York real estate to uninhabitable rubble. Business operations in these buildings obviously ceased, resulting in lost revenue and costly transitions to new facilities. The Pentagon also suffered substantial damage, not to mention the four commercial aircraft that were destroyed in the attacks. Insurance claims for these losses, combined with life insurance benefits for the thousands of individuals who lost their lives, totaled an estimated $40–50 billion.[2]

The attacks underscored the international reach of the insurance industry—in particular, the *reinsurance* industry, which provides insurance for insurance firms. Firms in the United States, the United Kingdom, Germany, Switzerland, and Australia, to name a few, all incurred substantial losses. Germany's Munich Re, the world's largest reinsurer, sustained losses of more than $3 billion. Lloyd's of London, which historically has operated the world's largest insurance market, incurred reinsurance losses of more than $1 billion.[3] The terrorist attacks sought to undermine American capitalism and in the process they highlighted the broad and deep integration of the global financial system. Insurance and reinsurance firms around the world are linked in a complex chain, and the strength of that chain suffered a grueling test in the weeks and months after the September 11 attacks.

As with banking and securities, the international spread of the reinsurance industry underscores the problem of systemic risk.[4] If a reinsurer is not adequately capitalized, it may not have sufficient funds to cover claims from its clients. The collapse of a reinsurer in one country could in turn lead to the collapse of an insurance firm in another. Ultimately, businesses and consumers pay the price—either because they are unable to collect on their legitimate insurance claims or because they are precluded from obtaining insurance for future projects. Fortunately, the world's largest reinsurers were able to withstand the losses from the September 11 attacks, but the fact remains that insurance firms are vulnerable to developments outside their home countries. The adequate capitalization of reinsurance firms is, at least in theory, an international issue. As the saying goes, a chain is only as strong as its weakest link. But as the previous chapters attest, the presence of systemic risk is not a helpful predictor of the emergence of international standards.

This chapter analyzes the recent efforts by insurance regulators to create international standards, focusing in particular on the issue of capital adequacy. I pay particular attention to the reinsurance industry, which is more international—and more prone to systemic risk—than the direct insurance industry. The locus of discussions among insurance regulators is the International Association of Insurance Supervisors (IAIS), a forum created in 1994 that now welcomes members from more than 180 jurisdictions. Much like the Basel Committee and IOSCO, the IAIS is not an international actor per se: it has no agency independent of its membership, which consists entirely of insurance regulators and supervisors.[5] It has a very small secretariat housed in leased office space in the Bank for International Settlements in Basel, Switzerland. It is newer than both the Basel Committee and IOSCO, and its accomplishments are more modest. Indeed, the IAIS has created guidelines for effective insurance supervision but no specific regulatory standards.

The IAIS emerged rather quietly in 1994, largely because the growing importance of the Basel Committee and IOSCO created pressure on insurance regulators to create their own international committee.[6] The work of the IAIS is conducted under the guidance of an Executive Committee, which itself established a Technical Committee to oversee member cooperation in areas such as solvency, disclosure and transparency, fraud, and financial conglomerates.[7] Members vote on technical standards and guidelines at the General Meeting, with a two-thirds majority required for adoption. In practice, members strive for consensus; open disputes at the General Meeting are rare.

The purpose of this chapter is to explain the relative absence of pressure to create international regulatory standards for the reinsurance industry.

As in the previous chapters, I view the weakly institutionalized IAIS as a reflection of national regulators' preferences, not as an independent influence on their behavior. Because there is no specific set of negotiations on which to focus, I explore the domestic environments of insurance regulators in the United States and the United Kingdom, which represent the largest reinsurance markets. The Japanese insurance market remains heavily protected, and Japanese insurance firms have not reached the international prominence of Japanese banks or securities firms.[8] I argue that insurance regulators have emerged only modestly as international actors because of the fragmented nature of insurance regulation in the United States and because international competition in reinsurance is relatively mild compared with banking and securities, and not nearly as nationalistic. As with other financial areas, appeals to the importance of systemic risk are not analytically useful in explaining patterns of international regulatory harmonization.

The regulatory environments in the United States and the United Kingdom were influenced by two "stability shocks": the liability crisis of the 1980s in the United States and the reinsurance crisis in the Lloyd's of London market in the early 1990s. The low levels of international competitive pressure, combined with regulators' efforts to fight fraud and malfeasance rather than create solvency requirements, prevented these episodes from triggering a push toward international regulatory harmonization. More recent efforts in the European Union—in particular, the Solvency II Directive—may lead to considerable harmonization within the EU countries, but these developments are unlikely to prompt additional harmonization outside the EU in the near future.

Insurance in the Global Economy

Insurance is one of the most important but least appreciated functions in the global economy. It serves as the foundation for most private economic activities and as a catalyst for economic growth and development. The insurance industry has expanded beyond national borders alongside banking and securities markets, and its top-grossing firms rank among the largest financial institutions in the world. Despite its prominence in economic activity, insurance receives short shrift in studies of the global economy by political scientists.[9] Indeed, there is scant mention of international insurance markets in the literature, especially compared with the more frequent treatments of banking and securities.[10]

In certain respects, insurance deserves to be segregated from banking and securities because of the nature of the transactions involved. As discussed in chapter 2, banks and securities firms channel funds from savers to borrowers, thereby expanding the pool of productive investment in an economy. The demand for bank deposits and securitized investments arises because individuals and businesses seek to earn a return on their savings, in the form of interest payments, dividends, or capital gains. An investor who purchases a security, or a bank that lends funds to a business, assumes speculative risk: the outcome of the investment may be a gain or a loss. Insurance markets, on the other hand, are markets for *pure risk*. A consumer purchases an insurance contract as a means of ceding risk to another entity, not as an instrument for earning a return on excess capital. The insurance firm, in turn, accepts the possibility of incurring a loss (but never a gain) in exchange for a premium from the consumer.

It should come as no surprise that consumers of all types are averse to pure losses. Asset holders—including the owners of automobiles, production facilities, and cruise ships—are generally eager to protect themselves against financial losses stemming from damage, theft, or catastrophe. Individuals are similarly averse to financial losses due to ill health or the death of a wage-earning family member. In an environment of risk aversion, gains from trade are possible because consumers are willing to pay insurers a hefty premium in order to transfer risk away from themselves. Insurers, in turn, pool risk from many clients to become profitable. The so-called law of large numbers gives insurance firms their advantage, because the mean risk ceded by their clients becomes arbitrarily close to the mean risk of the population as a whole. In other words, the greater the number of independent clients with similar loss exposures, the more predictable is the insurance firm's claims experience. An insurance firm with ten clients could easily go bankrupt in an unlucky year, but a firm with thousands of clients can collect premiums that will more than offset its predictable annual losses.

In practice, insurance firms are not always able to take advantage of the law of large numbers. In certain circumstances, the number of clients with similar loss exposures is small, as in the case of coverage for oil tanker accidents.[11] A more common problem is that clients' risk exposures are not independent. Consider, for example, the financial losses due to the successive hurricanes in Florida during the summer of 2004. The risk of loss for one Florida resident was not independent of the risk of loss for any other resident. The potential covariance of client claims—also called *locally dependent risks*—lead insurers to protect *themselves* against financial loss by ceding some of the risk to another insurer. In short, insurance companies often require their own insurance. The suppliers of insurance to insurance firms are known as reinsurers.

The International Reinsurance Industry

Reinsurers assume risk from primary (or "direct") insurers for a premium in much the same way as primary insurers assume risk from customers. In that role, they are critical in enhancing the financial performance and security of primary insurers. Virtually all direct insurers purchase reinsurance.[12] The IAIS delineates five specific areas in which reinsurance is critical: (1) capacity: allowing primary insurers to enter new lines of business of various sizes and types; (2) expertise: providing assistance to insurers with little experience in specific coverage areas or geographic regions; (3) stability: mitigating the possible fluctuations in primary insurers' underwriting results; (4) financial: helping to fund firm operations without the requirement of raising additional capital; and (5) protection: providing a shield against large claims resulting from catastrophic events.[13] The economic motivation for reinsurance stems from the fact that locally dependent risks, such as those arising from hurricanes and other natural disasters, may be globally independent. As the IAIS notes, reinsurers "can improve the risk profile and the financial soundness of primary insurers by diversifying and limiting territorial accumulations of exposure, and consequently creating underwriting capacity."[14] Reinsurers, with few exceptions, work with clients in many countries. Their international orientation enables them to pool locally dependent risks with other independent risks from other parts of the world.

The growth in the global market for reinsurance tracks the underlying market for direct insurance, which has grown at a healthy clip since the 1980s. Between 1987 and 1994, gross direct premiums written by insurance firms grew at an average inflation-adjusted annual rate of 4.5 percent, reaching approximately US$2 trillion at the end of 1994.[15] Between 1993 and 2002, gross direct premiums continued to grow at approximately 4 percent annually, reaching US$2.9 trillion in 2003.[16] The major national markets for direct insurance—the United States, the United Kingdom, Japan, France, and Germany—have remained fairly constant over the past two decades.

Global reinsurance markets have experienced a similar pattern of growth. Total reinsurance premiums increased from US$69 billion in 1990 to more than US$175 billion in 2003 (see table 6). Non-life reinsurance, which includes coverage for property, liability, and a variety of other areas, accounts for most of the annual totals.

The major reinsurance firms are located in Europe and North America. A survey conducted by the IAIS in 2003 revealed that slightly more than half

TABLE 6.
Global Reinsurance Premiums (billions of U.S. dollars)

	1990	1995	2000	2003
Non-life reinsurance	61.3	93.2	97.5	146.0
Life reinsurance	7.8	11.7	20.4	29.5
Total reinsurance	69.1	104.9	117.9	175.5

Source: Based on IAIS 2004b.

TABLE 7.
Gross Reinsurance Premiums Assumed/Ceded by Region, 2003
(billions of U.S. dollars)

	Gross assumed (1)	Gross ceded (2)	Net position (1)–(2)
Europe	77.1	(50.2)	26.9
North America	70.3	(86.3)	(16.0)
Asia and Australia	2.1	(9.1)	(7.0)
Africa, Near and Middle East	—	(1.5)	(1.5)
Latin America	—	(2.4)	(2.4)

Source: Based on IAIS 2004b.

of all reinsurance premiums were collected by firms domiciled in Europe, with slightly less than half received by North American firms (see table 7). North America constitutes the largest market for reinsurance: direct insurers in the region ceded more than $86 billion in premiums in 2003.

There are many reasons for the growth of the insurance and reinsurance markets. There is clearly a strong connection between economic development and the demand for insurance and reinsurance; indeed, insurance premiums tend to rise at a faster rate than national income.[17] As individual and business incomes grow and the value of assets increases, the demand for insurance and the funds available to pay the premiums rise in synch.[18] Moreover, the gradual liberalization of trade in services has facilitated cross-border insurance transactions and the development of a truly international market.[19] Many countries have dismantled virtually all restrictions on international reinsurance transactions, reflecting the inherently international foundation of the reinsurance process.[20] Nevertheless, the liberalization process is far from complete. Access to the historically closed Japanese market, for example, remains a top priority for U.S. and European insurance firms.

The Nature of Reinsurance Competition

For reinsurance to be effective in spreading risk, it generally must have an international component. Reinsurance firms seek to diversify their risks by contracting with clients in a variety of countries and regions.[21] Direct insurers, for their part, are also interested in ceding risk to a globally diversified reinsurance firm because reinsurers that are diversified are more stable and less likely to run into financial difficulty—and thus less likely to renege on their commitments in the event of a claim.

The desire for international diversification, on the part of both reinsurers and their clients, creates an unusual competitive environment. Unlike clients in the markets for banking services and derivatives, insurance clients may actually prefer to do business with foreign firms—pricing issues aside. Thus domestic reinsurance industries exhibit little of the nationalist sentiment found, for example, in the U.S. banking industry in the 1980s during the rise of Japanese banks. In the developed world, reinsurance industries are indeed proud of their foreign participants. Consider the stance of the Reinsurance Association of America, which boasts on its Web site that "40% of all U.S. reinsurance premiums, and two-thirds of all property catastrophe reinsurance premiums, are written by foreign reinsurance companies."[22] Such pride in foreign involvement in an industry is quite rare for a U.S. trade association.

The other unusual element in the competitive environment for reinsurance is the need for capacity. Reinsurance contracts tend to be quite large, covering millions or even billions of dollars of risk ceded by direct insurers. Reinsurance firms clearly must be large enough to accept such enormous risks. The capacity constraint creates incentives for reinsurance firms to grow—and indeed, the industry has undergone a wave of consolidation since the 1990s.[23] But more important is that direct insurers do not have the option of transacting with a domestic reinsurer with inadequate capacity. Direct insurers, in short, may require the larger capacity of foreign reinsurers. As Harold Skipper notes, "No one country's market can provide needed cover for property- and liability-loss exposure arising from oil refineries, tankers, offshore rigs, satellites, jumbo jets, environmental impairment, and the like. An international spread is essential if such large risks are to be insured."[24] Along with the demand for international diversification, the capacity constraint attenuates any nationalistic sentiment that might otherwise arise in the reinsurance industry.

Nevertheless, international competition exists in the reinsurance market. Firms use their knowledge bases, competitive pricing, and the cultivation of long-term relationships to gain international market share. Financial and human resources are invested to develop expertise in specific areas, such as marine, aviation, and transportation (collectively known as *MAT*), casualty, and professional liability. The pricing and structuring of coverage in each area is a complicated and sophisticated matter and requires the efforts of actuaries and financial analysts with specialized training. Firms that can overcome these barriers to entry are rewarded in the international marketplace.

Relationships with clients are also a critical element in the market for reinsurance. The longevity of relationships is in part driven by expertise, since reinsurance firms build up a level of specialized knowledge about their clients over time. More important, the reinsurance business is fundamentally about credibility. In the event that a client incurs a loss, the reinsurance firm is expected to honor the client's claim. However, the "recovery" process is fraught with transaction costs, loopholes, and the potential for divergent interpretations. In short, the criteria for filing a claim may not be clear-cut. Reinsurance analysts will scrutinize all claims from their clients, and they can and do refuse to accept liability if the cause of a client's loss is deemed to be beyond the scope of the reinsurance contract. Even successful claims settlements may require several months of technical investigation and legal negotiation.[25] However, a client with a strong relationship with a reinsurer will generally fare better in the recovery process.

The Regulation of Reinsurance Firms

The regulation of reinsurance focuses on the relationship between the solvency of the reinsurer and the solvency of the direct insurer. If a reinsurer collapses or does not have sufficient funds to pay a claim, the client (a direct insurer) may in turn not have sufficient funds to pay its own claims. The clients of the direct insurer—businesses and individuals—will therefore experience financial losses. If those losses are large or widespread, they could have a deleterious effect on the economy. Ensuring the stability of reinsurance firms is therefore critical in protecting the interests of ceding insurers and the public at large.[26]

Regulators have two main tools for regulating reinsurance firms. The first, which can be called "indirect" regulation, pertains to restrictions on direct insurers' choice of reinsurance firms.[27] Direct insurers generally receive balance-sheet credit for ceding risk to reinsurers, and regulators often require insurers to cede a certain percentage of their underwriting risk to protect against insolvency. Indirect regulation occurs when regulators grant balance-sheet credit to direct insurers only if they select reinsurers that meet certain criteria. The U.S. regulatory system relies primarily on indirect regulation to ensure the stability of the insurance market. Second, regulators can impose restrictions directly on reinsurers domiciled in their jurisdictions, such as capital requirements and portfolio guidelines. Direct regulation is often not feasible, however, since many reinsurance firms are located in foreign countries.

In the remainder of this chapter I discuss domestic developments in the insurance and reinsurance markets of the United States, the United Kingdom, and the European Union more generally. In the case of the United States I begin with an overview of the current regulatory environment and analyze the 1980s liability crisis as a potential stability shock to insurance markets. Ultimately, the low level of international competitive pressure and the absence of a single federal insurance regulator precluded any efforts at international harmonization. I then move on to a discussion of British regulation and chronicle the intriguing story of the LMX spiral, which threatened to bring down the venerable Lloyd's of London insurance market. That episode decimated the capital bases not of firms but of the wealthy individuals who formed the foundation of the Lloyd's market. It also amplified the demand for more national and international reinsurance capacity and therefore did not trigger any preemptive attempts at international harmonization by British regulators. Finally, I turn to a discussion of recent harmonization efforts within the EU, focusing on the European Commission's Solvency II insurance regulation directive.

Reinsurance Regulation in the United States

Domestic Fragmentation

Insurance and reinsurance firms are licensed and regulated separately by regulators in each of the fifty U.S. states. In the McCarran-Ferguson Act of 1945, Congress granted states the right to regulate and tax insurance and also provided the insurance industry with a limited exemption from federal antitrust laws. Despite periodic efforts by Congress to establish a centralized regulatory authority, there currently is no involvement by the federal government in the regulation of insurance. However, state regulators do not work in complete isolation. In 1871 they formed the National Association of Insurance Commissioners (NAIC) to coordinate their policies and share information. Today regulators work together in NAIC committees to develop "model laws" that individual states are encouraged to emulate. Leaders of NAIC also serve as representatives of the insurance industry in testimony before Congress and in international bodies such as the IAIS.[28]

Issues of centralization aside, state regulators are quite powerful within their jurisdictions. They can grant and suspend licenses, promulgate and retract regulations pertaining to firms and the businesses with which they transact, and examine and monitor the financial status and regulatory compliance protocols of licensed firms.[29] In the case of reinsurance firms, state regulators use a combination of direct and indirect regulation. Licensed reinsurance firms are subject to the same prudential regulations as primary insurers, including minimum capital and surplus requirements.[30] These regulations are direct in that they are imposed on the reinsurance firm and are monitored and enforced by the regulator. Direct regulations apply only to domestic firms and to foreign firms that have established subsidiaries in the United States. Recall, however, that capacity considerations often lead businesses to seek the services of reinsurance firms domiciled in foreign countries. State regulators enact indirect regulation on these foreign firms by controlling the mechanism through which domestic primary insurers receive credit for their reinsurance contracts. If a foreign reinsurer must meet certain criteria in order for a United States–based client to receive the blessing of its state regulator, then the reinsurer has little choice but to abide by the rules to attract domestic clients.

The use of the credit mechanism to regulate reinsurance firms works as follows. Since state regulators cannot extend their jurisdiction to include foreign reinsurers, their only alternative is to exert influence over firms that are licensed domestically. That influence comes in the form of balance-sheet incentives: when a primary insurer cedes risk to a reinsurer, it receives an accounting credit equal to the amount of liability ceded to the reinsurer.[31] This balance-sheet credit may be seen as a "reward" granted to the primary insurer for transacting with the "right crowd."[32] Primary insurers automatically receive statement credit for risk ceded to a reinsurer licensed and accredited in a U.S. state, unless that reinsurer is determined to be in a hazardous financial statement by state regulators. When the reinsurer is not licensed or accredited in the United States, the process is more complicated. Statement credit is granted only if the foreign reinsurer satisfies one of two conditions: it secures its obligations to all U.S. clients by establishing a multiple-beneficiary trust fund in a qualified U.S. financial institution, or it provides collateral by way of a trust or letter of credit to each U.S. client.[33] A state regulator, of course, has no legal ability to compel any foreign reinsurer to satisfy these criteria; instead, its power emerges through its influence on direct insurers' transaction decisions. Reinsurers that choose not to be licensed in the United States or satisfy the requirements for statement credit will be virtually ignored by U.S. primary insurers.

It is expensive and inefficient for foreign reinsurers to meet the collateral requirements established by U.S. regulators. Trust funds must be entirely liquid, and they earn little or no interest. Thus most foreign reinsurers choose to establish licensed subsidiaries in the United States, thereby bypassing the collateral requirements and ensuring that their clients will receive appropriate balance-sheet credit for transacting with them. However, foreign firms may still experience a cost disadvantage even after establishing a presence in the United States. Reinsurance firms themselves cede a portion of their risk to other firms in a transaction known as *retrocession*. If a foreign subsidiary in the United States wishes to retrocede a portion of its risk to its parent company, the same balance-sheet and collateral rules apply. Reinsurers such as Swiss Re therefore routinely set up collateral trust funds in the United States to back their retrocession arrangements, even though their reinsurance subsidiaries are licensed in the United States.[34]

The purpose of U.S. licensing and collateral rules is to enhance the stability of insurance firms and ultimately to protect consumers. On that count, U.S. regulations have been reasonably successful. However, bouts of instability have occurred in the insurance market, especially in the 1980s. The instability of the 1980s created pressure for more enforcement power and centralization of regulatory authority but not pressure for more stringent regulations. In the end, the fragmentation of the fifty state regulators made any push toward international regulatory harmonization highly unlikely.

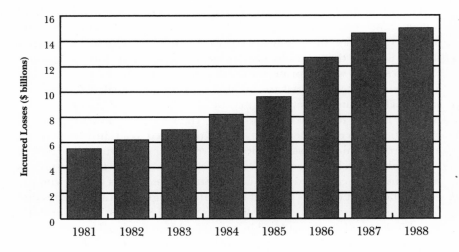

Figure 8. U.S. Insurance Firm Annual Losses, 1981–1988.
(Source: Based on Harrington 1991.)

The Liability Crisis of 1985–1986

In the view of many observers, the U.S. liability insurance market experienced a crisis in the mid-1980s. Insurance firms dramatically increased their premiums for liability coverage beginning in 1985—indeed, it was not atypical for clients to experience increases well in excess of 100 percent.[35] Some insurance firms refused to offer coverage to clients at any price. Clients reacted by purchasing less insurance coverage, accepting more exclusions for certain activities and risks, and in some cases continuing their operations without insurance coverage at all.

The most prominent cause of the crisis was the sharp fall in the profitability of insurance underwriting due to record-high liability claims. The 1980s marked the beginning of the "litigation explosion," and changes in legal doctrine encouraged lawsuits pertaining to medical malpractice, manufactured product liability, and the use of asbestos in residential and commercial construction.[36] The expansion of tort liability made million-dollar malpractice settlements relatively commonplace and caused an increase in both the number and payout of product liability lawsuits.[37] Insurance firms were hit hard by the lawsuits (see figure 8). Firms' annual incurred losses more than doubled between 1982 and 1986.[38]

The profitability of reinsurers roughly tracks that of direct insurers during this period. Figure 9 provides time-series data on the relative financial losses of reinsurers. The data are based on the industry's "combined ratio," the ratio of losses incurred and other underwriting expenses to premium income. A ratio of 1.0 is considered a break-even point, and underwriting

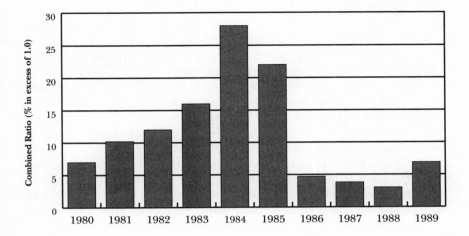

Figure 9. Relative Losses of U.S. Reinsurance Firms, 1980–1989.
(Source: Based on Berger, Cummins, and Tennyson 1992, 261.)

profitability decreases as the ratio increases.[39] To capture the dramatic increase in the losses incurred by reinsurance firms during the liability crisis, Figure 9 tracks percentage deviations from a 1.0 combined ratio from 1980 to 1989. Higher percentage deviations indicate greater relative losses.

While many firms were struggling with financial losses, new direct insurers entered the market to take advantage of the sudden rise in premiums and to provide service to customers who otherwise could not find coverage. Poor management and overly aggressive underwriting quickly led to a sharp rise in the number of insurance firm insolvencies. More than two hundred property/casualty firms failed during the period 1985–89.[40]

In response to the growing number of insolvencies, the congressional Subcommittee on Oversight and Investigations issued a damning report titled "Failed Promises: Insurance Company Insolvencies" in February 1990.[41] The report was remarkable not for its policy recommendations (it offered none) but rather for its dramatic revelations of fraud, mismanagement, and other forms of malfeasance at four insurance firms that failed in the late 1980s.[42] The legislators were alarmist in the report but clearly stated that the insurance industry was *not* in the midst of a crisis.[43] Four years later the subcommittee issued a follow-up report that advocated more federal government involvement in insurance regulation. Continuing the tone established by the prior report, the subcommittee referred to state regulators as "too many cooks without a recipe" and argued that the NAIC's lack of enforcement power made it ineffective as a central coordinator.[44]

The congressional investigations made it clear that insurance insolvencies were largely the result of shady business dealings and criminal behavior. The

1994 report in particular stated that insurance firm failures were "characterized by a flagrant disregard for insurance laws, sound business standards,
and honest reporting to regulators."[45] Legislators pushed for stricter enforcement of existing regulations rather than the promulgation of new rules. One
section of the report openly scoffed at the idea of creating new rules, stating:
"Normally, financial calamities are caused by gross mismanagement, fidu-
ciary breaches, and fraudulent behavior, all of which happen in spite of the
rules intended to prevent them."[46] The report concluded that a stronger enforcement mechanism was required at the national level, thereby laying the
foundation for the creation of a federal insurance regulator.

The NAIC urged Congress not to overreact based on an investigation
that was limited to four particularly egregious cases. The NAIC's vice president at the time, James E. Long, stated that the "breadth of regulatory resources and the capabilities of the existing regulatory system have been
underappreciated."[47] Nevertheless, the NAIC attempted to preempt the
nascent congressional effort to establish a federal insurance regulator by
expediting its own domestic harmonization processes. The group adopted
a series of model regulations for stricter reporting requirements, information sharing, and fraud prevention.[48] Another innovation was a formal certi-
fication program for state insurance regulators, which was clearly intended
to reduce the diversity of regulatory enforcement in the fifty states. Capital
requirements were still largely left to the discretion of individual state regulators, but the NAIC offered guidance on reserve requirements, including
restrictions on the use of junk bonds.[49]

In summary, the liability crisis led to a predictable dose of regulatory
tightening, led by the NAIC. In the process, the fifty state regulators moved
closer in terms of their rule books, and the NAIC's efforts at domestic harmonization helped ward off congressional attempts to create a unified
federal regulator. The crisis did not coincide with rising international
competitive pressures; indeed, domestic insurance firms were not able to
provide adequate capacity in the wake of the crisis and therefore were not
particularly alarmed by foreign involvement in the market. Rather than
seek international solutions to domestic regulatory challenges, state regulators turned to one another—through the NAIC—to enhance the solvency
of U.S. insurance firms.

Reinsurance Regulation in the United Kingdom

Lloyd's of London

The London market has a unique status in the international insurance industry as the main trading center for large industrial risks and global reinsurance coverage.[50] At the center of this market is the venerable Lloyd's of

London, an association of thousands of members who pool their resources into insurance syndicates. Until recently, members were wealthy individuals, known as *names*, who generally had no direct experience with insurance underwriting. Institutional reforms have since allowed for incorporated entities to join the ranks of the names, but the names' reliance on professional underwriters to select and initiate insurance coverage has remained constant. The Lloyd's market provides coverage for a variety of big-ticket risks, from natural disasters and oil tanker accidents to terrorist acts, and its club-like atmosphere belies its status as a leading innovator of insurance products and services.

In the years before 2001 an unusual division existed in London's regulatory environment between the Lloyd's market and the rest of the insurance industry. Lloyd's was largely self-regulated. As a society incorporated by the Lloyd's Act of 1871, the market was exempt from the investor protection clauses of the 1986 Financial Services Act and was granted the authority to oversee its own compliance with the solvency guidelines of the Insurance Companies Act of 1982.[51] On the other hand, insurance firms outside the Lloyd's market were subject to regulation by the Department of Trade and Industry (DTI), which included on-site inspections and "fit and proper" requirements. In 2001 the newly created Financial Services Authority assumed jurisdiction over the Lloyd's market and also took over the responsibilities of the DTI's insurance directorate.[52]

Unlike their counterparts in banking and securities, British insurance regulators showed little interest in international regulatory harmonization during the 1980s and into the 1990s. Regulators were able to navigate the precarious path between market stability and firm competitiveness without seeking an international solution. This is not to say that insurance markets in the United Kingdom have been completely stable. On the contrary, the Lloyd's market in particular has experienced several confidence shocks, the most prominent being the so-called LMX spiral of the late 1980s and early 1990s. I describe that episode next, noting how Lloyd's was able to alter its own regulations without concern for encroachment from foreign competitors.

The Lloyd's LMX Spiral

After nearly two decades of consistent profits, the Lloyd's market reported losses of over £500 million for the 1988 year of account and more than £2 billion in 1989.[53] Sizable losses continued into the 1990s, and some observers predicted that the market would not survive beyond the end of the decade.[54] The losses occurred as a result of the so-called loss market excess (LMX) spiral, which remains the most prominent crisis in the history of the British insurance market.

Loss market excess is a form of reinsurance for reinsurers, also known as retrocession. If governed properly, retrocession is a prudent activity that enables firms (or in the case of Lloyd's, syndicates) to cede some of their risk and protect themselves from catastrophic loss. However, in the late 1980s Lloyd's syndicates shifted their liabilities among themselves in the form of a vicious circle, or spiral. Instead of spreading risks prudently throughout the market, the syndicates accumulated liabilities by inadvertently *reaccepting* risk exposures that they had previously ceded to other syndicates. The result was a garbled chain of reinsurance contracts in which syndicates sometimes ceded risk and sometimes served as reinsurers for other syndicates.[55]

The LMX spiral collapsed in the wake of a number of catastrophic losses, including those caused by the crash of Pan American flight 103 over Lockerbie, the explosion of Occidental Petroleum's Piper Alpha oil rig in 1988, and Hurricane Hugo and the Exxon-Valdez oil-tanker disaster in 1989. Each of these disasters resulted in billions of dollars of insurance claims in a very short time, thereby taxing the capacity of Lloyd's loss reserves. The asbestos-related liability crisis in the United States in the mid-1980s also led to sizable reinsurance claims in the Lloyd's market. The LMX spiral rendered syndicates' reinsurance arrangements nearly worthless. Many Lloyd's syndicates, backed by names who were previously insouciant about their involvement in underwriting insurance risk, were financially devastated. Some were forced to sell their homes and liquidate assets to raise capital for their obligations.[56]

Lloyd's set up a task force in 1991, chaired by Securities and Investments Board chairman Sir David Walker, to make recommendations about how to rebuild the market.[57] There were two main responses to the crisis. The first, which came directly from the task force report, was to make institutional changes to facilitate the raising of additional capital. In 1994 Lloyd's expanded its capital base to include "corporate names" with limited liability.[58] In effect, the capital base of wealthy private individuals had been exhausted with the LMX spiral, so corporations had become eligible to invest in the market.[59] With the influx of corporate capital, the downward tend in Lloyd's underwriting capacity ended, albeit temporarily.[60]

The second response to the crisis resulted from decentralized market forces, not the overt decision of Lloyd's: underwriting capacity migrated to other British insurance firms.[61] As the capital base of Lloyd's shrank—or failed to grow at the rate of its competitors—businesses seeking insurance or reinsurance coverage sought the services of better-capitalized insurance houses. Indeed, after Lloyd's initial contraction in the early 1990s, its underwriting capacity remained virtually static throughout the decade, a remarkable development in light of the late 1990s economic boom. Fears of foreign competition were not prominent in the wake of the crisis because domestic firms did not have the capacity to handle additional business. In short, foreign capacity was needed to satisfy existing reinsurance demand.

The crisis at Lloyd's eventually changed the regulatory preferences of the names, who initially embraced the self-regulating market and its seemingly risk-free profit potential. As annual losses piled up through the 1990s, it became inevitable that the market would move under the umbrella of national insurance regulation, in part to protect the names from further losses and underwriting malfeasance. With the passage of the Financial Services and Markets Act of 2000, the Lloyd's market entered the jurisdiction of the newly created Financial Services Authority.[62]

Regulators and private market participants were ultimately able to shore up the Lloyd's market, but its scope and stature were greatly diminished. As with the liability crisis in the United States, foreign competition was not at the forefront of regulators' policy considerations in the wake of the LMX spiral. When the FSA gained jurisdiction over Lloyd's, the market's capacity had decreased significantly and the stringency of its regulatory environment was far behind that of the other major insurance markets in the United States and throughout Europe. The regulatory changes imposed on Lloyd's by the FSA, including core principles for insurance underwriting and basic capital requirements, simply served to bring the market up to the level of its foreign competitors. In short, insurance regulators were able to shore up confidence in the market with unilateral action; unlike some of their counterparts in banking and securities, they did not need to seek an international solution to their domestic regulatory challenges.

Recent Developments in International Insurance Regulation

Although insurance regulators did not emerge as international actors in the 1980s and early 1990, there have been significant recent attempts at international regulatory harmonization. As mentioned earlier, the IAIS developed a set of core principles for effective insurance supervision in 2003.[63] The principles do not constitute a standard (or standards), but they provide a benchmark for insurance regulators, especially those in developing countries with weakly institutionalized regulatory environments.

Regulatory developments at the regional level—in particular, within the European Union—have garnered more attention than those at the multilateral level. The European Commission has moved aggressively toward the creation of a single European market for insurance.[64] A full discussion of the entire suite of directives governing the EU insurance market is beyond the scope of this book. However, the current debate over a proposed insurance solvency directive, known as Solvency II, is worth discussing in some detail.

The goal of the proposed Solvency II Directive is to establish a capital adequacy framework that matches the actual risk profile of insurance and reinsurance companies. New developments in financial risk management and actuarial mathematics are driving the proposal, as is the desire to avoid the one-size-fits-all approach that ultimately hobbled the first Basel Accord for banks. Indeed, the newly promulgated Basel II agreement provides a much more sensitive risk-based approach to bank capital requirements, and insurance regulators are striving to emulate it. The emerging Solvency II Directive, which will replace the vague first Solvency Directive, will allow insurance firms to employ internal risk models to determine appropriate capital levels.[65] In short, insurance firms will direct their research departments to calculate the probabilities of financial stress situations such as financial losses due to portfolio allocations or operational problems due to information-technology breakdowns or criminal behavior. Managers will then derive a target capital level based on an aggregation of these expected losses. Smaller firms with more modest actuarial and research departments will employ a simpler, more conservative risk model.

If the European Commission ultimately promulgates Solvency II, it may put pressure on non-EU insurance regulators—such as those in the United States—to adopt a similar approach to capital adequacy. That said, insurance regulators currently show little interest in creating multilateral standards in the IAIS or any other body. The current secretary-general of the IAIS, Yoshi Kawai, recently stated that the group will continue to serve as an international forum for insurance regulators but that the creation of solvency standards is unlikely in the foreseeable future.[66]

Conclusion

Insurance regulation is puzzling because of the very limited efforts of regulators to create international standards. The industry, especially the reinsurance industry, is inherently international, leading to the familiar problem of financial interdependence: the possibility that the failure of a firm in one country could cause financial distress in other countries, with harmful effects on the real economy. Insurance regulators, however, have national jurisdictions, and their priorities lie in maintaining the often precarious balance between stability and competitiveness. Over the past two decades regulators have been successful in maintaining the balance without resorting to international solutions. This is not to say that insurance markets have always been stable or free of regulatory problems, but simply that regulators have been able to modify their regulations unilaterally in response to domestic problems.

The liability crisis in the United States and the LMX spiral in the United Kingdom are two examples of significant confidence shocks to the insurance market. Fears of encroachment by foreign firms were not prominent in each episode, in part because foreign capacity was needed to address shortfalls in the domestic industry. In each case, regulators were able to adapt to the changing insurance environment. In the U.S. case, the NAIC increased its harmonization efforts to bring the fifty state regulators in line and assuaged congressional concerns (albeit temporarily) about enforcement and implementation. In the U.K. case, insurance regulators eventually brought the Lloyd's market under their jurisdiction and ramped up its regulatory environment to national levels.

Balancing issues aside, there is an important institutional barrier to international harmonization in insurance that is not present in other financial industries: fifty separate state regulators in the United States. Regulatory harmonization is not complete *within* the country, and the international negotiating table is clearly not big enough for all fifty regulators to have a seat. The NAIC has taken steps to centralize its authority and to speak with a unified voice, but international standards are unlikely to emerge before the NAIC is subsumed by a federal insurance regulator. Until that time, the individual state regulators will remain largely insulated from direct congressional pressure and concerned only about their subnational jurisdictions.

In the future it is possible that new domestic developments in the major insurance markets may prove less conducive to unilateral regulatory responses. The creation of new insurance products could lead to stiffer international competition and more potential for risk and instability. Finite reinsurance, for example, is an innovative insurance product developed in the late 1980s as a result of the global retrenchment in reinsurance capacity. With finite reinsurance, an insurer obtains reinsurance coverage at a lower cost than traditional reinsurance but with a lower probability of loss to the reinsurer. Critics have argued that finite insurance is simply a tool for insurers to cover up weaknesses in their financial statements, and that might explain why the product has become popular in recent years.[67] Lawmakers and regulators, however, are beginning to pay attention to abuses of finite reinsurance, possibly triggering a bout of regulatory tightening, especially in the United States, where New York attorney general Eliot Spitzer is leading the charge. If regulators cannot maintain the balance between stability and competitiveness on this issue, we may see the first signs of an international discussion—and possibly the emergence of an international regulatory standard.

Chapter 7

Conclusion: The Future of International Regulatory Harmonization

The word *harmonization*, which connotes a sense of frictionless and mutually beneficial cooperation between actors, is tossed around frequently in discussions of international financial regulation. To outside observers, the term might appear appropriate for the ostensibly apolitical gatherings of financial regulators which often result in proclamations of "governing principles"—and occasionally financial standards—for the world economy. Alan Greenspan, the quintessential U.S. financial regulator, appeared unconstrained by the fray of electoral politics during his long tenure at the Fed, especially in his dealings with his peers in other countries. His successor, Ben Bernanke, appears similarly apolitical, swayed by his prior academic research rather than by current political tides. And international regulatory agreements, with their jargon and arcane concepts impervious to most observers, certainly seem to be the product of experts working harmoniously and in tune with the exigencies of global finance. But in its musical connotations the term *harmonization* does a disservice to the politics of international financial regulation. Episodes of shared interests among regulators are matched by acrimonious bouts of dissension, the latter frequently masked by anodyne coverage in the financial press and a lack of public transparency in regulators' interactions. Where prior observers have found regulators galvanizing to address international problems through the creation of global standards, this book has uncovered a more compelling motivation for harmonization rooted in variable domestic constraints and fueled by regulators' urgent attempts to survive in the face of globalization.

The historical record indicates that international financial instability is not sufficient to bring about international financial regulation. Functionalist arguments about international institutions are therefore largely unhelpful in explaining the emergence of global standards. In chapter 4 I told the story of the collapse of the Herstatt Bank in Germany in 1974, which led to a new era in the international interactions of national bank regulators. The Herstatt collapse sent the international foreign exchange market into a tailspin and brought into stark relief the risks and vulnerabilities of global capital markets in the post–Bretton Woods era. Bank regulators quickly huddled in Basel in an unprecedented display of multilateralism, but the immediate outcome of their discussions—the 1975 Concordat—proved to be a vaguely worded "gentlemen's agreement" rather than a pragmatic regulatory standard.[1] Securities markets experienced a more jarring bout of instability on Black Monday, the infamous 1987 stock market crash. Companies around the world saw their market capitalizations plummet, and securities firms struggled to execute trades and manage their own precarious capital bases. Securities regulators sprang into action and attempted to hammer out a regulatory agreement with the same zeal as their counterparts in banking, but their efforts crumbled in 1992 under the weight of divergent preferences and intractable distributional issues.

Why do some regulators demand international regulatory standards while others resist? If international systemic disruptions cannot explain regulators' varying demands for regulatory harmonization, then what can? This book has posed an alternative explanation for the creation of international financial standards based on domestic political constraints. The explanation focuses on the agents of harmonization—national financial regulators—and on their relationships with elected officials. Regulators continually walk a fine line between maintaining public confidence in financial institutions through regulatory stringency, and maintaining international competitiveness through regulatory flexibility. Elected leaders value both stability and competitiveness and will intervene in regulatory policy should levels of either decline significantly. Intervention is costly for both politicians and regulators. For politicians, intervention requires time (for hearings, public statements, and the like), resources (to draft legislation, if necessary), and the risk of being held accountable should legislative intervention exacerbate the underlying problems. Legislative intervention also threatens the policymaking autonomy of regulatory agencies and can harm regulators' future job prospects. Indeed, political intervention is the bane of a regulator's existence. The principal-agent relationship between elected leaders and regulators, combined with regulators' constant struggle to protect their own interests, creates a win-set for regulatory policy—a range of policy options that do not trigger legislative intervention or other career costs. This analytical framework generates hypotheses about regulators' demands for international financial standards.

As discussed in chapter 3, I expect regulators to demand international standards when their win-sets are shrinking. When the domestic financial sector loses international competitiveness due to the rise of a foreign rival, and when public confidence in financial stability declines due to the sudden collapse of financial institutions and extreme asset volatility, regulators' ability to satisfy their principals' demands for stability and competitiveness diminishes. As regulators' win-sets shrink, the probability of legislative intervention increases, and regulators are more likely to look to the international arena for a solution. International regulatory harmonization is therefore a strategy for regulators to expand their win-sets and maintain their autonomy. In short, harmonization relaxes the competitive constraint on regulators. When foreign regulators choose to match the stringency of regulations in the home country, the domestic regulator can satisfy the legislature's demands for stability without putting the international competitiveness of the financial sector in jeopardy.

This book employed a case-study research design to explore the connection between regulators' shrinking win-sets and demands for international regulatory harmonization. The first two case-study chapters explored the policy stances of regulators in the United States, the United Kingdom, and Japan in two important sets of negotiations. The first case was the negotiations over the harmonization of bank capital adequacy requirements, which led to the promulgation of the Basel Accord in 1988. There is a mature literature on the Basel Accord, but prior analytical studies generally treat the agreement in isolation. I therefore added a second case: the negotiations among securities regulators over capital adequacy for securities firms, which took place between 1988 and 1992 under the auspices of IOSCO. The IOSCO negotiations—which ended without an agreement—represent a "negative" case and have therefore been overlooked in academic circles despite their obvious parallels to the Basel negotiations. More important for this book is that the cases revealed puzzling variation in regulators' demands for an international standard. The U.S. Fed and the Bank of England were the primary advocates of an international capital standard for banks whereas Japanese regulators, representing seven of the ten largest banks in the world at the time, stood in staunch opposition. In the case of the negotiations over securities firm capital, the United Kingdom's Securities and Investments Board was the primary advocate of harmonization, with strong opposition from the U.S. Securities and Exchange Commission and, to a lesser extent, the Japanese Ministry of Finance. Rather than rely on functionalist reasoning or assume away the importance of regulators as actors, I argued that changes in regulators' win-sets—indicated by exogenous shocks to domestic financial stability (firm failures and asset price volatility) and international competitiveness—were the driving force behind the varying demands for international regulatory standards.

In the negotiations leading up to the Basel Accord, the Bank of England and the U.S. Federal Reserve faced shocks to stability from high-profile bank failures, along with shocks to international competitiveness with the rise of the Japanese banking sector. As domestic political pressure on these regulators began to mount, they looked to international harmonization as a solution, first by way of a bilateral agreement and then a multilateral accord through the Basel Committee. Japanese regulators, who did not face similar threats to stability and competitiveness, were adamantly opposed to an international regulatory agreement and served as the primary antagonists to harmonization. In the case of the negotiations over capital adequacy for securities firms, U.S. and British regulators found themselves on opposing sides. In the United Kingdom the SIB was struggling to survive after the Big Bang liberalization of 1986 and found itself presiding over a secular decline in market share in the derivatives business and a rise in asset price volatility with the stock market crash of 1987. In light of its concerns over financial stability, the SIB was in no position to consider more flexible regulations for domestic securities firms, but it also could not sit idly while U.S. derivatives providers swallowed up more and more of the worldwide derivatives market. The SIB's best strategy was to seek an international regulatory agreement that would lead to the adoption of stricter regulations for U.S. derivatives dealers. The U.S. SEC, fearing pressure for regulatory tightening of its dominant derivatives providers, became a staunch opponent of harmonization and brought the nascent negotiations to an abrupt halt. The Japanese MOF, preoccupied with its own collapsing asset markets and faltering firms, was in no condition to advocate any regulatory policies—international or otherwise—that would limit its flexibility to prop up the domestic financial sector. The MOF therefore took a backseat in the negotiations and enabled the SEC to oppose a regulatory agreement with minimal difficulty.

In the realm of insurance, regulators have only recently emerged on the international scene, and their efforts at creating international rules have thus far been modest. The initial puzzle in the insurance case is that regulators from the major markets have all been quiescent despite the internationalization of the industry and the possibility of systemic shocks. However, a closer examination of regulators' domestic environments reveals that regulators have generally been able to adjust to stability shocks with unilateral changes in regulation. The fragmentation of the U.S. insurance market, characterized by fifty separate state regulators, further explains the relative absence of international harmonization in insurance.

The underlying story in each of the cases is one of regulator survival in the face of economic globalization. In a closed economy, fulfilling the mandate of stable and competitive financial institutions is a relatively straightforward affair. Regulators simply find a degree of regulatory stringency that strikes a balance between financial-sector profitability and stability and then alter regulations as needed to compensate for changes in the risk profiles of financial institutions. In an open economy, however, these adjustments are fraught with difficulty when international discrepancies in regulations have important competitive implications. Regulators cannot simply tighten regulations in response to domestic financial instability if such changes will adversely affect the international competitiveness of the financial sector. Elected leaders, however, are not particularly sympathetic to the plight of regulators. They will continue to castigate their regulatory agents for bouts of financial instability due to insufficient regulations or for declining domestic market share due to the rise of a less stringently regulated foreign financial sector. The specter of political intervention in regulatory policy therefore increases, and regulators must struggle to maintain their autonomy—and, in some cases, to survive. The United Kingdom's Securities and Investments Board is an excellent example of the latter case: after its untimely genesis in 1986 in the midst of wide-scale liberalization and financial instability, the SIB ultimately was not able to strike a viable balance between stability and competitiveness. The regulator hung on for nearly a decade, enduring constant pressure from legislators, industry, and the financial press, but ultimately was dismantled in 1997 with the creation of the Financial Services Authority.

The policy positions of the regulators in these three cases do not constitute a large enough sample for a thorough test of this book's "shrinking win-set" hypotheses. But the case studies provide evidence of the relationship between changing domestic constraints and regulators' international efforts to create regulatory standards. Despite the relatively large literature on the Basel Accord, scholars have yet to present a compelling explanation of bank regulatory harmonization that explains the policy positions of all the relevant regulators. The literature on the negotiations over securities firm capital adequacy—a case that merits that same degree of scholarly attention as the Basel Accord—is almost nonexistent. And insurance remains a mostly overlooked industry in the globalizing economy. This book has brought these three important cases together to explore a generalizable analytical framework for harmonization and to provide a historical narrative for future research on international financial regulation.

Regulators as Agents of Harmonization

There are a number of ways in which regulations can converge in the global economy. One of the most visible methods is through international treaties, such as the General Agreement on Tariffs and Trade (GATT) and the Articles of Agreement of the International Monetary Fund. In treaty negotiations, heads of government and their representatives are the primary participants, and agreements must be ratified by domestic legislatures. The result is a "two-level game" in which the executive's foreign policy commitments are constrained by legislative ratification.[2] However, when regulatory convergence occurs outside an international legal process and in the absence of legislative ratification, the game is necessarily different. In this book I have argued that legislatures, with their dueling demands for financial-sector stability and international competitiveness, create constraints on regulators that prompt demands for international regulatory harmonization. Unlike the typical two-level-game scenario, regulators are international actors *because* of domestic constraints rather than international actors *constrained* by domestic politics.

Prior research on regulatory harmonization has often ignored the fact that regulators—agents of governments with at least some degree of autonomy—are often the primary actors in international negotiations over financial regulatory standards.[3] It is rare for heads of government to engage in direct discussions over the regulation of domestic financial industries. Instead, international committees of national regulators have formed over the past two decades to facilitate international harmonization. The committee structures themselves, I argue, are not particularly important; indeed, the Basel Committee has no formal bylaws or voting rules, and IOSCO is simply a forum for regulators from the largest financial markets to coordinate their activities as they deem necessary. (Former U.S. comptroller of the currency and Merrill Lynch executive John Heimann, known for his blunt and colorful assessments of the financial regulatory environment, quipped dryly that IOSCO is a "debating society.")[4] What is critical, however, is the fact that regulators are agents that respond to their changing domestic environment.

When governments enter into international negotiations on a policy issue, the requirement of legislative ratification necessarily implies that the negotiations will be relatively transparent and politicized. Legislators will demand information on the president's or prime minister's bargaining strategies as the negotiations unfold and will make their own preferences continually known. Once an agreement has been reached by the negotiators and ratified by legislatures, the domestic legal system in each participating country enforces compliance. In contrast, regulators who initiate international negotiations over harmonization do not face a ratification requirement and therefore can conduct themselves in a relatively opaque and seemingly apolitical environment. Once an agreement has been reached, decentralized market forces—sometimes in combination with the coercive influence of international institutions and powerful states—encourage compliance in varying degrees.[5]

The difference in the negotiating environments for governments and regulators has important implications for the study of international regulatory harmonization. An analytical framework to explain governmental behavior should encapsulate the welter of domestic interests and domestic and international institutions that shape the negotiators' strategies, as well as the institutional features of the legislatures that are ultimately responsible for ratifying the agreement.[6] For the international negotiations of regulators, the concern about legislative ratification is replaced by a new focus on international market pressures for compliance.

The number and scope of regulatory jurisdictions and independent regulators are increasing across the developed and developing world, and not just in the realm of finance. In the first half of the twentieth century, governments created bank and securities regulators, followed by regulators for insurance, commodities and futures, and other areas of finance. Outside finance, governments have delegated regulatory responsibility for a range of issues, including telecommunications, the environment, and health and safety. Any regulatory agency, regardless of its mandate, has incentives to survive and protect its decision-making discretion. And most regulatory agencies face dilemmas similar to those discussed in the cases in this book. Environmental regulators, for example, face opposing demands to preserve natural resources and to enhance the competitiveness of domestic industries.[7] The implication is that patterns of international regulatory cooperation across a broad spectrum of issues will increasingly be dependent on the domestic context of regulatory agencies. Regulators that face difficulty balancing competing demands for policy outcomes—such as industry competitiveness versus the preservation of domestic public goods—are likely to find themselves in international negotiations with their foreign counterparts.

While governments are increasingly delegating regulatory responsibility to subexecutive agencies, they are also restructuring existing agencies based on new market conditions and the changing economy. In 1997 the British government stripped the Bank of England of its bank regulatory responsibilities and created a new Financial Services Authority, which placed banking, securities, and insurance regulation under one roof. Governments have recently created similar FSAs in Japan, Australia, and Ireland, and other countries are considering following suit. The effects of these new "super-regulators" on international harmonization are uncertain. On the one hand, regulators with limited functional mandates (e.g., insurance) may be more vulnerable to political intervention than super-regulators. Given that FSAs combine authority for a range of financial issue areas, legislatures will find it difficult to divorce intervention in one issue from wholesale meddling in the financial regulatory environment. The differences in the political costs of legislative intervention imply that narrow, issue-specific regulators will face more threats to their autonomy and survival than FSAs and are therefore more likely to seek international regulatory agreements to keep their legislatures at bay. On the other hand, the creation of FSAs and other super-regulators coincides with the rise of financial conglomerates that combine the functions of banking, securities, and insurance in a single firm. It is increasingly difficult to impose regulations on one functional area without affecting the other areas. For example, the imposition of bank capital requirements on financial conglomerates influences not only credit intermediation activities but also securities underwriting and insurance activities. To the extent that legislatures view conglomerates as single entities governed by a coherent set of regulations, political intervention in FSAs may follow the same logic—and incur the same costs—as for narrow, issue-specific regulatory agencies. From this perspective, the implication is that super-regulators will be just as eager to establish international regulatory standards as their narrower, functionally specific predecessors but that the substance of those standards will encompass more functional areas. Sorting out the effects of the new super-regulators on international financial regulation requires further research and, just as important, more time for the regulators themselves to face changing constraints in their domestic political environments.

Regulator Autonomy and Legislative Response: The Empire Strikes Back?

I have presented a framework in which the behavior of regulators changes in response to implicit or explicit threats from the legislature. Politicians themselves are static in this framework: their demands for stability and competitiveness are fixed, and they allow regulators to "go international" without resistance. In reality, the story is more complicated. The growing prominence of international committees of national regulators, especially the Basel Committee on Bank Regulation, has prompted some elected leaders to balk at the idea of international regulatory "treaties" negotiated outside the normal legislative ratification process. Consider, for example, the recent attempts by the Basel Committee to revise the Basel Accord to take into account new developments in banking markets and risk-management techniques, discussed at the end of chapter 4. Members of the U.S. Congress have expressed opposition to the autonomy that the U.S. Fed and its foreign counterparts have displayed throughout the multiyear negotiations. The House Committee on Financial Services, chaired by Michael Oxley (R-Ohio), wrote an urgent letter to the Fed which cautioned federal regulators against "making important public policy decisions outside the political process."[8] The letter was enough to cause considerable concern among European regulators and to raise doubts about the viability of the new Basel II agreement.[9] Congressional objections to the Basel Committee's activities are part of a larger chorus of concern about the "democratic deficit" in the creation of international regulatory policy and of international policy more generally.[10] An analysis of the validity of these arguments is beyond the scope of this book. However, the prospect of a political backlash in response to international regulatory harmonization by autonomous regulators is an important consideration for future research.[11] Regulators become international actors in reaction to threats to their autonomy, but elected leaders may strike back by reining them in, especially if regulators miscalculate the balance between stability and competitiveness in their international negotiations.

Varieties of Harmonization

The analytical framework presented in this book, with its emphasis on the industrialized world, highlights an important set of distinctions that should be noted in the literature on harmonization. I argue that there are three broad types of international regulatory harmonization, apart from harmonization through international treaties. The first, *regulatory convergence*, is the organic process by which countries modify their regulations based on the policies of other countries, especially dominant countries like the United States, or simply converge on a common set of rules inadvertently.[12] A prime example is bank deposit insurance, which is common in many countries but was until recently a U.S. phenomenon.[13] The second type of harmonization, which I call *core harmonization*, is the process emphasized in this book in which a small group of advanced industrialized countries agree, through overt negotiation, to harmonize their regulations. The result of successful core harmonization is an international standard, often with a formal name (e.g., the Basel Accord). The creation of an international standard gives rise to the third type of harmonization, *peripheral harmonization*, in which countries outside the core group of industrialized countries choose whether to accede to the standard or to maintain divergent regulations. Third world countries, for example, often tout that they are "Basel-compliant" to increase investor confidence in their banking systems; other countries intentionally diverge from bank supervisory standards as a means of attracting capital from tax evaders and criminals.

Scholars should be clear about which type of harmonization is under investigation, since each requires a separate analytical approach. Analyses of regulatory convergence might look at epistemic communities, global economic and geopolitical conditions, and other factors that lead regulators and policymakers in multiple countries to adopt similar policies. Economic incentives in emulating a dominant country are also important, especially for countries with open markets. Core harmonization requires an analytical framework rooted in domestic politics—such as the one presented in this book—since the varying preferences of the small number of core countries are critical. And finally, peripheral harmonization focuses our attention on the coercive power of the core countries through international institutions and economic sanctions, as well as the economic incentives of the peripheral countries themselves in acceding to the international standard.[14]

The Basel Accord provides a useful example of the importance of these types. In the mid-1980s, before the existence of an international standard, there were strong incentives for countries to undercut each other with lax capital requirements, since doing so provided a competitive advantage. After the G-10 countries established the Basel Accord in 1988, however, these incentives largely disappeared, and Basel compliance became an important signal to investors of bank stability. For core harmonization of capital requirements, competitive pressures were a hindrance; but after the G-10 countries harmonized, competitive pressures actually *ensured* peripheral harmonization.[15]

In light of the global adoption of Basel capital requirements, it is easy to overlook the fact that compliance with international regulatory standards is not guaranteed. Regulatory laxity may be a competitive advantage in a variety of financial issue areas, depending on countries' involvement with the world economy. Consider the issue of money laundering, in which market actors attempt to disguise the origins of illegally obtained capital. Regulations designed to prevent money laundering, such as currency transaction reporting, increased data collection on customers, and the abolishment of anonymous accounts, are expensive and generally require additional human resources and information technology. They also stem the flow of capital from both legitimate market actors and criminals who seek attractive returns and financial secrecy. When it comes to money laundering, regulatory laxity may help an otherwise capital-poor country to attract funds into its banking sector. The countries of the G-7, eager to stop money laundering and the predicate criminal activities that fuel it, have led the charge in attacking the market confidence of countries that maintain lax regulations. The G-7's Financial Action Task Force (FATF) conducts periodic regulatory reviews of countries around the world and publishes the names of countries that do not comply with its "40 recommendations" to fight money laundering. By drawing attention to these countries, the FATF hopes to discourage investment in their markets and to encourage the spread of stringent anti-money-laundering regulations. The FATF's "name and shame" policy has been reasonably successful based on its published reports, but several countries remain steadfast in their opposition to regulatory tightening. These countries—such as the isolated island-nations Vanuatu and Nauru, and larger countries such as Egypt and Indonesia—pose a significant threat to the worldwide fight against illicit finance.[16]

The variation in compliance with international regulatory standards represents an interesting research puzzle. Egypt and Indonesia both tout their compliance with the Basel capital requirements but historically have not been swayed by the FATF's anti-money-laundering rules. Clearly, there are different market forces at work in the two areas—Basel noncompliance would presumably lead to a much more serious crisis of confidence among investors than FATF noncompliance—but that observation is only the beginning of an analytical explanation. When do investors—especially influential market movers like pension fund managers, insurance companies, and mutual funds managers—adopt international regulatory standards as determinants of their investment decisions? This question will be left to future research, but we have already seen several potential clues, such as the influence of international institutions and the presence of direct pressure from powerful governments eager to impose particular policy outcomes.

The Role of International Financial Institutions

The rules of global financial governance are increasingly the creation of international committees of regulators and private actors rather than heads of government acting in concert.[17] As a result, international regulatory standards often do not have the force of law, nor are they backed by dispute-settlement mechanisms or any source of coercive authority. Market pressures, alluded to earlier, are the primary means by which regulatory standards diffuse throughout the world economy, but international institutions have also begun to play an important role. The International Monetary Fund, for example, produces Reports on the Observance of Standards and Codes (ROSCs) for member countries, which analyze adherence to a variety of regulatory standards. ROSCs now cover twelve areas (see table 8), representing the full range of financial regulation. Many of these standards and codes were created by international committees of regulators (e.g., the Basel Committee, the International Association of Insurance Supervisors) or by private-sector groups (e.g., the International Accounting Standards Committee). ROSCs are particularly influential because they influence member countries' funding relationships with the IMF. If a ROSC uncovers a deficiency in a country's financial regulatory environment based on adherence to any of the recognized standards, the IMF might dictate regulatory improvements as a condition for future structural adjustment funding. IMF conditionality therefore adds teeth to international regulatory standards, particularly for emerging-market countries. Indeed, rather than impose its own policy views on member states, the IMF has increasingly become an enforcer of regulatory standards produced elsewhere.

TABLE 8.
Standards, Codes, and Principles Used in the IMF's Reports on the Observance of
Standards and Codes (ROSCs)

Regulatory area	Originating body	Name of standard/code
Data transparency	IMF	Special Data Dissemination Standard
Fiscal transparency	IMF	Code of Good Practices on Transparency
Monetary and financial policy transparency	IMF	Code of Good Practices on Transparency
Banking supervision	Basel Committee	Core Principles for Effective Banking Supervision
Securities	International Organization of Securities Commissions (IOSCO)	Objectives and Principles for Securities Regulation
Insurance	International Association of Insurance Supervisors (IAIS)	Insurance Supervisory Principles
Payments systems	Committee on Payments and Settlements Systems (CPSS)	Core Principles for Systematically Important Payment Systems
Anti-money-laundering and terrorism	Financial Action Task Force (FATF)	40 + 8 Recommendations
Corporate governance	Organization for Economic Cooperation and Development (OECD)	Principles of Corporate Governance
Accounting	International Accounting Standards Board	International Accounting Standards
Auditing	International Federation of Accountants	International Standards on Auditing
Insolvency and creditor rights	World Bank and UN Commission on International Trade Law	In progress

Source: International Monetary Fund (http://www.imf.org/external/standards/index.htm).

The strategy of using loan conditions as a means of enforcing regulatory standards is also employed by other international financial institutions, especially the affiliated institutions of the World Bank Group. The International Bank for Reconstruction and Development (IBRD) and the International Development Association (IDA), which grant low- or zero-interest loans to developing countries to foster sustainable development, both incorporate ROSC-style regulatory standards (in varying degrees of stringency) in their loan conditions. For countries that are otherwise shut out of international capital markets, World Bank lending is absolutely critical. Regulatory standards that are incorporated in World Bank lending programs therefore have substantial influence over national regulatory environments.

The coercive influence of international financial institutions has a feedback effect on market pressures to comply with international regulatory standards. Investors must decide which factors are important in driving their portfolio allocation decisions.[18] When regulatory standards developed, say, by the Basel Committee are subsequently incorporated in the lending conditions of the international financial institutions, investors have greater incentives to examine national compliance with those standards as a determinant of their investment decisions. The adoption of regulatory standards by the IMF and World Bank serves as a clear signal to market actors that compliance with certain standards is critical to development and financial stability. The influence of international financial institutions therefore operates through two channels: directly, through conditions on lending to developing countries; and indirectly, by signaling the importance of regulatory standards to market actors.

Core-Periphery Negotiations over Regulatory Standards

The confluence of market and institutional pressures for regulatory compliance complicates the negotiations of the most powerful countries in global finance. The presence of substantial pressures for worldwide compliance has two implications. First, the initial bargaining stage in which international standards are created will be fierce, lengthy, and contentious. James Fearon has elegantly argued that states have incentives to bargain harder for their preferred policy objectives as the enforcement stage of the agreement becomes more effective.[19] When international financial institutions stand ready to incorporate new standards in their lending decisions, with market actors making investment decisions accordingly, participants in regulatory negotiations realize that their decisions are often irrevocable. Contrary to studies that view negotiations among regulators as an organic convergence of views, Fearon's analysis implies that the myriad pressures for regulatory compliance in the world economy will lead to substantial difficulties in the creation of international standards. The cases in this book, which were marked by divergent preferences among the participants and acrimonious debate, support Fearon's view.[20]

The second implication of the worldwide pressures for regulatory compliance is that standards created by and for the most powerful countries are almost necessarily applicable to the developing world. The Basel Accord, created in 1988 by regulators from the G-10 countries and intended to standardize capital requirements only in the industrialized world, quickly reverberated throughout the developing world and became a truly global standard. Participants in the Basel negotiations were surprised by the accord's universal implementation; indeed, it was never their intention to create a globally applicable standard.[21] The global reach of the 1988 Basel Accord has influenced more recent attempts to revise the agreement to reflect new thinking on financial stability and new developments in financial markets.

Whereas the 1980s negotiations consisted of relatively secret discussions among a small set of regulators from the largest banking markets, the negotiations over Basel II included regular input from developing countries and therefore much more coordination between the core and periphery.[22] The evolution of the Basel agreement may prove to be an important trend: standards are initially created by the core financial countries, but subsequent revisions incorporate a larger and more contentious group of participants from the developed and developing worlds.

These developments may also influence the membership structure of the international financial institutions through which regulators negotiate international standards. International rule-making committees, such as the Basel Committee and IOSCO, tend to form with a select few members and then gradually expand to include other countries with a stake in the institutions' policy areas.[23] This pattern may accelerate if market pressures continue to enforce the widespread adoption of regulatory standards created by a small, core group of countries. If countries outside the core group join together to reject a new regulatory standard, the developing world may gain enough leverage to earn a place at the negotiating table and an official membership in the international rule-making bodies.

Regulatory harmonization, in its various forms, will continue to be a controversial topic for policymakers and scholars. The trend in many countries is toward the creation of more and more agents of government, with separate budgets, staffs, and varying degrees of policymaking autonomy. As these agents—or, more accurately, bureaucrats, despite the word's negative connotation—gain more autonomy over policy areas, they will increasingly find themselves in international negotiations as they adapt to the global economy. Scholars of international political economy who employ state-centric frameworks or who include only interest groups and formal political institutions in their analyses, will neglect the importance of the new open-economy bureaucratic politics and thus will overlook a powerful force behind regulatory harmonization.

Notes

1. Introduction: Financial Regulators and International Relations

1. See, for example, Eichengreen 1999. Prudential regulations pertain to the stability and solvency of financial institutions.

2. Cerny 1995.

3. See Simmons 2001; Drezner forthcoming.

4. See Kapstein 1989, 1994; Oatley and Nabors 1998; Reinicke 1995; Singer 2004.

5. Eichengreen (1999, 25) notes that the Basel Accord demonstrates "the feasibility of standard setting in the financial realm."

6. See Reinicke 1998; Slaughter 2004.

7. Kapstein 1989.

8. This view is similar to Edward Kane's "regulatory dialectic": banks find ways to bypass existing regulations, leading regulators to enact new, more stringent regulations. See Kane 1981.

9. I differentiate harmonization from the process of regulatory convergence that arises through market pressures or emulation. Here international regulatory harmonization implies an agreement between regulators—that is, the purposive creation of an international regulatory standard. See Singer 2004.

10. Slaughter 2004. See also Kapstein 1989; Porter 1993; Zaring 1998.

11. Cf. Kapstein 1989, which emphasizes international consensus among financial regulators.

12. Vogel 1996; Laurence 2001.

13. Vogel 1996.

14. There is also a voluminous literature on whether globalization causes a regulatory "race to the bottom" or some other process of convergence, absent any overt negotiation among rule makers. For an excellent overview, see Mosley 2003.

15. Analytical works focused exclusively on international banking regulation include Kapstein 1989, 1991, and 1994; Oatley and Nabors 1998; Reinicke 1995; and Wood 2005.

The Basel Accord features prominently in Murphy 2004, Porter 1993, Reinicke 1998, Simmons 2001, Singer 2004, and Underhill 1997.

16. Kapstein 1989. See also Kapstein 1994.

17. Oatley and Nabors 1998.

18. Keohane 1984.

19. Mishkin (2001) reflects this view for the Basel Accord, as does Underhill (1997) for international banking and securities regulation. On institutions more generally, see special issue, *International Organization* 55, no. 4 (2001).

20. Oatley and Nabors (1998) make this point in regard to Japan's resistance to the Basel Accord.

21. On systemic risk, see Herring and Litan 1995.

22. On systemic risk in various financial markets, see Herring and Schuermann 2005.

23. Garrett 1992; Krasner 1991.

24. Oatley and Nabors 1998. See also Susan Strange's (1983) critique of regime theory.

25. For an expression of this view in a domestic context, see Weingast 1984.

26. Interviews with current and former regulators at the Federal Reserve Bank of New York, U.S. Securities and Exchange Commission, Bank of England, and the (former) U.K. Securities and Investments Board, May–June 2002.

27. See, for example, Shepsle and Weingast 1987. On logrolling and the design of legislative institutions, see Carrubba and Volden 2000.

28. Slaughter 2004.

29. Simmons 2001.

30. On industry self-regulation, see Haufler 2001; on the delegation of authority to private-sector bodies, see Mattli and Buthe 2005a and 2005b; on private-sector participation in international regulatory efforts, see Mosley 2005.

31. See, for example, Martin 2000; Milner 1997; Putnam 1988.

32. For example, governors of the Federal Reserve Board are granted fourteen-year terms.

33. Goldstein et al. 2000.

34. Ibid.

35. See Eatwell and Taylor 2000 for a related normative argument.

36. Abbott and Snidal 2000.

37. Kapstein (1994, 13) emphasizes the importance of market pressures for international regulatory agreements.

38. On sovereignty costs, see Abbott and Snidal 2000.

39. Basel Committee on Banking Supervision 2004. The fierce bargaining over the Basel Accord is consistent with the expectation of *ex-post* adherence to the rules. See Fearon 1998.

40. Slaughter 2004. Other works in the transgovernmentalism literature include Cutler, Haufler, and Porter 1999; Hall and Biersteker 2002; Kahler and Lake 2003; Keohane and Nye 1989, Risse-Kappen 1995; and Rosenau and Czempiel 1992.

41. Slaughter 2004.

42. See Kahler and Lake 2003. On the characteristics of transgovernmental "regimes" for banking and securities, see Porter 1993.

43. For a useful typology of governance in the global economy, see Drezner 2005.

44. The interviews took place in London, Basel, Geneva, Boston, New York, and Washington, D.C., from 2002 to 2005. Interviews were off the record except where noted.

2. Capital Regulation: A Brief Primer

1. See OECD 1983 for a discussion of the risks in international banking.

2. On cross-border credit risk, see Smith and Walter 2003.

3. On the functioning of securities markets, see Sobel 1994.

4. An investor has a "long" position when she owns a security and a "short" position when she has sold a borrowed security. As an example of the latter, consider an investor who believes that the stock price of XYZ Corporation will decline. The investor, wishing to make a profit from the price movement, can "short" a predetermined number of shares of the stock and immediately obtain the proceeds from that sale. The investor must then "purchase" the stock at a later date (which amounts to returning the borrowed shares to the securities firm). If the stock price has indeed declined over that period of time, then the investor makes a profit.

5. Mishkin 2001.

6. See Friedman and Schwartz 1963 for a discussion of bank panics and economic recessions in the United States.

7. OECD 1991.

8. Moskow 1998, 15.

9. See Alexander, Dhumale, and Eatwell 2006.

10. See Haberman 1987; Walker 1992.

11. Dale 1996.

12. In the United States the SEC's net capital rule (SEC Rule 15c3–1) stipulates that a broker-dealer should have the capacity to wind down its operations and protect its customers within one month. See Haberman 1987.

3. Regulators, Legislatures, and Domestic Balancing

1. On systemic risk in financial markets, see Crockett 1997; Alexander, Dhumale, and Eatwell 2006; OECD 1991; Wyplosz 1999.

2. See, for example, Kapstein 1989; Simmons 2001.

3. See Weingast 1984; Ferejohn and Shipan 1990.

4. See, among others, Weingast 1984; Weingast and Moran 1983; Ferejohn and Shipan 1990.

5. See Bawn 1995; Khademian 1992; Majone 1994a; Radaelli 1999. On delegation to international organizations, see Barnett and Finnemore 2004.

6. Fiorina 1989. On financial policy and the avoidance of blame, see Pauly 1997.

7. For a formal review of the principal-agent framework, see Laffont and Martimort 2002.

8. For example, the U.S. Securities and Exchange Commission issued more than thirty "final rules" in 2005, including reporting requirements for asset-backed securities, classification rules for investment advisers, and application guidelines for international financial reporting standards.

9. This antipathy corresponds to the notion in the principal-agent literature that there are costs to the agent when its policy is overturned. See Ferejohn and Shipan 1990.

10. See Keech 1995 for a discussion of bureaucrat accountability.

11. SEC chairman Harvey Pitt objected to the creation of the PCAOB and tried to hobble its effectiveness by appointing an inexperienced financial regulator, former CIA director William Webster, as its first director. That decision, combined with the view that Pitt was partly responsible for the regulatory laxity that led to the Enron and Worldcom fiascos, ultimately brought about his dismissal as SEC chairman.

12. Walter 2003, 18.

13. On the "zone of acceptance" for bureaucracies, see Meier 1985a; on win-sets, see Putnam 1988. For the remainder of the text, I use the term *win-set*, but with some reluctance. First, the international regulatory agreements discussed in this book do not require domestic ratification or any formal voting procedures. Regulators' policies "win" to the extent that the legislature does not overturn them or otherwise intervene. Second, Putnam's use of

the term *win-set* as a range of policies that would gain acceptance (i.e., ratification) by the legislature is different from its usage in the formal modeling literature, in which a win-set refers to the set of points that would defeat a specific alternative in a vote. See Shepsle and Weingast 1987.

14. On bureaucratic decision making within limits set by the legislature, see Moe 1987.

15. By *realistic,* I mean policies that a financial regulator in the developed world might actually choose. Laxity, therefore, does not mean deregulation to the point that regulations do not exist; similarly, stringency does not imply such burdensome regulations that the industry can no longer function.

16. My view of competitiveness pertains to the market share of national firms in domestic and international markets but could also incorporate the attractiveness of a financial center for foreign (internationally oriented) firms.

17. Stigler 1971; Peltzman 1976.

18. Note that this line is not a *budget* constraint, as it does not address the costs of obtaining the various combinations of policy outcomes.

19. The congressional restructuring of S&L regulation is contained in the Financial Institutions Reform, Recovery, and Enforcement Act of 1989 (FIRREA), Public Law 101–73.

20. On the S&L crisis, see Kane 1989; Mayer 1990.

21. Kapstein 1989 and Oatley and Nabors 1998 are in agreement on the importance of market power in explaining the emergence of a multilateral agreement for bank capital adequacy. On the role of international institutions in the process of harmonization, see Simmons 2001.

22. This approach reflects a trend in the literature to focus on the "processes" of harmonization rather than on final outcomes. See Simmons 2001.

23. Interviews with current and former regulators, summer 2002.

24. See, among others, Kapstein 1989 and 1994; Murphy 2004; Oatley and Nabors 1998; Porter 1993; Reinicke 1995 and 1998; and Singer 2004.

25. Although academics may overlook the case, regulators and industry executives are quick to mention the securities capital adequacy negotiations as a striking counterexample to the Basel Accord. Interviews with current and former Basel Committee members, Basel, Switzerland, June 18–20, 2002.

26. On "structured, focused comparison," see George 1979.

27. Porter 1993.

28. This is not to argue that international organizations are unimportant in international regulatory harmonization more broadly, but rather to suggest that they are of secondary concern in explaining the international interactions of national regulatory agencies. On international organizations as actors in international relations, see Barnett and Finnemore 2004.

4. Banking: The Road to the Basel Accord

1. On the agreement as a landmark, see Kapstein 1989. See also Braithwaite and Drahos 2000; Kapstein 1991; Murphy 2004; Reinicke 1995; Singer 2004; and Tobin 1991.

2. On the end of Bretton Woods, see Gowa 1983.

3. Tobin 1991, 75.

4. U.S. Federal Reserve 1999.

5. James 1996; Lomax 1986.

6. James 1996, 353.

7. Spero 1980.

8. James 1996, 359.

9. Spero 1980, 111.

10. Spero 1980, 112.

11. On the failure of Franklin National, see Spero 1980.

12. See Helleiner 1994.

13. Quoted in Reinicke 1998, 104.

14. Fisher and Molyneux 1996.

15. Braithwaite and Drahos 2000; Kapstein 1989; Spero 1980.

16. Spero 1980, 159.

17. Ibid., 160.

18. U.S. Federal Reserve 2005.

19. Kapstein 1989, 329.

20. Underhill 1997.

21. Kapstein 1989, 330.

22. Quoted in Spero 1980, 163.

23. Spero 1980, 164.

24. The Basel Committee issued a revised Concordat in 1983.

25. This section relies on Smith and Walter 2003.

26. Commercial bank deposit data from U.S. Federal Reserve published data, http://www.federalreserve.gov/releases/h8/data.htm. Mutual fund data from *Forbes*, Sept. 8, 1986, Annual Mutual Funds Survey, pp. 104–226.

27. On the LDC debt crisis, see, among others, Cohen 1986; Helleiner 1994; James 1996; Kahler 1985; Lipson 1986; and Lomax 1986.

28. Oatley and Nabors 1998.

29. Personal interview, telephone, April 22, 2002.

30. International Lending Supervision Act 1983, 1280–81.

31. Oatley and Nabors 1998.

32. Ibid.

33. U.S. House of Representatives 1988.

34. Ibid.

35. Reinicke 1995.

36. Kapstein 1989.

37. See, for example, Mishkin 2001; Herring and Litan 1995; Porter 1993.

38. FDIC 1998, 66.

39. My focus in this section is on bank failures, not thrift (or "savings and loan") failures. On the many possible causes of the bank failures of the 1980s, see FDIC 1997.

40. FDIC 1997, 16.

41. Ibid., 111.

42. Ibid., 197.

43. FDIC 1998, 66.

44. The now-defunct Federal Home Loan Bank Board, which regulated savings and loans (S&Ls), is excluded from this discussion.

45. FDIC 1997, 111.

46. Ibid.

47. Wall 1983, 46.

48. See Wall 1983.

49. Reinicke 1995, 147.

50. See Oatley and Nabors 1998; Reinicke 1995.

51. Reinicke 1995, 140–50.

52. On the failure of Continental Illinois, see Sprague 1986 and Zweig 1985.

53. FDIC 1997, 44.

54. On the relationship between Penn Square and Continental, see Zweig 1985.

55. Sprague 1986, 149.

56. FDIC 1997, 244.

57. *New York Times,* Oct. 4, 1984, p. 18.

58. *Christian Science Monitor,* Sept. 19, 1984, p. 1, and *New York Times,* Sept. 19, 1984, p. 18.

59. FDIC 1997, 114.

60. Reinicke 1995, 150.

61. FDIC 1997, 16.

62. Ibid., 7.

63. HR 5565, 99th Cong., 2nd sess., *Congressional Record,* Oct. 10, 1986, E 3522.

64. See, for example, the statement by Rep. Parris, 99th Cong., 2nd sess., *Congressional Record,* Oct. 2, 1986, H 8890.

65. FDIC 1997, 92.

66. Ibid., 94.

67. Ibid., 96.

68. The legislation was the Competitive Equality Banking Act of 1987, Public Law 100–86.

69. *Wall Street Journal,* Sept. 18, 1987.

70. *Financial Times,* Jan. 31, 1986, p. 24.

71. Larry Armstrong, "What All of America's Japan-Bashing Can't Change," *Business Week,* Aug. 31, 1987, p. 63.

72. FDIC 1997, 114.

73. William Hall, "U.S. Banks Use More NIFs to Shift Lending," *Financial Times,* Sept. 26, 1986, p. 29. With an NIF a bank or group of banks agrees to underwrite a client's issue of short-term debt (notes) and to back up the facility with medium-term credit if the notes are not successfully sold on the market. If the notes are successfully sold, then no credit is actually extended to the client.

74. McCauley 1986.

75. Reinicke 1995, 151.

76. Ibid.

77. Cited in ibid.

78. Quoted in Joan Pryde, "Risk-Based Capital Rule Seen Helping Foreign Bank Letter of Credit Business," *American Banker,* May 30, 1986, p. 18.

79. Quoted in Solomon 1995, 414.

80. Nina Easton, "FDIC Study Says Risk-Based Plan Could Reduce Capital Overall," *American Banker,* April 21, 1986, p. 2.

81. Oatley and Nabors 1998.

82. Kapur 2000.

83. *Washington Post,* July 13, 1988, F1.

84. Monica Langley, "U.S. Regulators Move to Let Banks Enter Several New Businesses," *Wall Street Journal,* Dec. 29, 1986.

85. Hall 1999. See also Laurence 2001.

86. Penn 1989, 3.

87. Hall 1999, 3.

88. Penn 1989, 4.

89. On the secondary banking crisis, see Reid 1982.

90. Hall 1999, 6.

91. Penn 1989, 11.

92. Hall 1999, 7.

93. Quoted in Penn 1989, 13.

94. Hadjiemannuil 1996, 200.

95. See Cooper 1984, 213–17; Hadjiemannuil 1996, 197–200.

96. Hadjiemannuil 1996, 199.

97. Interviews, senior Bank of England officials, June 2002. See also Penn 1989, 1.
98. Estrella 2001, 8.
99. Grady and Weale 1986, 168.
100. Ibid.
101. Interviews, senior Bank of England officials, June 2002.
102. *Financial Times,* Oct. 6, 1984, p. 18.
103. Bank of England 1985a.
104. Grady and Weale 1986, 168.
105. *Financial Times,* Dec. 21, 1984, p. 1.
106. Geddes 1987, 109.
107. Moran 1986, 175.
108. Ellinger, Lomnicka, and Hooley 2002, 35.
109. Hall 1999, 34.
110. See Geddes 1987.
111. On the Banking Act of 1987, see Hall 1999.
112. Bank of England 1985b. See also Hadjiemannuil 1996, 201–2. In 1986 the Bank issued a consultative paper on the treatment of off–balance sheet risks which solicited the views of the banking sector.
113. Hadjiemannuil 1996, 203.
114. Quoted in Solomon 1995, 416.
115. Oatley and Nabors 1998.
116. Building societies are the United Kingdom's equivalent of thrifts in the United States.
117. Hawawini and Schill 1994, table 7.1.
118. See Solomon 1995.
119. Ibid., 416.
120. Solomon 1995.
121. On the international expansion of Japanese banks in the 1980s, see Amyx 2004.
122. Vogel 1996; see also Scott and Iwahara 1994.
123. Scott and Iwahara 1994, 8.
124. Solomon 1995, 424.
125. Vogel 1996.
126. Amyx 2004, 108.
127. Rosenbluth 1989, 129.
128. Ibid.
129. Ibid., 130.
130. Interviews, current and former bank regulators, New York and London, May–June 2002.
131. Kapstein 1989, 1991.
132. Quoted in Kane 1994, 106.
133. Kapstein 1989, 341.
134. Kapstein 1989, 1991; Oatley and Nabors 1998.
135. U.S. Shadow Financial Regulatory Committee 2000.
136. For an opposing view, see Scott and Iwahara 1994.
137. Ho 2002. It should be noted that the original Basel Accord has been amended since 1988. See www.bis.org.
138. A representative example is Eichengreen 1999.
139. Basel Committee on Banking Supervision 1988.
140. See U.S. Shadow Financial Regulatory Committee 2000 for a summary of critiques of the Basel Accord.
141. See Basel Committee on Banking Supervision 1999a for a review of the empirical literature on the effects of the Basel Accord.

142. Basel Committee on Banking Supervision 1996.

143. Ibid., 7.

144. Ibid., 2.

145. Basel Committee on Banking Supervision 1999b, 2001, and 2003.

146. See Basel Committee on Banking Supervision 2003.

147. Basel Committee on Banking Supervision 2005, 152. Also see chapter 2.

148. See Basel Committee on Banking Supervision 2005 for a discussion of these two pillars.

149. Ferguson 2003.

150. See King and Sinclair 2003.

151. Ferguson 2003.

152. The term *relaxation* may not be well received by some regulators and industry executives who emphasize the Basel II agreement's many enhancements to banks' risk-management practices. Indeed, risk management may be smarter and more sophisticated after Basel II, and it is possible that banks could be more stable as a result. However, the enhanced discretion granted to banks to implement these new risk-management processes strongly implies a degree of flexibility that was missing from the initial accord.

153. Ferguson 2003.

154. Chorafas 2004. For a broader critique of the new agreement, see King and Sinclair 2003.

155. Basel Committee on Banking Supervision 2006. This figure applies to "Group 1" banks, defined as internationally active banks with Tier 1 capital greater than 3 billion. Note that any estimates of the impact of Basel II should be taken with a grain of salt. Cross-country and cross-firm methodological differences in estimating the losses stemming from economic downturns could have a profound impact on the resulting Basel II capital charges. I thank Kim Olson for stressing this point.

156. FDIC data from http://www.fdic.gov/bank/historical/bank/index.html.

157. See Foot 2003.

158. On these bank failures, see Brewer et al. 2002.

5. Securities: Financial Instability and Regulatory Divergence

1. See, for example, Eichengreen 1999.

2. Interviews, Basel Committee and BIS staff, Basel, Switzerland, June 18–20, 2002; and former SEC senior staff member, New York, May 7, 2002.

3. Turner 1991.

4. Dale 1996, 2.

5. International Monetary Fund 2000.

6. Keohane and Milner 1996 is an example of an edited volume on globalization that omits any mention of derivatives.

7. Mishkin and Eakins 1998.

8. International Swaps and Derivatives Association 2003. This figure includes outstanding interest rate swaps, currency swaps, and interest rate options.

9. Global Derivatives Study Group 1993, 58. "Notional amounts," the most common method of measuring derivatives activity, refer to the principal amounts hedged by derivative contracts.

10. OECD 1991, 10.

11. Ibid., 9.

12. Chuppe, Haworth, and Watkins, 1989, 37.

13. Sobel 1994, 2.

14. Global Derivatives Study Group 1993, 3.

15. Dale 1996, 160.

16. Securities and Exchange Commission 1988, 3.6 and 3.12.

17. Hewitt 1992; Tobin 1991.

18. OECD 1991, 15.

19. For a comprehensive list of reports stemming from the 1987 stock market crash, see Tobin 1991, 282–83.

20. OECD 1991.

21. Simmons 2001, 612.

22. See Porter 1993; Tobin 1991.

23. Tobin 1991.

24. On the structure of IOSCO, see Porter 1993 and Tobin 1991.

25. Tobin 1991, 315.

26. Interviews, London and New York, summer 2002.

27. Quoted in Tobin 1991, 314.

28. The areas addressed by the working groups were international equity offerings, capital adequacy, off-market trading, clearing and settlement, accounting and auditing, futures markets, and enforcement. See International Organization of Securities Commissions 1989.

29. Tobin 1991.

30. International Organization of Securities Commissions 1989. U.K. stock exchanges, as self-regulatory organizations, were under the jurisdiction of the Securities and Investments Board.

31. Tobin 1991.

32. International Organization of Securities Commissions 1989.

33. On the Big Bang, see Laurence 1996, 2001; Moran 1988, 1991; Vogel 1996.

34. Laurence 1996.

35. On re-regulation, see Vogel 1996.

36. Solomon 1995, 97.

37. On the process of underwriting in the United Kingdom, see Smith and Walter 2003.

38. Solomon 1995, 97.

39. Ibid., 98.

40. Littlewood 1998.

41. Quoted in Solomon 1995, 98.

42. See, for example, *Boston Globe*, Oct. 16, 1989, p. 23.

43. *Guardian,* Oct. 16, 1989, p. 1.

44. See Reid 1988; Vogel 1996.

45. Reid 1988, 59.

46. Ibid.

47. The Financial Services Act of 1986 stipulated that the SIB would establish a set of core rules by which the SROs would abide. The primary SROs were the Securities and Futures Authority, the Investment Management Regulatory Organization, and the Personal Investment Authority. Other SROs were dismantled or were consolidated into other SROs. See Vogel 1996.

48. Vogel 1996, 111.

49. Laurence 1996.

50. Ibid., 329.

51. Euromoney Publications 1993.

52. Notional data on derivatives can be found in Swaps Monitor Publications 1994 and International Organization of Securities Commissions 1995.

53. Interviews, London and New York, summer 2002.

54. Reid 1988, 5.

55. Dale 1996.

56. On DPCs, see Dale 1996.

57. Interviews, London, summer 2002.

58. *Observer* (London), April 28, 1991, p. 31.

59. See, for example, *Independent,* Jan. 28, 1990, p. 4.

60. On the SIB's leadership in the negotiations, see *International Securities Regulation Report,* multiple issues (1989–92).

61. Dimson and Marsh 1996.

62. *International Securities Regulation Report,* Nov. 3, 1992. A "long position" means that a firm has ownership of a security whereas a "short position" means that a firm has "sold short" a security by delivering borrowed shares to the purchaser but has yet to cover its position by buying the shares in the market. Firms (and individuals) often take short positions to protect the profits in their long positions.

63. Dimson and Marsh 1996.

64. Ibid.

65. International Organization of Securities Commissions 1989.

66. Interview, former senior SIB official, London, June 2002. Such pressure is implied in Walker 1992.

67. *Financial Times,* March 8, 1990, p. 18.

68. *San Francisco Chronicle,* March 3, 1990, p. B1.

69. *Los Angeles Times,* March 3, 1990.

70. U.S. Senate 1990.

71. Ibid.

72. *Financial Times,* March 3, 1990, p. 2.

73. U.S. Public Law 101–432. Note that the legislation applied only to holding companies of broker-dealers. Bank holding companies were already subject to consolidated supervision in the United States.

74. *International Securities Regulation Report,* July 28, 1992.

75. Quoted in ibid.

76. *International Securities Regulation Report,* Nov. 3, 1992.

77. Interview, former senior SIB official, London, June 2002; see also Walker 1992.

78. Solomon 1995, 83.

79. On the negotiations over monetary policy in the wake of the crash, see Solomon 1995, 82–88.

80. Vogel 1996.

81. Ohama 1991.

82. Quoted in Solomon 1995, 90. See also Vogel 1996.

83. Laurence 2001.

84. Ibid., 155n.

85. Kato 1992.

86. On the expansion of Japanese firms in Canada, see *Toronto Star,* June 11, 1987, p. E4.

87. *Fortune,* Oct. 8, 1986. See also *New York Times,* Feb. 13, 1986, p. D1.

88. *New York Times,* Feb. 9, 1986, sec. 3, p. 1.

89. Ohama 1991.

90. Kato 1992.

91. Ohama 1991.

92. On the tight relationship between the Big Four and MOF policy, see Brown 1999.

93. The Nikkei recovered slightly toward the end of 1992 but remained stagnant throughout the mid-1990s and continued its fall later in the decade.

94. Laurence 2001.

95. *Gazette,* Aug. 14, 1991, p. F4.

96. *Economist,* Nov. 28, 1992, p. 88.

97. Agence Presse France, Nov. 25, 1992. On the declining capital levels of the Big Four, see *Financial Times,* May 18, 1992, p. 19.

98. See Vogel 1996 and Laurence 2001.

99. Vogel 1996.

100. Ibid., 187.

101. Laurence 2001.

102. *Financial Times,* Sept. 13, 1991, p. 19.

103. Ibid., Nov. 20, 1992, p. 28.

104. Millman 1995.

105. Laurence 2001.

106. Ibid.

107. International Organization of Securities Commissions 1995.

108. Interviews, London and New York, summer 2002.

109. *Economist,* Nov. 28, 1992, p. 88.

110. Ibid.

111. Ibid., Oct. 31, 1992. See also Steil 1994.

112. Interview, former SIB official, London, June 2001.

113. *International Securities Regulation Report,* July 28, 1992, and interviews, London and New York, summer 2002.

114. *International Securities Regulation Report,* July 28, 1992.

115. *Financial Times,* Oct. 28, 1992.

116. *Economist,* Oct. 31, 1992. In early 1992 the SEC requested that the Federal Reserve Bank of New York run a simulation of the 1987 stock market crash, assuming that U.S. firms were capitalized at the SIB's proposed level. The study found that the crash would have led to the collapse of one of the largest securities firms in the country. Interview with former senior SEC official, May 2002.

117. *Financial Times,* Oct. 28, 1992.

118. Ibid., Feb. 11, 1993.

119. Ibid., Oct. 19, 1995, p. 25.

120. See *Independent,* June 27, 1995, p. 21; *Economist,* July 20, 1996, p. 63; and *Business Week,* July 3, 1995, p. 42.

121. Interviews, London, New York, and Basel, summer 2002.

6. Insurance: Domestic Fragmentation and Regulatory Divergence

1. Artwork valued at more than $100 million is believed to have been lost in the attacks. *Insurance Day,* Oct. 11, 2001, p. 3.

2. There is no definitive tally of the losses stemming from the September 11 attacks. Indeed, as of late 2006 some claims have yet to be settled. The $40–50 billion figure was commonly cited in the financial press (e.g., *Financial Times,* May 24, 2002, p. 1).

3. Figures from BBC News, Oct. 8, 2001 ("Insurer Doubles Trade Center Losses"). Available at news.bbc.co.uk.

4. On systemic risk in insurance markets, see OECD 2003a and 2003b. For an opposing view from the reinsurance industry, see Swiss Re 2003.

5. The United States' National Association of Insurance Commissioners (NAIC) is a member of the IAIS, but only individual NAIC members have voting rights; the NAIC itself does not vote in IAIS affairs. See IAIS 2004a.

6. The Basel Committee itself urged insurance regulators to create the IAIS. See Zaring 1998.

7. See www.iaisweb.org for a full list of subcommittees.

8. On the limited international activity of Japanese insurance firms, see Skipper 1996, 175–77.

9. Two notable exceptions are Kenneth Meier (1985b), who has written on the politics of U.S. insurance regulation, and Virginia Haufler (1997), who has treated the management of international risk.

10. See chapters 4 and 5 for citations of the literature in these two areas.

11. Cummins and Weiss 2000, 7.

12. Skipper 1996, 156.

13. Quoted in Hall 2001, 19–20.

14. IAIS 2002, 3.

15. Swiss Re 1996.

16. Swiss Re 2004.

17. Skipper 2001, p. 8.

18. Ibid.

19. On the liberalization of insurance trade, see OECD 1999.

20. OECD 1999.

21. Despite the clear economic rationale for globally diversified reinsurance firms, direct insurers have in the past selected reinsurers based more on price and expediency, often at the expense of financial stability. For example, small, relatively undiversified reinsurance firms were able to thrive in the United States until the onset of the liability crisis of the mid-1980s, which quickly led to their demise.

22. Reinsurance Association of America Web site: www.reinsurance.org.

23. Cummins 2002.

24. Skipper 1996, 169.

25. Ibid., 179.

26. See Wang 2003.

27. See KPMG 2002, 41, and Wang 2003, 25.

28. The bylaws of the IAIS explicitly state that the NAIC is permitted to be a member along with national regulators. IAIS 2004a.

29. Clifford Chance 2002.

30. Hall 2001.

31. Hernandez and McEneaney 2002.

32. Ibid., 40.

33. Hall 2001, 27.

34. Interview, Swiss Re senior executive, Geneva, April 7, 2005.

35. Priest 1988.

36. Meier 1985b, 93.

37. For representative data, see Priest 1988.

38. Data from Harrington 1991.

39. Note that the ratio does not incorporate profits from investment activities, which are a significant part of a reinsurer's operations. Thus the combined ratio is useful only as a relative (not absolute) indicator of profitability.

40. A.M. Best 2002.

41. U.S. House of Representatives 1990.

42. The four firms were Mission Insurance Company, Integrity Insurance Company, Transit Casualty Company, and Anglo-American Insurance Company. See U.S. House of Representatives 1990.

43. The report stated, "The Subcommittee has found no evidence of an overall crisis threatening the existence of the insurance industry at the present time." U.S. House of Representatives 1990, 2.

44. U.S. House of Representatives 1994, 11 (quotation) and 9–10.

45. Ibid., 1.

46. Ibid., 7.

47. Quoted in *Business Insurance,* Aug. 6, 1990, p. 2.

48. The NAIC's model laws are available at www.naic.org. A useful summary of the NAIC's efforts in 1990 can be found in *Business Insurance,* Aug. 6, 1990, p. 2.

49. *Journal of Commerce,* June 8, 1990, p. 1A.

50. Swiss Re 2002.

51. For the specific requirements imposed on Lloyd's by the Insurance Companies Act, see Financial Services Authority 1998.

52. See Clifford Chance 2002.

53. *Financial Times,* June 20, 1992, p. 8.

54. *Guardian* (London), May 1, 1995, p. 16.

55. For an accessible discussion of the LMX spiral, see Luessenhop and Mayer 1995.

56. See ibid.

57. For more on Sir David Walker, see chap. 5.

58. See Financial Services Authority 1998.

59. Swiss Re 2002, 26.

60. Ibid.

61. See ibid., 14.

62. See www.Lloyd's.com. Lloyd's retains its own governing council, which is overseen by the FSA.

63. IAIS 2003.

64. On the evolution of EU (and EC) insurance regulation, see Clifford Chance 2002.

65. See Koller 2005 and Trainar 2005.

66. Kawai 2005.

67. See *Reactions* 25 (January 2005).

7. Conclusion: The Future of International Regulatory Harmonization

1. Kapstein 1989.

2. Putnam 1988.

3. Regulators are not always the primary actors, as the case of accounting standards demonstrates. But in the realm of banking, securities, and insurance—three pillars of finance—regulators are indeed the primary actors in international negotiations over regulatory standards.

4. Personal interview, telephone, April 22, 2002.

5. There is no legal requirement in the Basel Accord that national regulators enforce the standard; however, if and when regulators choose to enforce the standard domestically, that choice has the force of national law.

6. On the connection between legislatures and governments' foreign policy negotiations, see Martin 2000 and Milner 1997.

7. DeSombre 2000.

8. Reported in the *Financial Times,* Dec. 3, 2003, p. 23.

9. Ibid.

10. See Moravcsik 2004 on the democratic deficit in world politics.

11. I thank Devesh Kapur for this point.

12. Simmons and Elkins (2004) use the related term *diffusion* to refer to the international spread of liberal economic policies. See also Brune and Guisinger 2003.

13. Calomiris and White 1994.

14. See the framework offered in Simmons 2001.

15. This point contrasts with Simmons's (2001) categorization of the Basel Accord. On worldwide compliance with the Basel Accord, see Ho 2002.

16. On noncompliant countries, see the FATF's list of noncooperative countries and territories at www.oecd.org/fatf.

17. Kapur 2000.

18. See Mosley 2003.

19. Fearon 1998.

20. Of course, as mentioned earlier, regulatory compliance throughout the world economy is not guaranteed. Future work on the determinants of regulatory compliance (the enforcement stage) will shed light on variation in the success of standard creation (the bargaining phase).

21. Interviews with current and former regulators, Basel, London, and New York, summer 2002.

22. Developing-country regulators are not part of the Basel Committee, which still consists only of participants from the G-10 countries (plus Luxembourg, Spain, and Switzerland).

23. Kapur 2000.

References

Abbott, Kenneth W., and Duncan Snidal. 2000. "Hard and Soft Law in International Governance." *International Organization* 54(3):421–56.

Alexander, Kern, Rahul Dhumale, and John Eatwell. 2006. *Global Governance of Financial Systems: The International Regulation of Systemic Risk*. Oxford: Oxford University Press.

A. M. Best. 2002. "P/C Industry: 2001 Insolvencies." Special Report, Oldwick, N.J. June 18.

American Banker. 1989. *Top Numbers 1989*. New York: American Banker.

Amyx, Jennifer. 2004. *Japan's Financial Crisis: Institutional Rigidity and Reluctant Change*. Princeton, N.J.: Princeton University Press.

Bank for International Settlements. 1998. *Central Bank Survey of Foreign Exchange and Derivative Market Activity*. Basel, Switzerland: Monetary and Economic Department.

———. 2002. "Basel Committee Reaches Agreement on New Capital Accord Issues." Press release, July 10. Available at http://www.bis.org.

Bank of England. 1985a. *Annual Report*. London: Bank of England.

———. 1985b. "Off–Balance Sheet Risks: Note Issuance Facilities/Revolving Underwriting Facilities." BSD/1985/2, April. London.

Barnett, Michael, and Martha Finnemore. 2004. *Rules for the World: International Organizations and Global Politics*. Ithaca: Cornell University Press.

Basel Committee on Banking Supervision. 1988. "International Convergence of Capital Measurement and Capital Standards." Bank for International Settlements. Available at http://www.bis.org/publ/bcbs04a.pdf.

———. 1996. "Overview of the Amendment to the Capital Accord to Incorporate Market Risks." Bank for International Settlements. Available at http://www.bis.org/publ/bcbs23.pdf.

———. 1997. "Core Principles for Effective Banking Supervision." Available at http://www.bis.org/publ/bcbs30a.pdf.

———. 1999a. "Capital Requirements and Bank Behaviour: The Impact of the Basle Accord." Working Paper No. 1 (April), Bank for International Settlements. Available at http://www.bis.org/publ/bcbs_wp1.pdf.

———. 1999b. "A New Capital Adequacy Framework." Bank for International Settlements. Available at http://www.bis.org/publ/bcbs50.pdf.

———. 2001. "The New Basel Capital Accord: An Explanatory Note." Bank for International Settlements. Available at http://www.bis.org/publ/bcbsca01.pdf.

———. 2003. "Consultative Document: Overview of the New Basel Capital Accord." Bank for International Settlements. Available at http://www.bis.org/bcbs/cp3ov.pdf.

———. 2004. "International Convergence of Capital Measurement and Capital Standards: A Revised Framework." Bank for International Settlements. Available at http://www.bis.org/publ/bcbs107.pdf.

———. 2005. "International Convergence of Capital Measurement and Capital Standards: A Revised Framework." Bank for International Settlements. Available at http://www.bis.org/publ/bcbs118.pdf.

———. 2006. "Results of the Fifth Quantitative Impact Study." Bank for International Settlements. June 16. Available at http://www.bis.org/bcbs/qis/qis5results.pdf.

Bawn, Kathleen. 1995. "Political Control versus Expertise: Congressional Choices about Administrative Procedures." *American Political Science Review* 89(1):62–73.

Berger, Lawrence A., J. David Cummins, and Sharon Tennyson. 1992. "Reinsurance and the Liability Insurance Crisis." *Journal of Risk and Uncertainty* 5:253–72.

Braithwaite, John, and Peter Drahos. 2000. *Global Business Regulation.* Cambridge: Cambridge University Press.

Breeden, Richard C. 1992. "Reconciling National and International Concerns in the Regulation of Global Capital Markets." In *The Internationalisation of Capital Markets and the Regulatory Response*, ed. John Fingleton. London: Graham & Trotman.

Brewer, Elijah, Hesna Genay, William Curt Hunter, and George G. Kaufman. 2002. "The Value of Banking Relationships during a Financial Crisis: Evidence from Failures of Japanese Banks." Working Paper 2002-20. Federal Reserve Bank of Chicago, Chicago.

Brown, J. Robert, Jr. 1999. *The Ministry of Finance: Bureaucratic Practices and the Transformation of the Japanese Economy.* Westport, Conn.: Quorum Books.

Brune, Nancy, and Alexandra Guisinger. 2003. "The Diffusion of Capital Account Liberalization in Developing Countries." Working Paper. Yale University, New Haven, Conn.

Calomiris, Charles W., and Eugene N. White. 1994. "The Origins of Federal Deposit Insurance." In *The Regulated Economy*, ed. Claudia Goldin and Gary Libecap. Chicago: University of Chicago Press.

Carrubba, Clifford J., and Craig Volden. 2000. "Coalitional Politics and Logrolling in Legislative Institutions." *American Journal of Political Science* 44(2):261–77.

Caves, Richard E., Jeffrey A. Frankel, and Ronald W. Jones. 1999. *World Trade and Payments.* 8th ed. Reading, Mass.: Addison-Wesley.

Cerny, Philip G. 1995. "Globalization and the Changing Logic of Collective Action." *International Organization* 49(4):595–625.

Chorafas, Dimitris. 2004. *Economic Capital Allocation with Basel II: Cost, Benefit, and Implementation Procedures.* Amsterdam: Elsevier Butterworth-Heinemann.

Chuppe, Terry M., Hugh R. Haworth, and Marvin G. Watkins. 1989. *The Securities Markets in the 1980s: A Global Perspective.* Washington, D.C.: Securities and Exchange Commission.

Clifford Chance. 2002. *International Insurance Regulation: Current and Proposed Regulation Explained.* London: Reactions Publishing Group.

Cohen, Benjamin. 1986. *In Whose Interest? International Banking and American Foreign Policy.* New Haven, Conn.: Yale University Press.

Cooper, John. 1984. *The Management and Regulation of Banks.* New York: St. Martin's.

Crockett, Andrew. 1997. "Why Is Financial Stability a Goal of Public Policy?" Paper presented at the conference "Maintaining Financial Stability in a Global Economy," sponsored by the Federal Reserve Bank of Kansas City, Jackson Hole, Wyo., Aug. 28–30.

Cummins, J. David. 2002. "The Global Market for Reinsurance: Consolidation, Capacity, and Efficiency." Paper presented at the conference "Global Issues in Insurance Regulation," London, April 17–18.

Cummins, J. David, and Mary A. Weiss. 2000. "The Global Market for Reinsurance: Consolidation, Capacity, and Efficiency." In *Papers on Financial Services 2000,* ed. Robert E. Litan and Anthony M. Snatomero. Washington, D.C.: Brookings Institution.

Cutler, A. Claire, Virginia Haufler, and Tony Porter. 1999. *Private Authority and International Affairs.* Albany, New York: SUNY Press.

Dale, Richard. 1994. "International Banking Regulation." In *International Financial Market Regulation,* ed. Benn Steil. New York: Wiley.

———. 1996. *Risk and Regulation in Global Securities Markets.* New York: Wiley.

DeSombre, Elizabeth R. 2000. *Domestic Sources of International Environmental Policy.* Cambridge, Mass.: MIT Press.

Dimson, Elroy, and Paul Marsh. 1996. "Stress Tests of Capital Requirements." Working Paper 96-50. Wharton Financial Institutions Center. Philadelphia.

Dodd, Lawrence C., and Richard L. Schott. 1979. *Congress and the Administrative State.* New York: Wiley.

Drezner, Daniel W. Forthcoming. *All Politics Is Global: Explaining International Regulatory Regimes.* Princeton: Princeton University Press.

Eatwell, John, and Lance Taylor. 2000. *Global Finance at Risk: The Case for International Regulation.* New York: New Press.

Edwards, Franklin R. 1988. "The Future Financial Structure: Fears and Policies." In *Restructuring Banking and Financial Services in America,* ed. William S. Haraf and Rose Marie Kushmeider. Washington, D.C.: American Enterprise Institute.

Eichengreen, Barry. 1999. *Toward a New International Financial Architecture: A Practical Post-Asia Agenda.* Washington, D.C.: Institute for International Economics.

Eichengreen, Barry, and Peter Kenen. 1994. "Managing the World Economy under the Bretton Woods System: An Overview." In *Managing the World Economy: Fifty Years after Bretton Woods,* ed. Peter Kenen, pp. 3–57. Washington, D.C.: Institute for International Economics.

Ellinger, E. P., Eva Lomnicka, and Richard Hooley. 2002. *Modern Banking Law.* Oxford: Oxford University Press.

Estrella, Arturo. 2001. "Dealing with Financial Instability: The Central Bank's Toolkit." *Riksbank Economic Review* 2:34–49.

Euromoney Publications. 1993. *Derivatives Survey, 1993.* London: Euromoney Publications.

Fearon, James. 1998. "Bargaining, Enforcement, and International Cooperation." *International Organization* 52(2):269–306.

FDIC. 1997. *History of the Eighties: Lessons for the Future.* Vol. 1. Washington, D.C.: Federal Deposit Insurance Corporation.

———. 1998. "A Brief History of Deposit Insurance in the United States." Paper presented at International Conference on Deposit Insurance, Washington, D.C. September.

Ferejohn, John, and Charles R. Shipan. 1990. "Congressional Influence on Bureaucracy." *Journal of Law, Economics, and Organization* 6:1–21.

Ferguson, Roger. 2003. "Basel II: A Realist's Perspective." Speech at the Risk Management Association's Conference on Capital Management, Washington D.C., April 9. Available at http://www.federalreserve.gov/BoardDocs/Speeches/2003/20030409/default.htm.

Financial Services Authority. 1998. "The Future Regulation of Lloyds." Consultation Paper 16. Financial Services Authority, London.

Fiorina, Morris. 1989. *Congress: Keystone of the Washington Establishment.* New Haven, Conn.: Yale University Press.

Fisher, A., and P. Molyneux. 1996. "A Note on the Determinants of Foreign Bank Activity in London between 1980 and 1989." *Applied Financial Economics* 6(3):271–77.

Foot, Michael. 2003. "Protecting Financial Stability: How Good Are We at It?" Speech at the University of Birmingham, Birmingham, U.K., June 6. Available at http://www.fsa.gov.uk/Pages/Library/Communication/Speeches/2003/sp133.shtml.

Frieden, Jeffry A. 1987. *Banking on the World: The Politics of American International Finance.* New York: Harper & Row.

Friedman, Milton, and Anna J. Schwartz. 1963. *A Monetary History of the United States, 1867–1960.* Princeton, N.J.: Princeton University Press.

Garrett, Geoffrey. 1992. "International Cooperation and Institutional Choice: The European Community's Internal Market." *International Organization* 46(2):41–76.

Geddes, Philip. 1987. *Inside the Bank of England.* London: Boxtree.

George, Alexander L. 1979. "Case Studies and Theory Development: The Method of Structured, Focused Comparison." In *Diplomacy: New Approaches in History, Theory, and Policy,* ed. Paul Gordon Lauren. New York: Free Press.

Global Derivatives Study Group. 1993. *Derivatives: Practices and Principles.* Washington, D.C.: Group of Thirty.

Goldstein, Judith, Miles Kahler, Robert O. Keohane, and Anne-Marie Slaughter. 2000. "Introduction: Legalization and World Politics." *International Organization* 54(3):385–99.

Gowa, Joanne S. 1983. *Closing the Gold Window: Domestic Politics and the End of Bretton Woods.* Ithaca: Cornell University Press.

Grady, John, and Martin Weale. 1986. *British Banking, 1960–85.* London: Macmillan.

Grossman, Gene M., and Elhanan Helpman. 2001. *Special Interest Politics.* Cambridge, Mass.: MIT Press.

Haberman, Gary. 1987. "Capital Requirements of Commercial and Investment Banks: Contrasts in Regulation." *Federal Reserve Bank of New York Quarterly Review* (Autumn): 1–10.

Hadjiemmanuil, Christos. 1996. *Banking Regulation and the Bank of England.* London: LLP.

Hall, Debra J. 2001. "Reinsurance Regulation in a Global Marketplace: A View from the United States." *Journal of Reinsurance* 8(1):19–51.

Hall, Rodney Bruce, and Thomas J. Biersteker. 2002. *The Emergence of Private Authority in Global Governance.* Cambridge: Cambridge University Press.

Hall, Maximilian J. B. 1999. *Handbook of Banking Regulation and Supervision in the United Kingdom.* Cheltenham, U.K.: Edward Elgar.

Harrington, Scott E. 1991. "Liability Insurance: Volatility in Prices and in the Availability of Coverage." In *Tort Law and the Public Interest,* ed. Peter H. Schuck. New York: Norton.

Haufler, Virginia. 1997. *Dangerous Commerce: Insurance and the Management of International Risk.* Ithaca: Cornell University Press.

———. 2001. *A Public Role for the Private Sector: Industry Self-Regulation in a Global Economy.* Washington, D.C.: Carnegie Endowment for International Peace.

Hawawini, Gabriel, and Michael Schill. 1994. "The Japanese Presence in the European Financial Services Sector." In *Does Ownership Matter? Japanese Multinationals in Europe*, ed. Mark Mason and Dennis Encarnation, pp. 253–87. Oxford: Oxford University Press.

Heggestad, Arnold A., and B. Frank King. 1982. "Regulation of Bank Capital: An Evaluation." *Federal Reserve Bank of Atlanta Economic Review* 67:3.

Helleiner, Eric. 1994. *States and the Reemergence of Global Finance*. Ithaca: Cornell University Press.

Hernandez, Gary A., and Sean McEneaney. 2002. "Reinsurance Regulation in the United States: A Primer on the Regulator's Ability to Monitor Solvency." *Journal of Reinsurance* 9(4):37–54.

Herring, Richard J., and Robert E. Litan. 1995. *Financial Regulation in the Global Economy*. Washington, D.C.: Brookings Institution.

Herring, Richard J., and Til Schuermann. 2005. "Capital Regulation for Position Risk in Banks, Securities Firms, and Insurance Companies." In *Capital Adequacy beyond Basel: Banking, Securities, and Insurance*, ed. Hal S. Scott, pp. 15–86. Oxford: Oxford University Press.

Hewitt, Michael E. 1992. "Systemic Risk in International Securities Markets." In *Regulating International Financial Markets: Issues and Policies*, ed. Franklin R. Edwards and Hugh T. Patrick. Boston: Kluwer Academic.

Ho, Daniel E. 2002. "Compliance and International Soft Law: Why Do Countries Implement the Basle Accord?" *Journal of International Economic Law* 5(3):647–88.

IAIS. 2002. "Principles on Minimum Requirements for Supervision of Reinsurers." Available at www.iaisweb.org.

——. 2003. "Core Principles for Insurance Supervision." Available at www.iaisweb.org.

——. 2004a. "Bylaws of the International Association of Insurance Supervisors." Available at www.iaisweb.org.

——. 2004b. "Global Reinsurance Market Report 2003." Available at www.iaisweb.org.

International Finance Corporation. 1992. *Emerging Stock Markets Factbook*. Washington, D.C.: International Finance Corporation.

International Lending Supervision Act. 1983. *United States Statutes at Large*. Vol. 97. Washington, D.C.: U.S. Government Printing Office.

International Monetary Fund. 2000. "IMF Global Portfolio Investment Survey." Available at http://www.imf.org/external/np/sec/nb/2000/NB0008.htm.

International Organization of Securities Commissions. 1989. "Capital Adequacy Standards for Securities Firms." Report of the Technical Committee. Available at http://www.iosco.org.

——. 1995. "Public Disclosure of the Trading and Derivatives Activities of Banks and Securities Firms." Joint Report with the Basel Committee on Banking Supervision. November. Available at http://www.iosco.org.

International Swaps and Derivatives Association. 2003. "ISDA Market Survey." Available at www.isda.org.

James, Harold. 1996. *International Monetary Cooperation since Bretton Woods*. New York: Oxford University Press.

Kahler, Miles. 1985. "Politics and International Debt: Explaining the Crisis." *International Organization* 39(3):357–82.

Kahler, Miles, and David Lake. 2003. "Globalization and Governance." In *Governance in a Global Economy*, ed. Kahler and Lake. Princeton, N.J.: Princeton University Press.

Kane, Edward J. 1981. "Accelerating Inflation, Technological Innovation, and the Decreasing Effectiveness of Banking Regulation." *Journal of Finance* 36(2):355–67.

———. 1988. "How Market Forces Influence the Structure of Regulation." In *Restructuring Banking and Financial Services in America,* ed. William S. Haraf and Rose Marie Kushmeider. Washington, D.C.: American Enterprise Institute.

———. 1989. *The S&L Insurance Mess: How Did It Happen?* Washington, D.C.: Urban Institute Press.

———. 1991. "Tension between Competition and Coordination in International Financial Regulation." In *Governing Banking's Future: Markets vs. Regulation,* ed. Catherine England. Boston: Kluwer Academic.

———. 1994. "Incentive Conflict in the International Regulatory Agreement on Risk Based Capital." In *Global Risk Based Capital Regulations,* vol. 1, ed. Charles A. Stone and Anne Zissu. Burr Ridge, Ill.: Irwin Professional Publishing.

Kapstein, Ethan B. 1989. "Resolving the Regulator's Dilemma: International Coordination of Banking Regulations." *International Organization* 43(2):323–47.

———. 1991. *Supervising International Banks: Origins and Implications of the Basle Accord.* Essays in International Finance, no. 185. Princeton, N.J.: Department of Economics, Princeton University.

———. 1994. *Governing the Global Economy.* Cambridge, Mass.: Harvard University Press.

Kapur, Devesh. 2000. "Reforming the International Financial System: Key Issues." In *Global Financial Reform: How, Why, and When?,* ed. North-South Institute. Ottawa, Ont.: North-South Institute.

Kato, Takashi. 1992. "Japanese Securities Markets and Global Harmonization." In *Regulating International Financial Markets: Issues and Policies,* ed. Franklin R. Edwards and Hugh T. Patrick. Boston: Kluwer Academic.

Kaufman, Henry. 1998. "Preventing the Next Global Financial Crisis." *Washington Post,* Jan. 28, p. A17.

Kaul, Inge, Isabelle Grunberg, and Marc A. Stern, eds. 1999. *Global Public Goods.* New York: Oxford University Press.

Kawai, Yoshi. 2005. "IAIS Recent Developments and Future Work." Paper presented at the 21st Annual PROGRES Seminar, Geneva, Switzerland, April 7–8.

Keech, William. 1995. *Economic Politics: The Costs of Democracy.* New York: Cambridge University Press.

Keohane, Robert O. 1984. *After Hegemony.* Princeton, N.J.: Princeton University Press.

Keohane, Robert O., and Helen Milner, eds. 1996. *Internationalization and Domestic Politics.* New York: Cambridge University Press.

Keohane, Robert O., and Joseph S. Nye. 1989. *Power and Interdependence.* 2nd ed. New York: HarperCollins.

Khademian, Anne M. 1992. *The SEC and Capital Market Regulation: The Politics of Expertise.* Pittsburgh: University of Pittsburgh Press.

King, Michael R., and Timothy J. Sinclair. 2003. "Private Actors and Public Policy: A Requiem for the New Basel Capital Accord." *International Political Science Review* 24(3):345–62.

Koller, Michael. 2005. "Solvency II." Paper presented at the 21st Annual PROGRES Seminar, Geneva, Switzerland, April 7–8.

KPMG. 2002. "Study into the Methodologies for Prudential Supervision of Reinsurance with a View to the Possible Establishment of an EU Framework." Commissioned by the Internal Market Directorate General of the European Commission. Jan. 31. Available at http://ec.europa.eu/internal_market/insurance/docs/reinsurance/reins-sup_en.pdf.

Krasner, Stephen D. 1991. "Global Communications and National Power: Life on the Pareto Frontier." *World Politics* 43:336–56.

Laffont, Jean-Jacques, and David Martimort. 2002. *The Theory of Incentives: The Principal-Agent Model.* Princeton, N.J.: Princeton University Press.

Laurence, Henry. 1996. "Regulatory Competition and the Politics of Financial Market Reform in Britain and Japan." *Governance* 9(3):311–41.

——. 2001. *Money Rules: The New Politics of Finance in Britain and Japan.* Ithaca: Cornell University Press.

Lichtenstein, Cynthia C. 1985. "U.S. Response to the International Debt Crisis: The International Lending Supervision Act of 1983 and the Regulations Issued under the Act." In *A Dance along the Precipice: The Political and Economic Dimensions of the International Debt Problem,* ed. William Eskridge. Lexington, Mass.: Lexington Books.

Lipson, Charles. 1986. "Bankers' Dilemmas: Private Cooperation in Rescheduling Sovereign Debts." In *Cooperation under Anarchy,* ed. Kenneth Oye, pp. 200–225. Princeton, N.J.: Princeton University Press.

Littlewood, John. 1998. *The Stock Market: Fifty Years of Capitalism at Work.* London: Financial Times.

Lomax, David F. 1986. *The Developing Country Debt Crisis.* New York: St. Martin's.

Luessenhop, Elizabeth, and Martin Mayer. 1995. *Risky Business: An Insider's Account of the Disaster at Lloyd's of London.* New York: Scribner.

Macey, Jonathan R. 2000. "The 'Demand' for International Regulatory Cooperation: A Public Choice Perspective." In *Transatlantic Regulatory Cooperation,* ed. George A. Bermann, Matthias Herdegen, and Peter L. Lindseth. New York: Oxford University Press.

Majone, Giandomenico. 1994a. "The Rise of the Regulatory State in Europe." *West European Politics* 17:77–101.

——. 1994b. "Comparing Strategies of Regulatory Rapprochement." In *Regulatory Co-operation for an Interdependent World,* ed. OECD. Paris: OECD.

Mankiw, N. Gregory. *Macroeconomics.* 5th ed. New York: Worth.

Martin, Lisa L. 1992. "Interests, Power, and Multilateralism." *International Organization* 46(4):765–92.

——. 2000. *Democratic Commitments: Legislatures and International Cooperation.* Princeton, N.J.: Princeton University Press.

Mattli, Walter, and Tim Buthe. 2005a. "Accountability in Accounting: The Politics of Private Rule-Making in the Public Interest." *Governance* 18(3):399–429.

——. 2005b. "Global Private Governance: Lessons from a National Model of Setting Standards in Accounting." *Law and Contemporary Problems* 68(3):225–62.

Mayer, Martin. 1990. *The Greatest-Ever Bank Robbery: The Collapse of the Savings and Loan Industry.* New York: Scribner.

McCauley, Robert N. 1986. "Are Large U.S. Banks Moving International Activity Off Their Balance Sheets?" *Federal Reserve Bank of New York Quarterly Review* (Summer): 42–44.

McCubbins, Mathew D., and Thomas Schwartz. 1984. "Congressional Oversight Overlooked: Police Patrols versus Fire Alarms." *American Journal of Political Science* 2(1):165–79.

Meier, Kenneth J. 1985a. *Regulation: Politics, Bureaucracy, and Economics.* New York: St. Martin's.

——. 1985b. *The Political Economy of Regulation: The Case of Insurance.* New York: SUNY Press.

Milner, Helen. 1997. *Interests, Institutions, and Information.* Princeton, N.J.: Princeton University Press.

Millman, Gregory. 1995. *The Vandals' Crown: How Rebel Currency Traders Overthrew the World's Central Banks.* New York: Free Press.

Mishkin, Frederic S. 2001. "Prudential Supervision: Why Is It Important and What Are the Issues?" In *Prudential Supervision: What Works and What Doesn't,* ed. Mishkin. Chicago: University of Chicago Press.

Mishkin, Frederic S., and Stanley G. Eakins. 1998. *Financial Markets and Institutions.* Reading, Mass.: Addison-Wesley.

Moe, Terry. 1987. "An Assessment of the Positive Theory of Congressional Dominance." *Legislative Studies Quarterly* 12(4):475–520.

Moran, Michael. 1986. *The Politics of Banking.* 2nd ed. London: Macmillan.

——. 1988. "Thatcherism and Financial Regulation." *The Political Quarterly* 59, 1:20–27.

——. 1991. *The Politics of the Financial Services Revolution: The U.S.A., U.K., and Japan.* New York: St. Martins.

Moravcsik, Andrew. 2004. "Is There a 'Democratic Deficit' in World Politics?" *Government and Opposition* 39(2):336–63.

Moskow, Michael H. 1998. "Regulatory Efforts to Prevent Banking Crises." In *Preventing Bank Crises: Lessons from Recent Global Bank Failures,* ed. Gerard Caprio, William Hunter, George Kaufman, and Danny Leipziger. Washington, D.C.: World Bank.

Mosley, Layna. 2003. *Global Capital and National Governments.* Cambridge: Cambridge University Press.

——. 2005. "Private Governance for the Public Good? Exploring Private Sector Participation in Global Financial Regulation." Paper presented at the conference "Financial Innovations: Markets, Cultures, and Politics," London School of Economics, June 16–17.

Murphy, Dale. 2004. *The Structure of Regulatory Competition: Corporations and Public Policies in a Global Economy.* New York: Oxford University Press.

Oatley, Thomas, and Robert Nabors. 1998. "Redistributive Cooperation: Market Failure, Wealth Transfers, and the Basle Accord." *International Organization* 52(1):35–54.

Odell, John. 1982. *U.S. International Monetary Policy.* Princeton, N.J.: Princeton University Press.

OECD. 1983. *The Internationalisation of Banking.* Paris: OECD.

——. 1991. *Systemic Risks in Securities Markets.* Washington, D.C.: OECD.

——. 1999. *Liberalisation of International Insurance Operations.* Paris: OECD.

——. 2003a. *Assessing the Solvency of Insurance Companies.* Paris: OECD.

——. 2003b. *Insurance and Expanding Systemic Risks.* Paris: OECD.

Ohama, Shunsaku. 1991. "Capital Rules for Securities Companies." In *Japan's Financial Markets,* ed. Foundation for Advanced Information and Research. Tokyo: FAIR Japan.

Pauly, Louis. 1997. *Who Elected the Bankers? Surveillance and Control in the World Economy.* Ithaca: Cornell University Press.

Pecchioli, R. M. 1983. *The Internationalisation of Banking.* Paris: OECD.

Peltzman, Sam. 1976. "Toward a More General Theory of Regulation." *Journal of Law and Economics* 19:211–40.

Penn, Graham. 1989. *Banking Supervision: Regulation of the UK Banking Sector under the Banking Act of 1987.* London: Butterworths.

Porter, Tony. 1993. *States, Markets, and Regimes in Global Finance.* New York: St. Martin's.

Priest, George L. 1988. "Understanding the Liability Crisis." In *New Directions in Liability Law,* ed. Walter Olson. New York: Academy of Political Science.

Putnam, Robert. 1988. "Diplomacy and Domestic Politics: The Logic of Two-Level Games." *International Organization* 42(2):427–60.

Radaelli, Claudio. 1999. *Technocracy in the European Union.* New York: Longman.

Reid, Margaret. 1982. *The Secondary Banking Crisis, 1973–75: Its Causes and Course.* London: Macmillan.

——. 1988. *All-Change in the City: The Revolution in Britain's Financial Sector.* London: Macmillan.

Reinicke, Wolfgang H. 1995. *Banking, Politics, and Global Finance.* Washington, D.C.: Brookings Institution.

——. 1998. *Global Public Policy.* Washington, D.C.: Brookings Institution.

Rhee, S. Ghon. 1992. *Securities Markets and Systemic Risks in Dynamic Asian Economies.* Paris: OECD.

Risse-Kappen, Thomas, ed. 1995. *Bringing Transnational Relations Back In.* Cambridge: Cambridge University Press.

Rogers, David. 1999. *The Big Four British Banks.* London: Macmillan.

Rosenau, James N., and Ernst-Otto Czempiel, eds. 1992. *Governance without Government: Order and Change in World Politics.* Cambridge: Cambridge University Press.

Rosenbluth, Frances M. 1989. *Financial Politics in Contemporary Japan.* Ithaca: Cornell University Press.

Rosenbluth, Frances M., and Ross Schaap. 2003. "The Domestic Politics of Banking Regulation." *International Organization* 57(2):307–36.

Rourke, Francis E. 1976. *Bureaucracy, Politics, and Public Policy.* Boston: Little, Brown.

Scott, Hal S., and Shinsaku Iwahara. 1994. *In Search of a Level Playing Field: The Implementation of the Basle Accord in Japan and the United States.* Washington, D.C.: Group of Thirty.

Securities and Exchange Commission. 1988. "Internationalization of the Securities Markets." Report to the Senate Committee on Banking, Housing, and Urban Affairs. Washington, D.C.: Securities and Exchange Commission.

Shepsle, Kenneth, and Barry Weingast. 1987. "The Institutional Foundations of Committee Power." *American Political Science Review* 81(1):85–104.

Simmons, Beth. 2001. "The International Politics of Harmonization: The Case of Capital Market Regulations." *International Organization* 55(3):589–620.

Simmons, Beth, and Zachary Elkins. 2004. "The Globalization of Liberalization: Policy Diffusion in the International Political Economy." *American Political Science Review* 98(1):171–89.

Singer, David Andrew. 2004. "Capital Rules: The Domestic Politics of International Regulatory Harmonization." *International Organization* 58(3):531–65.

Skipper, Harold J. 1996. "International Trade in Insurance." In *International Financial Markets: Harmonization versus Competition,* ed. Claude E. Barfield. Washington, D.C.: AEI Press.

——. 2001. *Insurance in the General Agreement on Trade in Services.* Washington, D.C.: AEI Press.

Slaughter, Anne-Marie. 2004. *A New World Order.* Princeton, N.J.: Princeton University Press.

Smith, Roy C., and Ingo Walter. 2003. *Global Banking.* 2nd ed. New York: Oxford University Press.

Sobel, Andrew. 1994. *Domestic Choices, International Markets.* Ann Arbor: University of Michigan Press.

——. 1999. *State Institutions, Private Incentives, Global Capital.* Ann Arbor: University of Michigan Press.

Solomon, Steven. 1995. *The Confidence Game: How Unelected Central Bankers Are Governing the Changed World Economy.* New York: Simon & Schuster.

Spero, Joan. 1980. *The Failure of the Franklin National Bank.* New York: Columbia University Press.

Sprague, Irvine H. 1986. *Bailout: An Insider's Account of Bank Failures and Rescues.* New York: Basic Books.

Steil, Benn. 1994. "International Securities Market Regulation." In *International Financial Market Regulation,* ed. Steil. New York: Wiley.

Stessens, Guy. 2000. *Money Laundering.* Cambridge: Cambridge University Press.

Stigler, George J. 1971. "The Economic Theory of Regulation." *Bell Journal of Economics and Management Science* 2:3–21.

Strange, Susan. 1983. "Cave! Hic Dragones: A Critique of Regime Analysis." In *International Regimes,* ed. Stephen Krasner, pp. 337–54. Ithaca: Cornell University Press.

Swaps Monitor Publications. 1994. *The World's Major Derivatives Dealers.* New York: Swaps Monitor Publications.

Swary, Itzhak, and Barry Topf. 1992. *Global Financial Deregulation: Commercial Banking at the Crossroads.* Cambridge: Blackwell.

Swiss Re. 1996. "World Insurance in 1994." *Sigma* no. 4.

——. 2002. "The London Market in the Throes of Change." *Sigma* no. 3.

——. 2003. "Reinsurance: A Systemic Risk?" *Sigma* no. 5.

——. 2004. "World Insurance in 2003." *Sigma* no. 3.

Terrell, Henry S., Robert S. Dohner, and Barbara R. Lowrey. 1990. "The Activities of Japanese Banks in the United Kingdom and in the United States, 1980–88." *Federal Reserve Bulletin* 76(2):39–50.

Tobin, Glenn Patrick. 1991. "Global Money Rules: The Political Economy of International Regulatory Cooperation." Ph.D. dissertation, John F. Kennedy School of Government, Harvard University.

Trainar, Philippe. 2005. "What Is at Stake with EU Solvency II Reform?" Paper presented at the 21st Annual PROGRES Seminar, Geneva, Switzerland, April 7–8.

Turner, Philip. 1991. "Capital Flows in the 1980s." BIS Economic Papers, no. 30. Basel, Switzerland: Bank for International Settlements.

Underhill, Geoffrey R. D. 1997. "Private Markets and Public Responsibility in a Global System: Conflict and Cooperation in Transnational Banking and Securities Regulation." In *The New World Order in International Finance,* ed. Underhill, pp. 17–49. New York: St. Martin's.

U.S. Federal Reserve. 1999. "International Activities of U.S. Banks and in U.S. Banking Markets." *Federal Reserve Bulletin* (September). Prepared by James V. Houpt.

——. 2005. "Share Data for U.S. Offices of Foreign Banks." Available at http://www.federalreserve.gov/releases/iba/Share/SHRTBL4.html.

U.S. House of Representatives. 1987. *Risk-Based Capital Requirements for Banks and Bank Holding Companies.* Hearing, Committee on Banking, Finance, and Urban Affairs, Subcommittee on General Oversight and Investigations. Statement by Paul Volcker. 100th Congress, 1st session, April 30.

——. 1988. *Risk-Based Capital Requirements for Banks and Bank Holding Companies.* Hearing, Committee on Banking, Finance, and Urban Affairs, Subcommittee on General Oversight and Investigations. 100th Congress, 2nd session, April 21.

——. 1990. "Failed Promises: Insurance Company Insolvencies." Report by the Subcommittee on Oversight and Investigations, Committee on Energy and Commerce. February.

——. 1994. "Wishful Thinking: A World View of Insurance Solvency Regulation." Report by the Subcommittee on Oversight and Investigations, Committee on Energy and Commerce. October.

U.S. Senate. 1990. Hearing, Committee on Banking, Housing, and Urban Affairs, on the subject of Drexel Burnham Lambert. 101st Congress, 2nd session, March 2.

U.S. Shadow Financial Regulatory Committee. 2000. *Reforming Bank Capital Regulation.* Washington, D.C.: AEI Press.

Varian, Hal R. 1999. *Intermediate Microeconomics: A Modern Approach.* 5th ed. New York: Norton.

Vogel, Steven. 1996. *Freer Markets, More Rules.* Ithaca: Cornell University Press.

Walker, Sir David. 1992. "Major Issues Relevant for Regulatory Response to the Internationalisation of Capital Markets." In *The Internationalisation of Capital Markets and the Regulatory Response*, ed. John Fingleton. London: Graham & Trotman.

Wall, Larry D. 1983. "Will Bank Capital Adequacy Restrictions Slow the Development of Interstate Banking?" *Federal Reserve Bank of Atlanta Economic Review* 68(5).

Walter, Ingo. 2003. "Financial Integration across Borders and Sectors: Implications for Regulatory Structures." In *Financial Supervision in Europe*, ed. Jeroen J. M. Kremers, Dirk Schoenmaker, and Peter J. Wierts. Northampton, Mass.: Edward Elgar.

Wang, Wallace Hsin-Chun. 2003. *Reinsurance Regulation: A Contemporary and Comparative Study*. London: Kluwer Law International.

Weingast, Barry R. 1984. "The Congressional-Bureaucratic System: A Principal-Agent Perspective (with Applications to the SEC)." *Public Choice* 44:147–91.

Weingast, Barry R., and Mark J. Moran. 1983. "Bureaucratic Discretion or Congressional Control? Regulatory Policymaking by the Federal Trade Commission." *Journal of Political Economy* 91(51):765–800.

White, Lawrence J. 1996a. "Competition versus Harmonization: An Analytical Overview of International Regulation of Financial Services." In *International Financial Markets: Harmonization versus Competition*, ed. Claude E. Barfield. Washington, D.C.: AEI Press.

——. 1996b. "International Regulation of Securities Markets: Competition or Harmonization?" In *The Industrial Organization and Regulation of the Securities Industry*, ed. Andrew W. Lo. Chicago: University of Chicago Press.

Wilson, James Q. 1975. "The Rise of the Bureaucratic State." *Public Interest* 41:77–103.

——, ed. 1980. *The Politics of Regulation*. New York: Basic Books.

Wood, Duncan. 2005. *Governing Global Banking: The Basel Committee and the Politics of Financial Globalisation*. Burlington, Vt.: Ashgate.

Wyplosz, Charles. 1999. "International Financial Instability." In *Global Public Goods: International Cooperation in the Twenty-first Century*, ed. Inge Kaul, Isabelle Grunberg, and Marc A. Stern, pp. 152–89. New York: United Nations Development Program.

Zaring, David. 1998. "International Law by Other Means: The Twilight Existence of International Financial Regulatory Organizations." *Texas International Law Journal* 33(2):281–330.

Zweig, Phillip L. 1985. *Belly Up: The Collapse of the Penn Square Bank*. New York: Crown.

Index

Italic page numbers refer to tables and figures.

Amyx, Jennifer, 59
Asian financial crisis, 1, 65
asymmetric information, 13–15, 17
Australia, 73, 96, 120

bank failures: and decline in confidence,
36; in Japan, 59, 65–66; systemic
consequences of, 17; in United Kingdom,
55–56, 57, 61, 65, 117; in United States,
45–49, 47, 51, 53, 61, 65, 117, 133n39
Bank for International Settlements (BIS),
39, 97
Banking Act of 1979 (U.K.), 55
Banking Act of 1982 (Japan), 60
Banking Act of 1987 (U.K.), 56
banking industry: and Basel Accord, 2,
5, 37; and capital adequacy standards
negotiations, 33; cross-border influences
on, 6; cross-national regulatory differences
in, 22; evolution of capital regulation in,
19; and financial instability, 45–49, 51–52,
55, 65; global banking markets in 1970s,
37–41; intermediary function of, 13; and
international competitiveness, 45, 49–54,
57–58, 57, 58, 59, 61; internationalization

of, 70; and prudential regulations, 46, 50,
54, 55, 56; and risk, 6, 14, 16
banking regulators: and Basel Accord,
2, 5; and debt crisis of 1982, 43; as
international actors, 37, 39, 40; and
international regulatory harmonization,
33, 36–37; and stability/competitiveness
balance, 36–37, 40, 45, 66; variations in
preferences of, 3, 4, 5–6, 36, 64, 118
Bank of England: and bank failures, 56, 57,
61, 117; and Basel Committee, 39–40; and
British Petroleum share price, 78; and
capital adequacy regulations, 3, 33, 36, 56,
57, 116, 135n112; charter of, 94; regulatory
environment of, 54–57, 58, 81, 120
Bank of Japan, 33, 59, 88
Barclays, 57, 58
Basel Accord of 1988: amendment of,
63–64, 65, 135n137; and banking
industry, 2, 5, 37; and capital adequacy
regulations, 5, 36, 41, 60; compliance
with, 61–62, 123, 124, 141n5; and
consolidated supervision, 81; criticism of, 37,
62–63, 112; effect of U.S. politics on, 44;
effect on securities regulators, 76, 82;

Basel Accord of 1988 *(cont.)*
  as example of international regulatory
    harmonization, 2, 33, 68, 116, 123; and
    International Association of Insurance
    Supervisors, 97, 139n6; and International
    Organization of Securities Commissions,
    74, 116; and market power, 60–61;
    negotiations over capital adequacy, 10,
    11, 36, 44; and prudential regulations,
    67; studies of, 5, 6, 8; and variation in
    banking regulators' preferences, 36, 118
Basel Committee: and Anglo-American
    agreement of 1987, 60; creation of,
    39, 40; and global regulation, 2; and
    International Organization of Securities
    Commissions, 92, 95; negotiations within,
    4, 10, 34, 40–41, 44, 64, 73, 117, 127,
    130n39; and qualitative impact study, 65,
    136n155; structure of, 119, 121, 127
Basel II: "gaming" of, 65, 66; and large
    versus small banks, 64–65; negotiations
    over, 127; and relaxation of specificity,
    65, 136n152; risk-based approach of, 112;
    and shortcomings of original agreement,
    37, 62, 63–64; viability of, 121
Bernanke, Ben, 114
Berrill, Kenneth, 80
Big Bang reforms, 76, 77, 79–80, 81, 117
Blunden, George, 39, 40
Breeden, Richard, 86, 87, 93
Bretton Woods international monetary
    system, 1, 34, 37, 70
British Petroleum (BP), 76, 77–78
building-block approach, 63, 83–84, 87

Canada, 73, 89
capital: definition of, 16, 44, 46, 47, 59, 61,
    74; and risk, 16–17, 62–64
capital adequacy, cross-national differences
    in, 19, 64
Capital Adequacy Directive (CAD), 78, 79,
    81, 82, 83
capital adequacy regulations: and
    Anglo-American agreement of 1987,
    58–59; and Bank of England, 3, 33,
    36, 56, 57, 116, 135n112; and Basel
    Accord, 5, 36, 41, 60; and derivatives
    markets, 81; and financial regulators,
    22; and insurance industry, 97, 112; and
    International Organization of Securities
    Commissions, 68, 73–74, 83, 87, 91;
    and Japanese Ministry of Finance, 59;

  negotiations over, 2, 3, 10, 11, 32, 33–34,
    45; and risk, 34, 49, 74; role of, 13, 61;
    and securities regulators, 11, 67–68, 117;
    and stability/competitiveness balance,
    11, 42–43; and U.K. Securities and
    Investments Board, 77, 79; and U.S.
    banking failures of 1980s, 45–48
capital decisions, 17–19
capital markets, 20, 70–71, 115
capital requirements, 8, 11, 18, 19, 28, 82
Citicorp, 53, 57, 79
Concordat of 1975, 40–41, 74, 115
Conover, Todd, 48
consolidated supervision, 81–82, 84, 86, 87,
    91–92, 93
Continental Illinois, 48, 56
contingent liabilities, 42
Cooke, Peter, 39
core harmonization, 122–23
core-periphery relationship, 126–27. *See also*
    less-developed countries (LDC)
Corrigan, Gerald, 53, 60
credit risk, 14, 16, 63, 64
cross-border lending, 41–42

Dai-Ichi Kangyo Bank, 53
Daiwa, 88, 89, 90
Dale, Richard, 71
debt crisis: of 1982, 43–45, 48; of
    less-developed countries, 5, 38
Depository Institutions Deregulation and
    Monetary Control Act (DIDMCA),
    49–50
derivatives markets: capital charges on
    derivatives trading, 84; increasing
    prominence of, 69–70, 71, 79, 80, 136n8;
    and international competitiveness, 80–81,
    83; and Japanese securities industry, 91;
    and notional amounts, 70, 136n9; and
    prudential regulations, 81, 82; and stock
    market crash of 1987, 69, 71–72, 75; and
    U.S. securities industry, 84–85, 91–92, 93,
    94, 117
derivatives products companies (DPCs), 82,
    83, 90
Dodd, Christopher, 86
domestic regulation: and capital
    requirements, 19; country studies of,
    4–5; and exogenous shocks, 68–69;
    international regulatory harmonization
    balanced with, 4, 5, 7, 11, 12, 21, 31, 114,
    118; and international relations, 8, 41

Dow Jones Industrial Average (DJIA), 71,
78–79
Drexel Burnham Lambert, 85–86

Egypt, 123, 124
Enron, 22, 131n11
European Commission, 111–12
European Union: insurance regulation
in, 98, 103, 104, 111–12; and regulation
developments, 2; and securities
regulation, 76, 78, 81, 82
exchange rates, volatility of, 15, 37, 38, 70, 71
exogenous shocks: and capital adequacy
regulations, 34; to financial stability,
26–27, 27, 28, 29, 31, 34, 35, 37, 59,
68–69, 75, 76, 85–86, 116, 117; to
international competitiveness, 27–28, 27,
28, 29, 31, 34, 35, 37, 59, 68–69, 75, 117;
and principal-agent relationship, 21; and
role of capital adequacy, 2; simultaneous
stability/competitiveness shocks, 3, 7,
11, 28–29, 29, 31, 36, 37, 69; and win-set,
25–30, 26, 27, 28, 29, 75

Fearon, James, 126
feasibility constraint, and win-set, 25, 26–27,
26, 27, 28, 29, 30
Federal Deposit Insurance Corporation
(FDIC), 45, 46–47, 47, 48, 49, 50
Federal Financial Institutions Examination
Council (FFIEC), 46
Federal Home Loan Bank Board (FHLBB),
30, 133n44
Federal Reserve Bank of New York, 51, 53,
60, 78, 139n116
Ferguson, Roger, 64, 65, 66
Financial Action Task Force (FATF), 123,
124
financial conglomerates, 121
financial instability: cross-border
domino effect in, 2; effect of
international regulations on, 3; effect
on financial regulators, 4; effect on
international relations, 8; effect on
securities regulators, 68, 75–76, 95;
insurance industry response to, 12;
and international competitiveness, 42;
and principal-agent relationship, 22; in
U.K. banking industry, 55, 65; in U.K.
securities industry, 75, 76, 77; in U.S.
banking industry, 45–49, 51–52, 65; in
U.S. insurance industry, 105

financial institutions: and principal-agent
relationship, 22; and risk, 13–16;
and spillover effects of decisions,
17–18; unpopularity of capital
requirements, 19
financial markets: and Basel Accord, 60–61;
and debt crisis of 1982, 43; and global
banking in 1970s, 37–38; globalization of,
1–2, 5, 8, 20, 21
financial regulators: analytical framework
for policy positions, 20, 21–30, 33, 35;
as international actors, 3, 4, 9, 10–11, 12,
119, 122, 141n3; and internationalized
financial markets, 1–2, 20; and
international regulatory harmonization,
3, 21, 30–31, 32, 35, 36, 118–21;
and negotiations over international
standards, 32–33; and political issues, 9,
11, 21, 22, 25, 28, 31, 32, 114, 115, 118,
120, 121–22; realistic range of policy
choices, 23, 25, 132n15; and role of
capital, 19; and stability/competitiveness
balance, 3, 9, 23, 45, 115; super-regulators,
120–21; variation in preferences of, 3–4,
5, 6, 7, 11, 23, 30, 31, 32, 33, 35, 126;
win-set of, 25, 26–29, 26, 27, 28, 29, 30,
116. *See also* banking regulators;
insurance regulators; principal-agent
(PA) relationship; securities regulators
Financial Services Act of 1986 (U.K.), 76,
78, 79, 82, 83, 109, 137n47
Financial Services and Markets Act of 2000
(U.K.), 94, 111
financial stability: and Bank of Japan,
59; Basel Accord promoting, 5, 61;
and capital requirements, 8, 11, 18;
effect of bank failures on, 36; effect of
regulations on, 23, 24, 25; exogenous
shocks to, 26–27, 27, 28, 29, 31, 34, 35,
37, 59, 68–69, 75, 76, 85–86, 116, 117;
and principal-agent relationship, 21,
23; and prudential regulations, 20, 23;
and U.K. securities industry, 77–79;
and U.S. insurance industry, 105; and
U.S. securities industry, 85–86. *See also*
stability/competitiveness balance
First National Bank of Bellaire, 47–48
foreign exchange markets, 15, 37, 38–39,
131n4
France, 61, 73, 78, 100
Franklin National Bank of New York, 39
fraud, 82, 123

FTSE (Financial Times Stock Exchange), 71, 77, 79
functionalist framework, 5–8, 34, 115

Garn St-Germain Depository Institutions Act (U.S.), 50
Garrett, Geoffrey, 6
General Agreement on Tariffs and Trade (GATT), 34, 118
Germany, 73, 78, 96, 100
Glass-Steagall prohibition, 17–18, 92
global economy: balancing competing interests in, 5; convergence of regulations in, 118–19; financial instability in, 1; insurance in, 98–104, 118; and purpose of financial regulation, 13; role of regulators in, 3, 117–18, 127
globalization: and derivatives markets, 69–70; domestic ramifications of, 34; and enforcement of national laws, 72; of financial markets, 1–2, 5, 8, 20, 21
Goldman Sachs, 69, 80, 81, 82
Gramm-Leach-Bliley Act of 1999 (U.S.), 17–18
Greenspan, Alan, 114
Group of Seven (G-7), Financial Action Task Force, 123
Group of Ten (G-10): and Basel Accord, 36, 61, 81, 123, 126; and Basel II, 65; and capital adequacy regulations, 60; and creation of Basel Committee, 40; and Standing Committee on Banking Regulations and Supervisory Practices, 39

Hadjiemannuil, Christos, 57
Haufler, Virginia, 140n9
hedging, 93
Heimann, John, 43, 119
Heinz, John, 86
Herstatt Bank, 38, 39, 115
Hill Samuel, 38
Hokkaido Takushoku Bank, 65
Hong Kong, 71, 73

indifference-curve diagram, and win-set, 25, 26, *26*
Indonesia, 123, 124
ING Bank, 94
in-house model, 63–64
Insurance Companies Act of 1982 (U.K.), 109

insurance industry: evolution of capital regulation in, 19, 33–34; in global economy, 98–104, 118; global links in, 96–97; global regulation for, 2; and international regulatory harmonization, 98, 103, 111–12, 113, 117; lack of international standards for, 3, 112; regulation in U.S., 104–5; and risk of financial losses, 14, 16, 17. *See also* reinsurance industry
insurance markets, 1, 6, 17, 99, 100, 101, 103
insurance regulators: as international actors, 98, 111–12, 117; and liability crisis of 1980s, 98, 106–8; and Lloyd's of London reinsurance crisis of 1990s, 98, 110, 111, 113; as primary actors in international negotiations, 119, 141n3; and reinsurance industry, 103–4; and stability/competitiveness balance, 12, 34, 112; structure of U.S. regulation, 104–5, 107–8, 113, 117; variations in preferences of, 4
Inter-American Association of Securities Commissions and Similar Organizations, 72–73
interest rates, volatility in, 15, 16, 71
internal-ratings-based (IRB) approach, 64–65
International Association of Insurance Supervisors (IAIS): core principles of, 111; and global regulation, 2; negotiations within, 4, 34; on reinsurance, 100; structure of, 97, 104, 112, 139n5
International Bank for Reconstruction and Development (IBRD), 125
international competitiveness: and Basel II, 64–65; and capital requirements, 11, 19, 28, 82; and cross-national regulatory differences, 20, 22, 30; and derivatives markets, 80–81, 83; effect of regulations on, 3, 5, 10, 20, 23, *24*, 25, 37, 44, 132n16; exogenous shocks to, 27–28, *27, 28, 29,* 31, 34, 35, 37, 59, 68–69, 75, 117; and financial instability, 42; and international securities regulations, 74; and Japanese banking industry, 59, 61; of national banking sectors, 41–42; and national regulatory agencies, 8; and principal-agent relationship, 21, 23; and reinsurance industry, 98, 101–3, 140n21; and securities regulators' preferences, 68,

74–76; in U.K. banking industry, 57–58, *57, 58*; and U.K. securities industry, 76, 79–82, 83; in U.S. banking industry, 45, 49–54; and U.S. securities industry, 76–77. *See also* stability/competitiveness balance

International Development Association (IDA), 125

international institutions: distributional nature of, 6; domestic legal principles used in, 9; enforcement role of, 124–26; and functionalist framework, 5–6; redistributive nature of, 6, 7

International Lending Supervision Act (ILSA), 43–44, 48, 49

International Monetary Fund (IMF), 43, 118, 124, *125*, 126

International Organization of Securities Commissions (IOSCO): and capital adequacy regulations, 68, 73–74, 83, 87, 91; formation of, 73; and global regulation, 2; and International Association of Insurance Supervisors, 97; and international regulatory harmonization, 67, 68, 87, 116; and Japanese Ministry of Finance, 89–90; negotiations within, 4, 34, 68, 74–75, 79, 84, 87, 91, 92–93, 116; as rule-making body, 94–95; structure of, 119, 127; Technical Committee of, 73–74, 83, 87, 92, 93; and U.K. securities industry, 83, 91; and U.S. securities industry, 87, 91; working groups of, 73, 87, 89, 92, 137n28

international regulatory harmonization: balanced with domestic regulation, 4, 5, 7, 11, 12, 21, 31, 114, 118; and Basel Committee, 40; and Basel II, 65; and capital adequacy regulations, 36, 49, 74; and debt crisis of 1982, 43–44; distinguished from regulatory convergence, 129n9; financial regulators' use of, 3, 21, 30–31, 32, 35, 36, 118–21; and insurance industry, 98, 103, 111–12, 113, 117; and legislature-focused argument, 6–7; negotiating environment's role in, 119–20; outcomes versus processes of, 32–33, 132n22; and political issues, 31, 114, 117, 122, 127; role of market power in, 2, 21, 32, 132n21; and securities regulators, 33, 67, 68, 74, 95, 116, 118;

typology of, 12, 122–24; U.K. regulators' demands for, 53–54, 58; and U.K. Securities and Investments Board, 69, 75, 82–84, 86–87, 91, 93, 116; U.S. regulators' demands for, 53–54, 58; U.S. Securities and Exchange Commission's opposition to, 33, 67, 68, 84–87, 91, 93, 94, 95, 116, 117; and win-set, 30, *31*, 116

international regulatory standards: enforcement of, 9, 10, 119, 120, 124–26, 141n5, 142n20; and international relations, 8–11; negotiations over, 32–33, 126–27; and reinsurance industry, 97; variation in emergence of standards across industries, 2–3, 5, 8

international relations, 8–11, 41

international treaties, 118–19

Ireland, 120

Italy, 73

Japan: and Basel Accord, 61; and capital adequacy negotiations, 2; competition with U.K. banking industry, 57–58, *57, 58*; competition with U.S. banking industry, 45, 49, 50–51, 53; and debt crisis of 1982, 43; domestic regulatory changes in, 5, 120; insurance industry growth in, 100; insurance market in, 98, 101; and internationalization of securities market, 69, 73; location of banks' assets, 51, *52*; recession in, 65–66; resistance to capital standards, 58–59, 61; rise of banks in 1980s, 27–28, 37, 50–51, *51*, 52, 53, 59; stock market capitalization of, 69, *70*

Japanese Ministry of Finance (MOF): and Anglo-American agreement of 1987, 59, 60; and Basel Accord, 61; and capital standards for securities industry, 3, 67, 69, 75, 87–92, 93, 94, 95, 116, 117; jurisdiction of, 2; as opponent of capital adequacy standard for banking industry, 3, 33, 36, 59, 117; and prudential regulations, 59–60, 88, 89–90; and stock market crash of 1987, 75

Japanese Securities and Exchange Law, 92

Johnson Matthey Bankers Limited (JMB), 55–56, 57, 61

junk bonds, 85–86, 108

Kaifu, Toshiki, 90

Kane, Edward, 129n8

Kapstein, Ethan, 5, 40, 60, 132n21
Kawai, Yoshi, 112
Keohane, Robert, 5
Kleinwort Benson, 94
Knight, Jeffrey, 73
Krasner, Stephen, 6

Latin America, 1, 38, 43
Laurence, Henry, 4–5
Laurie Milbank, 79
law of large numbers, 99
Law of the Sea Tribunal, 9
legalization in world politics, 9
legislatures: and constraints on regulators, 31, 119, 121–22; creation of regulatory bodies by, 29–30; and international negotiations, 7, 119, 120; and international regulatory harmonization, 31; intervention of, 29, 31, 115, 116, 120; legislature-focused argument, 6–7, 9; preferences of, 23, 61; and regulatory environment changes, 94. *See also* principal-agent (PA) relationship
Lehman Brothers, 80
Leigh-Pemberton, Robin, 59
less-developed countries (LDC), 5, 38, 42, 43, 62
liquidity risk, 15
Lloyd's Act of 1871 (U.K.), 109
Lloyd's of London, 96, 98, 103–4, 108–11
locally dependent risks, 99, 100
London Stock Exchange, 76, 79–80
Long, James E., 108
long position, 83–84, 87, 93, 138n62
Long Term Credit Bank of Japan, 65
loss market excess (LMX) spiral, 103, 109–11, 113

market power, 2, 21, 32, 36, 60–61, 132n21
market pressures, 9–10, 124, 126, 127
Market Reform Act of 1990 (U.S.), 85, 86, 87, 138n73
market risk, 14–15, 18, 63, 64
McCarran-Ferguson Act of 1945 (U.S.), 104
McMahon, Christopher, 56
Meier, Kenneth, 140n9
Merrill Lynch, 80, 91
Mexico, 43, 63
Milken, Michael, 85
Mitsui Bank, 60

money market mutual funds, 42, 45, 50
Moody's, 64, 90
Morgan Grenfell, 78, 79
Morgan Guaranty, 38
Morgan Stanley, 80, 81, 82
Moskow, Michael, 18
multinational banks, 46, 48
Munich Re, 96

Nabors, Robert, 6–7, 132n21
National Association of Insurance Commissioners (NAIC), 104, 107, 108, 113, 139n5
national regulatory agencies. *See* financial regulators
Nauru, 123
negotiable order of withdrawal (NOW) accounts, 50
Net Capital Rule, 81, 84
Netherlands, 73, 78
New York Stock Exchange, 71, 85, 91
Nikkei, 71, 87, 88, 90, 138n93
Nikko, 88, 89, 91
Nippon Credit Bank, 65
Nixon, Richard, 37
Nomura Securities, 69, 88, 89, 91
note issuance facilities (NIFs), 51, 134n73

Oatley, Thomas, 6–7, 132n21
Occidental Petroleum, 110
OECD countries, 63, 72
off-balance sheet activity, 51–52, 55, 57
Office of the Comptroller of the Currency (OCC), 46, 47–48, 52
Office of Thrift Supervision (OTS), 30
operational risk, 15–16
Oxley, Michael, 121

Penn Square Bank, 48
peripheral harmonization, 122, 123
Phillips & Drew, 79, 80
political issues: and Basel Accord, 6, 44; and effects of globalization, 34; and financial regulators, 9, 11, 21, 22, 25, 28, 31, 32, 114, 115, 118, 120, 121–22; and international regulatory harmonization, 31, 114, 117, 122, 127; and international relations, 9; and legislature-based arguments, 6–7; and national regulatory agencies, 21, 22; and securities market, 71; and stability/competitiveness balance,

3, 6, 115; and U.K. securities industry, 78, 83, 94, 95; and U.S. securities industry, 86, 95

principal-agent (PA) relationship: and delegation of regulatory responsibility, 21–22, 25; and financial regulator-legislature relationship, 11, 20–21, 22, 23, 25, 116, 131n9; and international regulatory harmonization, 31; and win-set for regulatory policy, 115

private standard-setting organizations, 8

prudential regulations: and Basel Accord, 67; and Basel Committee, 39; and derivatives markets, 81, 82; and financial stability, 20, 23; and Japanese Ministry of Finance, 59–60, 88, 89–90; and political issues, 6; and reinsurance industry, 104; re-regulating markets with, 5; setting of, 1, 129n1; and stability/competitiveness balance, 37; and stock market crash of 1987, 75; and supervisory protocols, 22; and U.K. banking industry, 54, 55, 56; and U.K. Securities and Investments Board, 76, 79, 84, 94; and U.S. banking industry, 46, 50; and U.S. securities industry, 76–77, 85

Public Company Accounting Oversight Board, 22, 29–30, 131n11

pure risk, 99

Quinn, Brian, 57, 78

regulatory adjustment cycle, 3, 4

regulatory convergence, 122, 123

Reid, Margaret, 81

Reinsurance Association of America, 102

reinsurance industry: and capacity restraint, 102, 104; capital requirements for, 11–12, 97, 104; and combined ratio, 106–7, *107*, 140n39; and finite reinsurance, 113; function of, 99–100; growth in, 100, *100*, 101; and insurance regulators, 103–4; and international competitiveness, 98, 101–3, 140n21; international orientation of, 96, 99–101, 112; location of, 100–101, *101*; regulation in United Kingdom, 108–11; regulation in United States, 104–8; and risk, 97, 102; role of international regulatory standards, 97

Reports on the Observance of regulations and Codes (ROSCs), 124, 125, *125*

Richardson, Gordon, 39–40

risk: and banking industry, 6, 14, 16; and capital, 16–17, 62–64; and capital adequacy regulations, 34, 49, 74; and capital standards, 52, 53; cross-border risks, 6; and derivatives markets, 71, 72; and financial institutions, 13–16; of global markets, 71; and insurance industry, 14, 16, 17; international systemic risk, 7, 20, 33, 66, 67, 68, 97; management of, 64–65, 136n152; pure risk, 99; and reinsurance industry, 97, 102; and securities industry, 6, 14–15, 16, 18, 67, 72, 74; weighting of, 59, 60, 61–64

risk aversion environment, 99

risk buckets, 62–63

Rosenbluth, Frances, 5, 23, 25

Rothschild (merchant bank), 77, 94

St. Germain, Fernand, 48

Sarbanes-Oxley Act of 2002 (United States), 30

Schaap, Ross, 23, 25

Schumer, Charles, 44

Scrimgeour Kemp-Gee, 79

Seccombe Marshall Campion, 79

Securities Exchange Act (U.S.), 86

securities industry: and capital adequacy negotiations, 33, 132n25; and capital adequacy requirements, 11, 19; cross-border influences on, 6; intermediary function of, 13; and international competitiveness, 76–77, 79–82, 83; lack of international regulations in, 2–3; and political issues, 78, 83, 86, 94, 95; and risk, 6, 14–15, 16, 18, 67, 72, 74

securities markets, 1, 69–76, 115

securities regulators: effect of Basel Accord on, 76, 82; and interdependencies of securities markets, 72; international cooperation of, 72–73; and international regulatory harmonization, 33, 67, 68, 74, 95, 116, 118; as primary actors in international negotiations, 119, 141n3; variations in preferences of, 3, 4, 67, 68, 74–75, 95, 115

Seidman, William, 53

self-regulating organizations (SROs), 80, 137n47

September 11, 2001, terrorist attacks, 1, 96–97, 139n2
SG Warburg, 69, 78, 80, 94
short position, 83–84, 87, 93, 138n62
Shumway, Norman, 44
Simmons, Beth, 7, 72
Simon & Coates, 79
simplified portfolio approach, 83
Singapore Exchange, 91
Skipper, Harold, 102
Slaughter, Anne-Marie, 7, 10
Solomon, Steven, 77, 88
Solomon Brothers, 91
Solvency II Directive, 98, 104, 111–12
sovereign bonds, 63
sovereign risk, 38
sovereignty costs, 10
Spero, Joan, 41
Spitzer, Eliot, 113
Sprague, Irvine, 48
stability/competitiveness balance: and banking regulators, 36–37, 40, 45, 66; and Bank of England, 58; and Basel Committee, 40; and Basel II, 65; and capital adequacy regulations, 11, 42–43; and feasibility constraint slope, 25; and financial regulators, 3, 19, 23, 45, 115; in insurance industry, 34; and insurance regulators, 12, 34, 112; and international regulatory harmonization, 4, 21; and principal-agent relationship, 21, 23; and prudential regulations, 37; and rise of Japanese banks, 52; and risk, 17; and securities regulators, 68–69; and U.K. Securities and Investments Board, 76–77, 78, 80, 82, 83, 94, 117, 118; and U.S. banking failures of 1980s, 46, 49; and U.S. banking regulations, 53; and U.S. Congress, 50; and win-set, 23, 24, 25, 94, 116
Standard & Poor's, 64, 79
Standing Committee on Banking Regulations and Supervisory Practices, 39. See also Basel Committee
stock exchanges: interdependence of, 71; volatility of, 78–79, 82, 88, 95
stock market crash of 1987: and capital market integration, 71; and derivatives markets, 69, 71–72, 75; effect on Japan, 88; effect on United Kingdom, 75, 76, 77–78, 79, 80; and effects of financial instability, 8; and International

Organization of Securities Commissions, 73; and securities markets, 1, 69, 115; simulation of, 93, 139n116
subordinated debt, 46, 61
Sumitomo Bank, 53
Sweden, 73
Swiss Bank Corporation, 94
Swiss Re, 105
Switzerland, 73, 79, 96

Teikoku Data Bank, 90
Thatcher, Margaret, 76, 78, 79
Tokyo Financial Futures Exchange, 91
Tokyo Stock Exchange, 88, 89, 91
transgovernmentalism, 4, 6–7, 10, 34
Turkey, 63
two-level game scenario, 9, 119

Union Bank of Switzerland, 79, 80
United Kingdom: Anglo-American agreement of 1987, 58–59, 60; banking industry in, 54–58; and Basel Accord, 37; and capital adequacy negotiations, 2; capital requirements in, 28; and debt crisis of 1982, 43; distribution of bank assets, 57; domestic regulatory changes in, 5, 54–55; and formation of Basel Committee, 39; insurance industry growth/losses in, 96, 100; and internationalization of securities market, 69, 73; and international regulatory harmonization, 53–54, 58; liberalizing reforms in, 89; loss market excess spiral, 103, 109–11, 113; reinsurance regulation in, 103, 108–11; and secondary banking crisis of 1973–75, 54–55; stock market capitalization of, 69, 70
United Kingdom Department of Trade and Industry (DTI), 109
United Kingdom Financial Services Authority (FSA), 94, 109, 111, 118, 120
United Kingdom Securities and Investments Board: and capital adequacy standard, 3, 33, 67, 68, 75, 77, 91, 93; and international regulatory harmonization, 69, 75, 82–84, 86–87, 91, 93, 116; rules of, 80, 83, 137n47; and stability/competitiveness balance, 76–77, 78, 80, 82, 83, 94, 117, 118
United States: Anglo-American agreement of 1987, 58–59, 60; banking competitiveness problem, 49–54;

banking instability in 1980s, 45–49; and Basel Accord, 37; and capital adequacy negotiations, 2; and creation of Basel Committee, 40; and debt crisis of 1982, 43; insurance firm losses in 1980s, 106, *106*; insurance industry growth/losses in, 96, 100; insurance regulation system in, 103; and internationalization of securities market, 69, 73; and international regulatory harmonization, 58–59; and liability crisis of 1980s, 98, 103, 105, 106–8, 110, 113, 140n21; reinsurance regulation in, 104–8; stock market capitalization of, 69, *70*
U.S. Congress: and autonomy of regulators, 121; and bank failures of 1980s, 49, 61; and capital adequacy regulations, 48; and international regulatory harmonization, 43, 44; and Regulation Q, 50; Subcommittee on Oversight and Investigations, 107–8, 140n43
U.S. Federal Reserve: autonomy of, 121; and banking instability of 1980s, 45, 48, 52–53, 117; and Basel Accord, 61; and Basel II, 65; and capital adequacy standard, 3, 33, 36, 47, 116; jurisdiction of, 2
U.S. savings and loan (S&L) crisis of 1980s, 26–27, 30
U.S. Securities and Exchange Commission: and capital regulations for securities industry, 3, 67, 83, 84, 87, 131n12; and derivatives market, 69, 72, 81–82; Net Capital Rule, 81, 84; opposition to capital adequacy standard, 33, 67, 68, 75, 84–87,

91, 93, 94, 95, 116, 117; and political issues, 22, 131n11; and reporting requirements, 131n8; and stock market crash of 1987, 75, 93, 139n116

value at risk calculation, 63
Vanuatu, 123
Vogel, Steven, 4–5, 80, 90
Volcker, Paul, 45, 59

Walker, David, 83, 110
Walter, Ingo, 23
Webster, William, 131n11
win-set: and exogenous shocks, 25–30, *26, 27, 28, 29,* 75; of financial regulators, 25, 26–29, *26, 27, 28, 29,* 30, 116; and indifference-curve diagram, 25, 26, *26*; and international regulatory harmonization, 30, *31,* 116; and Japanese banking regulations, 59, 61; and minimum thresholds, 25, 30; and principal-agent relationship, 115; and stability/competitiveness trade-off, 23, *24,* 25, 94, 116; and U.K. securities regulations, 77, 82, 83, 84, 94; and U.S. banking regulations, 53, 61; use of concept, 131–32n13; and U.S. securities regulations, 84; and zone of acceptance, 23
World Bank Group, 125, 126
Worldcom, 22, 131n11
World Trade Organization (WTO), 9, 34
Wriston, Walter, 38

Yamaichi, 88, 90
Yingling, Edward L., 53